hRac

D1062446

OKLAHOMA's MOST NOTORIOUS CASES

Machine Gun Kelly & The Urschel Kidnapping

United States vs. David Hall

The Girl Scout Murders

The Karen Silkwood Case

The Sirloin Stockade Murders

The Oklahoma City Bombing

KENT FRATES

THE ROADRUNNER PRESS
OKLAHOMA CITY

Copyright © 2014 by Kent Frates

Cover Photo by Petretei / Shutterstock.com
Cover Design: Jeanne Devlin
All rights reserved.

In accordance with the U.S. Copyright Act of 1976,
scanning, uploading, or electronic sharing of any part of this book, audio, written,
or e-published is strictly prohibited and unlawful. No part of this book may be
reproduced in any form or by any means, including photocopying, electronic,
mechanical, recording, or by any information storage and retrieval system
without permission in writing by the copyright owner.

The RoadRunner Press
Oklahoma City, Oklahoma
www.TheRoadRunnerPress.com
Bulk copies or group sales of this book available by
contacting orders@theroadrunnerpress.com or calling (405) 524-6205.

FIRST EDITION PRINTED AUGUST 2014
Printed in the USA
by Maple Press, York, Pennsylvania

Library of Congress Control Number: 2014948576
Publisher's Cataloging-In-Publication Data
(Prepared by The Donohue Group, Inc.)

Frates, Kent F.
  Oklahoma's most notorious cases : Machine Gun Kelly & the Urschel kidnapping, the
United States vs. David Hall, the Girl Scouts murders, the Karen Silkwood case, the Sirloin
Stockade murders, the Oklahoma City bombing / Kent Frates. -- First edition.

  pages : illustrations ; cm

  Issued also as an ebook.
  Includes bibliographical references.
  ISBN: 978-1-937054-33-5 (hardcover)
  ISBN: 978-1-937054-32-8 (eBook)

1. Law--Oklahoma--Cases. 2. Trials--Oklahoma--Case studies. 3. Murder--Oklahoma--Case
studies. 4. Kelly, Machine Gun, 1897-1954--Trials, litigation, etc. 5. Silkwood, Karen,
1946-1974--Trials, litigation, etc. 6. Hall, David, 1930---Trials, litigation, etc. 7. Oklahoma
City Federal Building Bombing, Oklahoma City, Okla., 1995. I. Title.

HV6793.O5 F73 2014
364.1/09766349.766   2014948576
                          10 9 8 7 6 5 4 3 2 1

For my brother Rod, who always encouraged my writing

Oklahoma's Most Notorious Cases

Contents

The Sirloin Stockade Murders

The Oklahoma City Bombing

Notorious: *well-known or famous especially for something bad: generally known and talked of; especially: widely and unfavorably known: from the Latin* noscere *to come to know*

Introduction

The title of this book isn't meant to be tricky. It's designed to tell you what this book is about. But, does it do the job? For a lawyer, a straightforward statement is usually the best way to communicate.

That's not necessarily true for a writer of history.

Legal cases are, of course, about events, but they are more about people. They have heroes, and they have villains . . . sometimes *really* bad villains. Who the good guys and the bad guys are goes to the heart of any good legal case, or true story. How often has someone picked up the newspaper or turned on the television and asked himself, How could anyone do that? How could anyone be that evil?

It may well be fortunate that we cannot know the thought process of the most vicious criminals, but it would be disingenuous to pretend their crimes do not catch and hold our attention. As much as we'd like to understand what drives the villains, we are equally, if not more so, enamored by the heroism, resourcefulness, and pure tenacity of the law enforcement professionals who bring down these same criminals. It is somehow this ying and yang of our justice system that creates memorable cases.

In a world of instant news and constant communication we must remember it was not always like this. The shrill buzz of 24/7 coverage is a relatively new phenomenon. Newspaper stories, word-of-mouth accounts, radio bulletins, and early-day television reports spread the news in less graphic and slower ways. Trials remain a source of mass entertainment, but there was a time when people actually traveled from town to town to attend them, as fans today might travel for a sporting event.

The language used by reporters then was also different. Who could ignore a news story like the one that appeared on the front page of the *Tulsa World* on December 2, 1934, that began: "A fantastic pattern of crime that might have been woven by a drug-crazed denizen of the underworld, but instead was the product of the thrill mad sons of two of Tulsa's most prominent families proved the solution yesterday to the slaying shortly after midnight Thanksgiving of John F. Gorrell Jr." Such melodramatic reporting rarely failed to stir the hearts and minds of readers. Indeed, it created huge public interest in cases.

Those who solve crimes today have benefited from new developments in technology (wire taps, hidden cameras) and science (DNA analysis, forensic research). And the journalists who cover trials have benefited from the evolution of technology and electronic communication, particularly television.

Still the fundamentally important American tradition of trial by jury remains. That is the important and time-honored way we protect the rights of all American citizens.

Yet trials also produce the human drama that makes for notorious cases. For all the theories about how twenty-four-hour news coverage has impacted the way we observe and perceive trials, such coverage is unlikely to influence a trial's outcome.

What can influence the verdict? Good police work, improved forensic science, changes in law or procedure, and public opinion. The impact of each of these can be found in at least one case in this book.

What then makes for a notorious case? Some trials are so universally well known, we simply refer to them as the "Trial of Galileo" or the "Scopes Trial." But to rise to the level of notorious requires that a case be more than just ubiquitous, think "Lizzie Borden" or "Charles Mason," "John Hinckley Jr.," or "O.J. Simpson." Such cases carry a hint of evil, an indifference to one's fellowman not found in your average murderer or corrupt politician or thief.

In Oklahoma, cases that rise to that standard might be the "Machine Gun Kelly Case," "The Sirloin Stockade Murders," or "The Girl Scout Murders." How to recognize such a case recalls what U.S. Supreme Court Justice Potter Stewart once said in reference to pornography, "I know it when I see it."

The cases chosen for this book cover a wide swath of Oklahoma history from 1933 to 2004. Some older cases were rejected because of the lack of sufficient reliable records. No test or particular criteria was used to determine which cases to include: the choices were more intuitive based on a familiarity with Oklahoma history and a life of talking to lawyers and judges. Certainly other notorious Oklahoma crimes and cases exist and could have been included. Oklahoma has, after all, been a state for more than a hundred years now—plenty of time for way too much tragedy to find its way here and into court.

Still the six cases included here would seem to fit the bill: notorious, with enough evidence on record to illustrate it.

Each chapter in this book covers the account of at least one trial: The Urschel kidnapping generated two trials, as did the murderous acts of Roger Dale Stafford. And the Oklahoma City bombing case produced three trials, involving two perpetrators.

The lack of a trial also precluded the inclusion of the Mullendore murder case, which to this day remains unsolved. The Silkwood case, which is included, is the only case in this book involving a civil, rather than a criminal trial, but that trial was internationally publicized and included mysterious circumstances that mesmerized the public both then and now.

If the choice of cases found here is largely subjective, then you are entitled to know who it is that has made these choices. I am an Oklahoman by birth and with the exception of college and military service, have lived in Oklahoma my entire life. It is above all else, my home. A lawyer by trade for almost fifty years, I have tried cases all over the state; the courthouse is my natural habitat. History is my avocation and writing, a part of me I cannot deny. It is from this background that the cases included in the book come.

I have arranged the cases chronologically from the oldest to the most recent with the State's most notorious and infamous crime of all time, the bombing of the Alfred P. Murrah Federal Building, providing the final chapter.

In each case the backdrop is the historical era in which the events occurred from the Dust Bowl of the 1930s, through World War II, to the beginning of the twentieth-first century. I believe you will find all of the cases unique and memorable in some way.

In the case of the Machine Gun Kelly trial, it not only brought to justice one of the most notorious gangsters of the turbulent thirties, but also marked a number of firsts: It was the first case prosecuted under the Lindbergh Kidnapping Law. The first time movie cameras were allowed in a federal courtroom. The first time a suspect was transported by airplane, and the first big conviction for the United States' fledging Federal Bureau of Investigation.

The Gene Leroy Hart case equally captured the attention of the public some years later, if only because of its juxtaposition of horror and innocence. The crime was horrific; the victims, the essence of innocence. Add to that a Cherokee suspect who stayed on the run for years, and it is little wonder that folklore grew up around the case and Hart, who because of the contradicting narrative painted by some of the evidence became a scapegoat, or even a legend, to some.

In an era rife with political corruption highlighted by the Watergate Scandal in Washington, Oklahoma Governor David Hall would go on trial for bribery. His trial played out in the manner of a Shakespearean tragedy as a man of great natural talent and charisma fell from a lofty position of high office to disgrace and prison.

In the case of Karen Silkwood, her life, death, and, subsequent notoriety were more a matter of timing and circumstance. She became in death a martyr for the anti-nuclear movement and a symbol for the

Introduction

women's rights movement, giving the trial regarding her exposure to plutonium international implications.

In 1978, when six innocent people, four of them younger than eighteen years, were found slaughtered in an Oklahoma City restaurant, it marked the worst mass killing in Oklahoma history. The subsequent investigation and trial were more fascinating than most fictional plots, and the case became known as "The Sirloin Stockade Murders."

This book closes with the Oklahoma City bombing on April 19, 1995, the worst act of domestic terrorism in the history of the United States. To this day, it remains the most heinous terrorist crime ever perpetrated in America by a U.S. citizen.

Each of the six cases in this book helped shape the history of Oklahoma. Each in its own way tells us not just the story of a crime, but something more about Oklahoma and Oklahomans. The significance may lie in the case's impact on politics, law, law enforcement procedures, the mood of the times, or conflicts left unresolved. I hope by any definition you will find them notorious.

—**Kent Frates**
August 2014

Machine Gun Kelly &
The Urschel Kidnapping

"Several years ago, thousands of our citizens shivered
in fear of a kidnapper whose name had much to do with the
terror he engendered: he was called Machine-gun Kelly.
However, there was someone far more dangerous than
Machine-gun Kelly. That was Machine-gun Kelly's wife."

—J. Edgar Hoover, *Persons in Hiding*, 1938

CHAPTER ONE

The Kidnapping

CHARLES URSCHEL NEVER had need to shout to be heard. Quiet, polite, and private, he was respected for his intelligence, business acumen, and proven bravery. He was wealthy for his time and ours. Yet it was not his affluence that made him special, but rather the calm heroism he displayed in the face of death.

Ironically Urschel would have been happy to live his life without any public recognition, but his kidnapping by George "Machine Gun" Kelly made that impossible. His abduction launched him into the public spotlight and there he would remain.

. . . . .

The kidnapping had been planned for weeks. And on July 22, 1933, a quiet, sultry summer night in Oklahoma City, the plan was launched at 11:15 p.m., while Charles and his wife, Berenice, and Walter Jarrett and his wife, Clyde, played bridge on the screened porch of the Urschel mansion at 327 N.W. Eighteenth Street. The men wore shirtsleeves and the women, summer dresses. In their stately neighborhood, known today as Heritage Hills, a barking dog was cause for excitement.

As the cards were dealt, the porch door from the Urschel backyard flew open. Two men burst into the room—one armed with a submachine gun, the other with a six-shooter.

Unmasked, the intruders commanded, "Hands up! Don't move or make a sound, or we'll blow your heads off."

One of the gunmen, later identified as Kelly, nervously pointed his machine gun at the bridge players and demanded, "Which one of you is Urschel?"

Neither man at the bridge table responded.

The second gunman, Albert Bates, leveled his revolver at Urschel's head. Neither Urschel nor Jarrett flinched. Still uncertain as to who was who, Kelly barked, "We'll take you both."

With that the gunmen forced both men out of the house, but not before Kelly warned their wives not to report the crime if they wanted to ever see their husbands alive again.

. . . . .

Two worlds had by design collided. One, that of the gangster, a breed of man spawned by the Great Depression and the Dust Bowl, a reckless criminal who stormed across the Southwest robbing, kidnapping, and killing. The other, a man of great wealth, a man who had made his fortune in the oil business at a time when successful wildcatters were little more than sophisticated crapshooters searching for oil on guts and instinct.

It should come as no surprise then that Urschel, forty-three years old at the time and wealthy beyond most people's dreams, was a target for kidnapping.

His was a very Oklahoma story. After growing up on a farm in Ohio, he served in the Army during World War I and then returned home. Inspired by tales of the oil boom, he moved to Oklahoma where he landed in Cushing and entered a partnership with Tom Slick, a man already known by then as the "King of the Wildcatters."

Slick had discovered the Cushing oil field in 1912, but he and Urschel would develop the field together. For eight years the Cushing field was the nation's largest oil field; in 1919, it accounted for seventeen percent of the United States and three percent of world production of oil (in 1979 cumulative production had exceeded 450 million barrels of oil).

The duo discovered more oil in Oklahoma and Texas, growing wealthier with each new gusher. In 1929, when Slick sold his oil properties for a reported $35 million, Urschel owned a stake in the sale and reaped a bonus of $2 million for handling the transaction. After the sale, Slick wasted no time getting back into the oil business. As his partner, Urschel handled Slick's business in Oklahoma.

In 1930, Slick died at the age of forty-seven, and Urschel continued on alone in the business. After his wife's death, he married Slick's widow, Berenice, a union that combined two fortunes—both Slick's and Urschel's.

The Urschel home, which still stands today, was an elegant mansion in Oklahoma City's most exclusive residential neighborhood. Although not particularly flashy or flamboyant, Berenice was known to wear expensive jewelry and furs, and the couple collected fine art of the highest quality. And the vast extent of Slick's estate was widely known thanks to a fight with the State of Oklahoma over more than a million dollars owed in estate taxes.

There is little doubt that the kidnappers knew the Urschels were not your typical well-to-do Oklahoma City couple.

. . . . .

Kelly and Bates forced the two men through Urschel's backyard and into a waiting car, then fled Oklahoma City. In the countryside, the kidnappers identified Urschel by going through the men's wallets.

Jarrett was dumped near Luther, about twenty minutes northeast of the city. He walked to a main road, thumbed a ride back to Oklahoma City, and eventually returned to the Urschel house about four the next morning.

Unbeknownst to Urschel, his captors included one of the most famous gangsters of the prohibition era. George Barnes, aka George "Machine Gun" Kelly, was born in Chicago on July 17, 1900, but had grown up in Memphis, a product of an unremarkable middle-class family. Kelly began bootlegging whiskey while still in high school and soon married Geneva Ramsey, the daughter of a prominent local businessman. He tried working for his father-in-law in a legitimate business, but the straight life didn't suit him, and he turned again to bootlegging. A divorce came next, then a move to New Mexico. All the while his rap sheet grew longer.

In 1927, Kelly served time for a prohibition violation in a New Mexico state prison. In 1928, he was arrested for selling bootleg whiskey on an Indian reservation in Oklahoma and served two and a half years in the federal penitentiary at Leavenworth.

While in prison Kelly met a number of the criminals who had roamed the Midwest during the Golden Age of Bank Robbery, including Wilbur "Mad Dog" Underhill, Verne Miller, and Frank "Jelly" Nash. On his release Kelly traded bootlegging for bank robbing, committing numerous bank robberies in small towns across at least six states in the South and Southwest.

That fateful night in Oklahoma City, Kelly was joined by Albert Bates of Denver, Colorado. Bates was known as "The Man of Many Names" for his use of a long string of aliases. Bates's convictions included petty theft, burglary, bank robbery, safe cracking, and carrying a concealed weapon. He had also broken out of prison two times, in Utah and Colorado. He was suspected of having murdered a pair of burglary accomplices but he was never charged.

As impressive as the criminal dossiers of both Kelly and Bates were, neither was the leader of the gang. She wasn't along for the ride. History may not have made her a household name, like her husband, but Kelly's wife, Kathryn, was the force behind the Urschel kidnapping plot—from the planning stage to the execution of the crime. Gifted with a cunning and calculating mind, Kathryn manipulated both her husband and his criminal career to further her own ambitions.

Born Cleo Mae Brooks in 1904 in Saltillo, a small town in northeast Mississippi, she changed her name to Kathryn, considering it more stylish. Kelly was her fourth husband. The death of her third husband, Charlie Thorne, while ruled a suicide, left behind significant evidence suggesting that he had been murdered.

Kathryn liked expensive cars, jewelry, and clothes, and she hung out in speakeasies in Fort Worth, Texas. It was there that she had met Kelly and married him in 1930. While some women dream of a man who'll be home every night at five o'clock for dinner, Kathryn aspired to a marriage with a real-life gangster. No petty thief or small-time bank robber would do for Kathryn, and so she pushed her husband to rob more and bigger banks. It was Kathryn who purchased the machine gun that Kelly carried on those heists, and it was Kathryn who coined his nickname: Machine Gun Kelly.

In an attempt to further her husband's notoriety, she was known to carry spent machine-gun cartridges with her, handing them out among the denizens of the speakeasies she frequented as souvenirs of his many bank robberies.

There is actually no evidence that Kelly ever shot anyone, with a machine gun or otherwise. Such details didn't stop Kathryn. She forced her husband to practice his shooting at her stepfather's ranch, and, like any good spin-doctor, both concocted and spread stories about Kelly's prowess with the machine gun, or "Chicago typewriter" as it was known in gangland. According to Kathryn, George could shoot walnuts off a fence and spell his name with bullets.

The fact that on the biggest caper of his career, Kelly could not even recognize the man he had been sent to kidnap should come as no real surprise despite his reputation. He and Kathryn had attempted two previous kidnappings and failed badly at both. In one case they exchanged an Indiana banker for a bogus IOU.

At first blush, the Urschel kidnapping appeared to have been extensively planned and well executed, but as the case unfolded the general incompetence of the perpetrators would quickly become evident.

CHAPTER TWO

Not Your Normal Hostage

A S THE GETAWAY CAR sped toward the gangsters' hideout, Urschel began the methodical mental process that would ultimately lead to his kidnappers' downfall. Although bound, gagged, and blindfolded, he applied all of his senses to try and pinpoint the location of his captivity, the direction of their route, and the identity of his captors.

When the car stopped for fuel Urschel listened carefully to the gas-station attendant, and overheard him make a comment about a drought in the area that had hurt some crops but "didn't hurt the broomcorn any." At one point the getaway car slid off the road; another time the driver stopped to ask for directions. Urschel was able to estimate the timing of his trip from the sound of roosters crowing at dawn. He also remembered being on paved roads and leaving them for a rough dirt road just prior to reaching their destination.

Although the kidnappers had tried to make Urschel think they were traveling north, their destination was actually the Shannon Ranch in Wise County, Texas, northwest of Fort Worth, not too far from the town of Paradise. Owned by R.G. "Boss" Shannon, who was married to Kathryn's mother, Ora, the ranch was used as a hideout for criminals on the run, an arrangement facilitated by a corrupt sheriff on the take, who let Boss operate without interference in the county.

Upon arrival, Urschel committed himself to learning as much as possible about where he was held. Though he was blindfolded almost the entire time, he did not let that deter him from gathering what clues he could. He was put in what he believed to be a tin-roofed garage, something he deduced from hearing rain ping on the roof and picking up the smell of gasoline and oil.

Having grown up on a farm Urschel recognized the sounds of horses, cattle, dogs, chickens, guineas, and quail. When taken from the garage, he counted the steps to the next structure, which he ascertained to be a house. This was the first of a number of calculations and deductions he made regarding his place of captivity, and later they were what allowed him to construct a detailed map of the premises that proved remarkably accurate.

After being moved from the garage to the house, Urschel was taken for a short automobile ride to a small shack on the property where Boss's son, Armon "Potatoes" Shannon, lived. During his captivity, Urschel overheard the nicknames of both Shannons, as well as scraps of conversation about nearby neighbors, including a supposed young prostitute.

At the new location, Urschel was chained to a metal bed. Other than to write a ransom note, he remained blindfolded for his entire captivity. And he continued to collect more clues. He convinced his guards to allow him to shuffle around the room in the name of his health, and by doing so, identified not only furniture but also the dimensions and characteristics of the shack where he was being held. He left his fingerprints on as many spots as possible, and scratched marks into the metal bed.

Afterwards, he would recall drinking water with a strong sulfur taste from a tin cup with a broken handle. He made note that the accents of his captors were Oklahoma or Texas drawls. He identified all of the animals kept on the farm, and by random questioning of the somewhat simple-minded Potatoes, learned how many of each animal there were. He recognized that at times he was being guarded by an older man, a man Urschel would later identify by his voice as Boss Shannon.

One could be forgiven for wondering how the size of a room or the taste of water could matter in a high profile kidnapping such as Urschel's, but, in fact, all of the clues that Urschel collected would prove to be helpful in solving the crime.

The single most important clue came the day he heard an airplane fly over and then later that same day, a plane fly back in the other direction. After counting how long he could hear the noise of the airplane and then asking questions of his guards, he established that the plane flew over each day at 9:45 in the morning and 5:45 in the afternoon. On Sunday, the plane did not fly over in the morning. This fact would prove to be essential in locating the Shannon Ranch.

CHAPTER THREE

The FBI

WHILE URSCHEL WAS BEING held for nine days at the Shannon Ranch in rural Texas, another side of the story was unfolding in Oklahoma City. Berenice Urschel had quickly called the police after the crime, despite Kelly's threat. And, because she had just read a *Time* magazine article in which citizens were urged to inform the FBI of any kidnapping, she also contacted the FBI and spoke directly with its new thirty-eight-year-old director, J. Edgar Hoover. Hoover assigned one of his best agents, Gus Jones, a former Texas Ranger to the case. Jones hurried from Texas to Oklahoma City to take control of the hunt for Urschel and his kidnappers.

The entry of the FBI into kidnapping cases marked a new era in law enforcement. Formed in 1908, the FBI had until now limited the role of its agents to acting as low profile investigators for the U.S. Justice Department. FBI agents traditionally had little to do with violent crimes, which were handled on a local basis by sheriffs and police.

The role of the FBI changed in 1932, when Charles Lindbergh's young son was abducted and killed. Congress quickly reacted to the tragedy by passing the Lindbergh Act, making kidnapping a federal crime punishable up to life imprisonment. In 1934, the death penalty would be authorized as punishment for kidnapping, but it was not an available punishment at the time of the Urschel case.

Prohibition and the Great Depression had made some criminals sympathetic in the eyes of the public. Then the Lindberghs lost their son and later four lawmen died in the 1933 Kansas City Massacre—killed, along with Frank "Jelly" Nash, in a failed attempt by three machine-gun-toting hoods to free Jelly from prison. Prior to the Lindbergh case and the Kansas City Massacre, even respectable members of the public had maintained an ambivalent attitude toward some criminals, often seeing bank robbers as Robin Hood-type characters, fostered by desperate economic times and bank failures. There was, however, no public tolerance for kidnapping or murder, and overnight it became politically expedient to press the prosecution of these crimes.

The U.S. Justice Department led by Franklin D. Roosevelt's new attorney general, Homer Stille Cummings, joined wholeheartedly in what Roosevelt called "the war on crime." Among other actions, Cummings appointed Assistant Attorney General Joseph B. Keenan as special counsel to assist local district attorneys with the prosecution of particularly heinous crimes. Keenan, who had a reputation as an aggressive trial lawyer, was described by one contemporary newspaper as "fat and fierce." He became the director of Justice's criminal division, and he later gained international stature as chief prosecutor for the International Military Tribunal for the Far East after World War II, in charge of prosecuting Japanese war criminals.

Needless to say, when Berenice made her call to the FBI, she mobilized the formidable investigative and prosecutorial forces of the U.S. Justice Department on a case that would prove to be the department's first high profile victory in the war on crime, though victory was no given in the beginning.

Upon Jones's arrival in Oklahoma City he was faced with a chaotic scene at the Urschel mansion: Police guarded the house and the entire neighborhood was overrun by reporters and curious onlookers. The Urschel family was also besieged by bogus contacts from crackpots and opportunists providing false information or demanding ransom money. Jones and the local agent in charge, R.H. Colvin, had to sort through the false contacts, and, despite their best efforts, a thousand dollars was paid to one phony kidnapper.

CHAPTER FOUR

The Ransom

THREE DAYS AFTER the kidnapping, the real ransom note was finally delivered. Oilman and Urschel friend John Catlett received an anonymous package at his home in Tulsa. The package contained three letters—two were in Urschel's handwriting, signed by him, one addressed to Berenice and the other to either Arthur Seeligson or E.E. Kirkpatrick. Seeligson was Urschel's brother in law and one of three trustees handling Tom Slick's multimillionaire dollar estate. Kirkpatrick was a trusted business associate of Urschel, who would figure prominently in the delivery of the ransom money. Also included in the package were Urschel's identification cards.

The third letter was typewritten by the kidnappers and contained detailed instructions regarding the ransom. The letter demanded the sum of two hundred thousand dollars to be delivered in twenty-dollar bills, the equivalent of around $3 million in today's currency and the highest known ransom sum ever demanded at the time. The letter went on to threaten to kill Urschel for any kind of "Double XX" or attempt to record the serial numbers on the bills.

As a signal that the ransom money would be paid, the letter directed that a blind ad be run in the real estate section of the *Daily Oklahoman* for one week setting out the specific terms for the sale of a small farm. All further communications would be to the post office box assigned by the *Daily Oklahoman*. There was no doubt this ransom note was real, and in spite of the vast sum demanded, Berenice immediately directed Seeligson to arrange for the money. Urschel would later say his first draft of a letter had advised Catlett, "If the amount they [ask is] excessive not to attempt to raise it, but let it go, and it would be okay with me." That had infuriated the kidnappers, who made Urschel tear up the note and write another, which they dictated with a gun to his head. The ransom money was obtained and, despite the warning to the contrary, the serial numbers laboriously recorded by hand. Many innocent inquiries were received about the farm property and then an airmail special delivery letter addressed to Kirkpatrick arrived, postmarked Joplin, Missouri.

The letter instructed Kirkpatrick to place the money in a "light colored leather bag" and proceed alone to Kansas City on the MKT line, Train 28 (*The Sooner*), on Saturday, July 29. Kirkpatrick was to ride on the observation platform and watch for a fire alongside the tracks. If he saw the fire and then a second fire, he was to throw the bag from the train at the point of the second fire. If he did not see a fire, he was to go to the Muehlebach Hotel, check in under the name E.E. Kincaid, and await further instructions. The letter carried the threat,

> Remember this—if any trickery is attempted you will
> find the remains of Urschel and instead of joy there will
> be double grief—for, someone very near and dear to the
> Urschel family is under constant surveillance and will
> likewise suffer for your error.

Law enforcement authorities agreed that for Urschel and his family's safety, Kirkpatrick should follow the plan without any intervention or surveillance from them. So on Saturday at 10:10 p.m., Kirkpatrick boarded the train as instructed. However, fearful that someone might try to hijack the money, he carried a concealed automatic pistol. Additionally, Catlett snuck on to the train with an identical bag stuffed with newspapers to be used if a hijack was attempted.

The trip was tense but uneventful. No fires were observed, and Kirkpatrick, accompanied by Catlett, checked into the Muehlebach as directed. "Mr. Kincaid" received a telegram Sunday morning from "C.H. Moore" stating he would receive a phone call around six.

At 5:30 a.m., the phone rang, and Kirkpatrick was ordered to come to a location near the LaSalle Hotel and to walk down the street carrying the bag with the ransom money. Kirkpatrick said he had a friend with him who he wanted to accompany him, but was advised that the kidnappers knew about the friend and ordered Kirkpatrick to come alone and unarmed.

Kirkpatrick followed their instructions, and Catlett remained at the hotel. Kirkpatrick was walking down the street near the LaSalle Hotel when he was accosted by a tall, well-dressed man who demanded the bag. Kirkpatrick asked when Urschel would be returned and was told Urschel would be released within twelve hours.

During the exchange Kirkpatrick got a good look at the pickup man. He dropped the bag on the sidewalk and, as ordered, turned and walked away to the sound of a car door slamming and a car speeding away. It was later learned that an accomplice had Kirkpatrick covered during the entire exchange and at any false move he had been prepared to shoot Kirkpatrick.

CHAPTER FIVE

The Hunt

KIRKPATRICK HUSTLED BACK to the hotel, relieved but still uncertain about Urschel's fate. He delivered the news of the ransom payoff to Berenice by telephone and returned to Oklahoma City by train. At the Urschel mansion he joined a tense vigil with Berenice and her entire family. There were no assurances that Urschel would return or even if he was still alive, but given the circumstances all they could do was hope.

When Urschel did not show up within twelve hours as promised, doubt began to set in. Finally, at 11:30 p.m., Monday, July 31, a gaunt and disheveled Urschel presented himself at his own front door to a policeman guarding the house. Unrecognized by the guard, Urschel was only admitted after Arthur Seeligson identified him. The FBI was anxious to question Urschel, but at Berenice's insistence the debriefing was delayed until the next morning.

That Urschel was alive and home at all was almost an accident. Evidence at Kathryn Kelly's trial later revealed that she had wanted to kill Urschel to eliminate any possibility he might have information to use against the kidnappers. It was only after an argument with George and Bates that she was overruled. Whether the kidnappers feared a murder charge or had more devious motives is not known. Possibly they reasoned that if this victim was killed they would never be able to extract ransom in any future kidnappings or, maybe, George just wasn't a murderer at heart. In any event, Kathryn's assessment of Urschel's danger to them as a witness proved correct.

Jones and Colvin begin to debrief Urschel the next morning and quickly learned that he was full of information that could assist in apprehending his captors. After reciting the details of his release near Norman some twenty-five miles south of Oklahoma City, Urschel began disclosing the evidence he had meticulously accumulated about the kidnappers' hideout during his captivity.

The agents were particularly fascinated by his account of the plane flights and immediately set to work using that clue to pursue finding the location of the hideout. Since this was long before global positioning satellites or other sophisticated GPS-like tracking devices were available, the search for the interrupted plane flight had to be carried out by sheer hard work. On the other hand, airplane travel was far less common in 1933 and so not as many flights required checking.

The FBI chose flights within a radius of six hundred miles of Oklahoma City based on the duration of Urschel's trip from the hideout back to Norman. The records of commercial flights were checked, as was the daily weather within the target area. By cross-checking these records it was determined that a flight from Dallas to Amarillo had been delayed and then rerouted on the date Urschel had missed hearing the morning plane.

The conversation Urschel had overheard on his trip to the hideout about a drought also helped confirm that he had traveled south from Oklahoma City on the night he was taken. This information allowed the agents to identify Wise County, Texas, as the likely location of the hideout. An open biplane was flown over the suspected area looking for a farm similar to what Urschel had described. An agent, posing as a banker offering to refinance mortgages, canvased the area with a map of the hideout reconstructed from the information Urschel had supplied to Jones. The agent visited the Shannon Ranch and verified that it matched Urschel's description. His visit also confirmed one of Urschel's other clues when the agent was offered a drink of water in a cup with a broken handle. The water tasted of sulfur.

On August 12, the FBI organized a raid on the ranch that included federal agents and Texas lawmen. In a unique move the FBI allowed Urschel, armed with a shotgun, to accompany the posse. Jones moved quickly, fearing a tip-off that might alert the suspects. At dawn, the raiders on foot approached the ranch. They found a man asleep on the porch of the house. Nearby was a machine gun and under his pillow they found a pistol. Covered by the heavily armed group, the startled suspect was identified as Harvey Bailey, one of the most notorious criminals of the day.

A known killer, Bailey was a suspect in the Kansas City Massacre. Three months before the Urschel kidnapping, Bailey had led a breakout from the Lansing Prison in Kansas, kidnapping the warden and killing a guard. He also had taken part in the robbery of the Lincoln Trust Company in Omaha, Nebraska, a holdup in which the robbers got away with $2 million, at the time the biggest heist in U.S. history. Recuperating at the ranch from a gunshot wound suffered in the prison break it was Bailey's bad luck to be caught with $680 of the ransom money in his possession. Although he probably had nothing to do with Urschel's actual kidnapping he would go down for the rap.

The posse quickly rounded up Boss, Ora, and Potatoes and his wife. Although told to keep his mouth shut, Potatoes immediately spilled his guts, identifying Kelly and Bates as the kidnappers and admitting his part in holding Urschel prisoner. The posse released Potatoes's wife after determining that she had played no part in the crime.

Urschel confirmed the ranch as the location of his captivity and was able to identify both Boss and Armon by their voices. He thanked Ora for the fried chicken dinner she had cooked and served him (his only real meal as a hostage), and joined the FBI in celebrating the capture of at least some of the gang. The real kidnappers, however, were still on the loose, and given their repeated threats, a danger to Urschel and his family that triggered a nationwide manhunt.

Bailey and the others were transported to the "unbreakable" Dallas County Jail. The local sheriff bragged that his jail was the safest in the country, and Bailey was housed in its most secure area, behind seven different metal doors. In spite of gangland threats, the sheriff was sure Bailey couldn't break out. His overconfidence was unwarranted. The jail itself may have been secure, but the sheriff's personnel weren't. Ten thousand dollars in bribes spread between a deputy sheriff and a jailer was all it took to spring Bailey. Someone sawed the bars on his cell and even provided him with a pistol. Bailey then took an unsuspecting guard hostage, forced his way out of the jail at gunpoint, and commandeered the car of another jailer, who he also used as a hostage.

His escape didn't last long. Bailey headed north toward Oklahoma, but rainy conditions forced him to travel the main roads. In Ardmore, just across the Oklahoma state line, an alert police chief intercepted the fleeing bank robber and a high speed chase ensued. Bailey was apprehended when his car turned over during the chase. He was immediately taken to Oklahoma City, where he was jailed along with Boss, Ora, and Potatoes. This time the Feds took no chances and set up twenty-four-hour guards armed with machine guns and teargas bombs. Bailey had made his last escape on the FBI's watch.

While Bailey was housed in the Dallas jail, Bates had been arrested in Denver for suspicion of car theft. Authorities found some of the ransom money on Bates and recognized him as a suspect in the Urschel kidnapping. He was quickly transported to Oklahoma City, joining his buddies in the county slammer. The crafty Bates, however, had gotten word to a woman companion to hide the rest of his share of the ransom money. Pressure was put on Bates to make a deal and reveal the location of the cash, but he refused to cave, although some of Bates's ransom money was later discovered.

Meanwhile, the government pressed ahead on two fronts: A criminal case was filed in U.S. District Court for the Western District of Oklahoma and all of the suspects, including the Kellys, were indicted by a grand jury. Bates, Bailey, and the Shannons were set for trial on September 18, along with seven men from the Minneapolis area charged with laundering part of the ransom money.

In keeping with the times, wanted posters of the Kellys were plastered all over the country, and law enforcement organizations were alerted to be on the lookout for George and Kathryn.

CHAPTER SIX

On the Run

A SEPARATE DRAMA WAS playing out between George and Kathryn. The couple was careening back and forth across the United States, covering some twenty thousand miles and criss-crossing a dozen or more states with stops from Cleveland to Chicago and San Antonio to Biloxi, Mississippi.

George had dyed his hair blonde and Kathryn was wearing a red wig. The couple frequently bought and exchanged cars—one day driving a sixteen cylinder Cadillac in Cleveland and a few days later steering a pickup in Louisiana. Their behavior was increasingly as erratic as their travels.

George, drinking heavily, had become paranoid and fearful, insisting they move on the slightest hint that someone might have identified them. For her part, Kathryn was enraged with the government for arresting and prosecuting Ora and Boss. Increasingly she blamed George for all this, especially for not killing Urschel. Obsessed with trying to also help her mother, Kathryn addressed a letter to Joseph B. Keenan, the federal special prosecutor, which stated in part:

The entire Urschel family and friends and all of you will be exterminated soon. There is no way I can prevent it. I will gladly put George Kelly on the spot for you if you will save my mother, who is innocent of any wrongdoing. If you do not comply with this request, there is no way in which I can prevent the most awful tragedy. If you refuse my offer I shall commit some minor offense and be placed in jail so that you will know that I have no connection with the terrible slaughter that will take place in Oklahoma City within the next few days.

After the Shannon trial began, Charles received another letter:

Ignorant Charles: Just a few lines to let you know that I am getting my plans made to destroy your so-called mansion, and you and your family immediately after this trial. And you fellow, I guess you've begun to realize your serious mistake. Are you ignorant enough to think the Government can guard you forever. I gave you credit for more sense than that, and figured you thought too much of your family to jeopardize them as you have, but if you don't look out for them, why should we. I dislike hurting the innocent, but I told you exactly what would happen and you can bet $200,000 more everything I said will be true. You are living on borrowed time now.

You know that the Shannon family are victims of circumstances the same as you was. You don't seem to mind prosecuting the innocent, neither will I have any conscious qualms over brutally murdering your family. The Shannons have put the heat on, but I don't desire to see them prosecuted as they are innocent and I have a much better method of settling with them. As far as the guilty being punished you would probably have lived the rest of your life in peace had you tried only the guilty, but if the Shannons are convicted look out, and God help you for he is the only one that will be able to do you any good. In the event of my arrest I've already formed an outfit to take care of and destroy you and yours the same as if I was there. I am spending your money to have you and your family killed—nice eh? You are bucking people who have cash—planes, bombs, and unlimited connections both here and abroad. I have friends in Oklahoma City that know every move and every plan you make, and you are still too dumb to figure out the finger man there.

If my brain was no larger than yours, the Government would have had me long ago, as it is I am drinking good beer and will yet see you and your family like I should have left you at first—stone dead.

I don't worry about Bates and Bailey. They will be out for the ceremonies—your slaughter.

Now I say it is up to you; if the Shannons are convicted, you can get another rich wife in hell, because that will be the only place you can use one. Adios, smart one.

Your worst enemy,

 Geo. R. Kelly

I will put my fingerprints below so you can't say some crank wrote this.

Give Keenan my regards and tell him maybe he would like to meet the owner of the above.

See you in hell.

Keenan, Hyde, and Judge Vaught also received death threats signed by Kelly. Later, evidence at the Kelly trial indicated Kathryn had authored the letters.

CHAPTER SEVEN

The First Trial

THE TRIAL OF BATES, BAILEY, and the Shannons, and the money launderers, began in the federal court in Oklahoma City on September 18, as scheduled. The magnificent ceremonial courtroom where the trial took place is preserved today and now houses the U.S. Bankruptcy Court. The large room with its vaulted ceiling looks like what a court should, paying homage to justice and the prestige and power of the federal courts.

Joining Keenan in the prosecution was Herbert Hyde, the U.S. district attorney for the Western District of Oklahoma. At the time, the thirty-five-year-old Hyde was the youngest U.S. district attorney in the country. A real firebrand he sensed this was a trial of a lifetime and hungered for a conviction. Together these two men would fiercely prosecute all of the defendants.

Presiding over the trial was Judge Edgar S. Vaught. A stern, law-and-order judge, Vaught was sixty years old and had been on the bench for five years. He would serve as a federal judge until 1956. Previously, he had been superintendent of Oklahoma City Public Schools before deciding to become a lawyer. He never attended law school but educated himself by reading the law and was admitted to the Oklahoma Territorial Bar in 1905.

In those days federal juries were referred to as "blue ribbon" juries. How they were picked was not fully known even to trial lawyers, but they were uniformly conservative and composed of twelve white males. Not exactly a judge and jury a defendant wanted to face in a criminal trial.

As for the trial, it was historic for a number of reasons. It was the first kidnapping case tried under the Lindbergh Law and the first case in which moving picture cameras were allowed in a federal courtroom. The case was also important to the newly constituted FBI, a chance to prove that the Bureau could investigate, arrest, and convict major dangerous criminals.

The trial received international attention from the press, and the courtroom was packed to overflowing every day with spectators who lined up hours beforehand to obtain a seat or even a chance to stand in the back of the court, a departure from usual decorum. Because of the threats made by the Kellys, the courthouse was ringed with armed guards and the Urschels, the prosecutors, and the judge were all heavily guarded, both in and out of court. The defendants were transported to and from the jail in an armored car.

Prior to and during the course of the Bates Bailey trial and the subsequent Kelly trial, the FBI, led by Hoover, kept up a constant barrage of publicity. Kelly was branded as a dangerous killer even though he had never killed anyone, and Hoover categorized the defendants as "dirty yellow rats." At the same time the government and the FBI were portrayed as heroes in a relentless fight against crime. The media bought into Hoover's description and sensationalized the case by characterizing Bates, Bailey, and Kelly as vicious killers.

The highlight of the trial itself was the testimony of Charles Urschel. Undaunted by the threats to him and his family, he took the stand and calmly buried the defendants under an avalanche of facts.

He meticulously documented the details of his captivity and specifically identified Bates, Boss, and Potatoes. Berenice and Mrs. Jarrett also confirmed the identification of Bates. Potatoes admitted his part in the crime and identified Bates and Kelly as the kidnappers and Boss as one of Urschel's guards.

The Shannons, faced with so much undisputable evidence of their involvement, asserted that they were forced to take part in the crime by Kelly and Bates under fear for their lives. Ora said they had been threatened with machine guns and forced to participate. Boss testified that he did not call the police for fear that his family would be murdered.

Bailey, while not actually involved beyond being caught with a little ransom money, did not mount a defense. Given his criminal record he could ill afford to take the stand, and simply resigned himself to his fate. Regardless of the outcome of the trial he was headed back to prison for a long time, due to his prior convictions and recent escapes. Bates also did not take the stand.

As the trial progressed it became increasingly clear that Judge Vaught believed the government's case and had little use for the defendants or their stories. When he instructed the jury he advised the jurors that the Shannons' excuses for holding and guarding Urschel "did not constitute a defense at law."

In closing arguments, Hyde and Keenan urged the jury to send a message to the underworld that kidnapping would not be tolerated. And that is exactly what the jury did, finding Bates, Bailey, Boss, Ora, and Potatoes all guilty of kidnapping, although they recommended leniency for Potatoes. Two of the money launderers were convicted; five others were found not guilty.

Judge Vaught set sentencing for the next morning and then he made a brief but telling statement before pronouncing judgment. His words included the following: "Something is more at stake in the trial of this case than the mere punishment . . . The question before the American people today is whether or not crime will be recognized as an occupation or a profession, or whether the people will enforce the laws of the nation as they are written. So far as this court is concerned, it is its purpose to try to enforce the laws as they are written."

The judge delivered his real message by sentencing Bates, Bailey, Boss, and Ora to life imprisonment. Potatoes was given a ten-year suspended sentence and placed under the supervision of his attorney. The verdicts and sentences were later affirmed on appeal.

CHAPTER EIGHT

Capturing the Kellys

WHILE THE BATES BAILEY trial proceeded, the Kellys remained at large. Their erratic behavior had helped in avoiding arrest, but their luck would not last. George and Kathryn decided to split up for a while. During their separation, Kathryn picked up the hitchhiking Arnold family: Luther, his wife Flossie, and their twelve-year-old daughter, Geraldine. Typical of many out-of-work, homeless families displaced by the Depression, the Arnolds gladly accepted Kathryn's aid, even after she disclosed her identity.

For her part, Kathryn used the Arnolds for cover and as messengers. She sent Luther to Fort Worth to tell an attorney to advise prosecutors she would trade George for the release of her mother. When this offer was rejected, Luther was dispatched to Oklahoma City to hire an attorney for Ora and Boss. After Kathryn reunited with George, the couple borrowed Geraldine as cover and continued their travels north to Chicago and then back south into Texas.

George found a place to hide out in his hometown of Memphis, contacted his ex-brother-in-law, Langford Ramsey, and convinced him to take Geraldine with him and to retrieve some of the ransom money, which was buried on the Texas farm of Cass Coleman, Kathryn's cousin. Coleman refused to cooperate, and Geraldine was returned to her parents in Oklahoma City.

Involving the Arnold family proved to be the Kellys' undoing. Luther couldn't keep his mouth shut and was picked up in Oklahoma City by authorities after bragging about his connection to the Kellys. Geraldine was able to identify Memphis as the whereabouts of George and Kathryn, and the FBI began to close the trap.

On the morning of September 26, while the Bates Bailey trial progressed in Oklahoma City, a heavily armed posse burst into the house where George and Kathryn were staying in Memphis. Although armed with a handgun, George immediately surrendered when a deputy sheriff rammed a shotgun into his stomach. Kathryn was asleep in the bedroom, but was awakened and arrested.

In spite of their bravado, the Kellys had been taken without a fight, though not without a scene. Kathryn, enraged, raved against the government for prosecuting her mother. She was cuffed and chained along with George and taken to the Memphis jail. The Kellys were flown to Oklahoma City, marking another legal milestone, the first time criminal defendants in the U.S. were transported by airplane.

The FBI fostered a story that George had thrown his hands in the air and shouted "Don't shoot G-men, don't shoot," thus coining a term that would become popular for years to come when describing FBI agents. Although contrary to the facts, the story stuck and was often repeated in the press, helping to enhance the stature of the FBI and its agents. Hoover was ecstatic and did nothing to dispel this apocryphal account.

CHAPTER NINE

The Kelly Trial

UPON LANDING IN Oklahoma City, the Kellys were greeted by an army of lawmen accompanied by Charles and Berenice. Both of the Urschels identified George as one of the kidnappers. After being checked into the Oklahoma City jail, the Kellys made their first court appearance at the same time as the sentencing of the Bates Bailey defendants. It was widely believed the couple would plead guilty, and both the prosecutor and the judge were angered by their not guilty pleas. A trial for the Kellys was set for just nine days away.

Based on information furnished by Geraldine, Jones and other agents had proceeded to Cass Coleman's farm. Coleman cooperated with the agents and identified the field and place where the Kellys had buried the ransom money. The agents then began to dig. They recovered $73,250, buried in a thermos jug and a coffee can.

The government juggernaut was rolling now, and with Vaught's cooperation there would be no let up. The judge received yet another threatening letter, this one anonymous. His reaction was to once again deny motions for continuances and change of venue and instead start the Kellys' trial as scheduled before a new jury on October 9. Once again Urschel took the stand, this time identifying George as one of his kidnappers. He was never questioned about Kathryn, and had he been, he wouldn't have had anything to say as he had no personal evidence or knowledge of her involvement.

There was, however, extensive testimony from the Arnold family about statements that Kathryn had made regarding the kidnapping and Urschel. According to Mrs. Arnold, Kathryn had told her that she "would like to kill the son of a bitch herself." Mr. Arnold testified that the Kellys had also discussed how they should have "took him out in Arizona and buried him." Geraldine stated that Kathryn said she was going to kill "Judge Vaught, Keenan, Urschel, and Hyde."

Kathryn was also implicated by members of the Cass Coleman family who recited a conversation at the Coleman farm the day before the kidnapping, in which George predicted a kidnapping in Oklahoma City and Kathryn told the couple "we're going to be in the big money before long." She was also tied to the spending of the ransom money.

Although not necessary for conviction, a piece of evidence that later proved dubious was introduced. Two of the threatening letters sent by George to Urschel were attributed to Kathryn by a somewhat goofy handwriting expert. How much this testimony aided the prosecution is, of course, unknown, but it would open the door for questioning the fairness of the trial at a later date.

As if the case was not already sensational enough, George provided even more fireworks. He became involved in an altercation with an FBI agent near the elevator in the lobby outside the courtroom and was pistol-whipped across the head by one of the agents. The beating produced a cut and knots on his head, leaving George to view most of the proceedings with a bloody handkerchief pressed to his wounds. George did not testify and was largely quiet during the trial, although he did renew his threats against Urschel and at one point made a motion with his finger slitting his throat as he faced Charles.

The climax of the trial was Kathryn's testimony in her own defense.

She denied any pre-knowledge of the crime and said she was forced to participate under fear for her life. She tried to characterize herself as an innocent victim in fear of her safety and painted George as a dangerous murderer armed with a machine gun. Her testimony was melodramatic and punctuated by tears. Years later in a petition to the U.S. Board of Parole, Gus Jones recalled Kathryn and described her thusly: "The writer [referring to himself] had occasion to observe and study Kathryn Kelly, while she was incarcerated in the Oklahoma County Jail and in the courtroom during the trial of the case. She is, putting it mildly, an enigma. She is a consummate actress possessed of a dual personality. I honestly believe that she is the most dangerous woman I have ever handled."

Kathryn was also a difficult and temperamental prisoner, complaining often about her treatment in jail and the jail food. Judge Vaught found her to be untruthful and gave the jury the unusual instruction that he believed Kathryn not to be "wholly truthful" and with "knowledge of the abduction conspiracy," though he did advise that the jury could disregard his remarks. The jury agreed with the judge, taking only an hour to find both George and Kathryn guilty. Once again, Judge Vaught put the hammer down and sentenced both of the Kellys to life imprisonment. After sentencing, Kathryn reportedly remarked, "If my Pekinese dog had been on trial he would have been given a life sentence." The Kellys' conviction and sentence were affirmed on appeal.

When Kathryn was told Urschel was going to file suit against her and try to obtain her jewelry for what he and his family had been put through, she told Colvin, "It won't do him any good. He hasn't much longer to live."

Remarkably, all of the perpetrators of the Urschel kidnapping were caught, tried, and convicted in only eighty-one days from the date the crime was committed. Although all of the guilty parties were in prison, aspects of the case would persist for many years.

CHAPTER TEN

Aftermath

A BREAKTHROUGH REGARDING recovery of more of the ransom money occurred more than a year later in November 1934. The FBI had received leads indicating that some of the money was located in the Pacific Northwest. In the aftermath of an auto accident, a suspect who was injured in the crash was found to be in possession of about thirteen hundred dollars of Urschel's ransom money. His arrest led to the further apprehension of Bates's female companion, or "wife," Clara Davis/Feldman/Bates.

The FBI recovered more parcels of the money from Davis and other suspects, and Urschel and Kirkpatrick flew to Oregon to help question Davis. After interrogation by the FBI and long conversations with Urschel and Kirkpatrick, Davis finally led agents to a deep canyon thirty-six miles northwest of Portland where she had buried $28,600 in a thermos jug. Agents dug up the buried money and along with the other monies recovered a total of $44,000. Judge Vaught later gave Clara Davis and her associates suspended sentences based on their co-operation with the government.

After sentencing, Kelly, Bailey, Bates, and Boss were taken to the federal penitentiary in Leavenworth, Kansas. Bailey, Bates, and Kelly were later transferred to Alcatraz in the San Francisco Bay when it opened, billed at the time as the nation's most secure prison. Kathryn and Ora did time at several women's prisons, eventually landing at a federal prison in Alderson, West Virginia.

Oddly, both Kelly and Bates wrote letters to Urschel from prison. Kelly had such respect for Urschel that on April 11, 1940, he wrote asking for advice in connection with making an oil and gas lease on the Shannon Ranch. In his lengthy letter, Kelly bemoaned his fate but also found time to poke fun at the oilman:

> How is your bridge game? Are you still vulnerable? I don't mean that as a dirty dig but you must admit you lost your bid on the night of July 22, 1933.

Contrary to some reports, Urschel never replied to Kelly's letter.

On June 19, 1942, Bates wrote Urschel, finally admitting the receipt of $93,750 of the ransom money. The purpose of his letter was to request clemency for Ora, who he stated took no part in the crime.

Urschel apparently responded, as Bates refers to a letter from Urschel in a second correspondence dated September 29, 1942. In his second letter, Bates discloses the split that was made between the two. Kelly first took $11,500 off the top of what Bates called the "nut" as expenses. The two men each then took $94,250, but each gave $500 to Bailey who was present at the ranch.

Why Bailey was paid is not explained nor is it known whether the Shannons received a part of the nut. Bates goes on to say he spent some of the money, but left $91,000 for Clara to hide.

This remains the best explanation of the disposal of the ransom funds available. Various accounts report that between $126,000 and $141,000 were recovered by Urschel, but the exact recovery is unknown.

Bates died in Alcatraz in 1948. Kelly was returned to Leavenworth and died there on his fifty-ninth birthday in 1954. Bailey was paroled from federal prison in 1962. He was transferred to the Kansas State Prison to serve his term for his 1933 escape, but his sentence was commuted and he was released in 1965. Thereafter he resided in Joplin, Missouri, where he worked as a cabinetmaker, lived at the YMCA, and died in 1979 at the age of ninety-one.

After his sentence was commuted to twenty years, Boss was paroled in 1944. He returned to his ranch and died in 1956.

CHAPTER ELEVEN

Kathryn & Ora Set Free

THE POSTSCRIPT FOR Kathryn and Ora is far more complicated and controversial. After repeated attempts at parole were
denied, the two women were able to persuade Washington,
D.C., attorney James J. Laughlin to attempt to reopen the case and obtain a new trial. In 1958, Laughlin filed a petition in district court on
behalf of Kathryn and Ora, alleging that they had failed to receive a fair
trial on a variety of grounds, including inadequate assistance of counsel, use of testimony known to be false, denial of compulsory service of
process, and conduct of the trial in an atmosphere that prevented a fair
and impartial trial.

A hearing was held in Oklahoma City and some of the participants
in the Kelly trial testified again under oath, including Hyde and Kathryn's defense attorney, James Mather. During the hearing, Laughlin
made a request for all the files the justice department had relating to
the prosecution of the Kelly case. Presiding Judge W.R. Wallace re-
cessed the hearing and after some deliberation ordered the government
to produce the files. In spite of this order, the government refused to do

so. Wallace then vacated the defendants' sentences, granted them a new trial, and set bond for them. Ora and Kathryn were released on bond. Judge Wallace's ruling was later reversed on appeal by the Tenth Circuit Court of Appeals, but the government never produced the files, and Kathryn and Ora were never arrested and returned to jail, remaining free for the rest of their lives.

Later it was learned through the discovery of an internal U.S. Justice Department memo that the testimony given by the handwriting expert identifying two of the threatening letters as being written by Kathryn was flawed and known to be questionable by the FBI before it was offered at trial. The letters had first been reviewed by internal FBI experts who did not believe they were written by Kathryn. In spite of this, the expert was allowed to testify to the contrary. There was no evidence that the prosecutors knew of the FBI's prior analysis, but given this inflammatory fact, the FBI chose not to release its files and the matter was never aired in court or publicized.

After their release, both Ora and Kathryn remained in Oklahoma. Kathryn worked as a bookkeeper and took care of her mother, who died in 1980. Kathryn died in 1985 while living in Tulsa. She steadfastly maintained her innocence until her death.

Charles Urschel went on to live a long and productive life. Always extremely private, he stayed away from any personal publicity and remained cautious about the safety of his family. In 1944, to take advantage of the lack of a personal income tax in Texas, he and Berenice moved to San Antonio, where he died in 1970 at the age of eighty. He was preceded in death by Berenice, who had died a few months earlier.

After Urschel's death, it was learned that he had provided support to Kathryn Kelly's daughter, Pauline, paying her way through East Central State College in Ada. The money was administered through Judge Vaught so that Urschel could remain anonymous. His only motive appears to be sympathy for the innocent young woman, collateral damage from her mother's criminal ambitions. Until Urschel's death, Pauline thought Judge Vaught was her benefactor.

The Urschel case remains one of the most famous in the history of the FBI. Aspects of the case also remain controversial. Clearly, Kelly and Bates were guilty and Boss complicit. It is also clear that Bailey had nothing to do with the actual kidnapping, although given his criminal record, he could hardly bemoan his imprisonment and served his time like a standup guy. Ora's involvement was at most peripheral, and her sentence was probably unnecessarily harsh. She was carried along in the tide of Judge Vaught's desire to send a message to gangsters that kidnapping would not be tolerated in this country.

Kathryn's role in the crime is less clear. Urschel, Kirkpatrick, Jones, Hyde, Keenan, Judge Vaught, and, most importantly, the jury believed that she was directly involved in the planning and execution of the kidnap plot.

Kathryn had certainly enjoyed spending the ransom money and had been cold heartedly ready to give up George for her mother. Yet, she was also most certainly, as Jones said, "an enigma," and long after her death some still believe her tale of woe. She remains one of those fascinating characters who dot history and make real life far more complex than fiction.

United States vs. David Hall

"Money is the mother's milk of politics."

—Statement attributed to Jesse "Big Daddy" Unruh,
Speaker of the California State Assembly, 1961-1969

CHAPTER TWELVE

The Road to Success

DAVID HALL WILL BE remembered as one of Oklahoma's most charismatic politicians and as one of the state's greatest disappointments. Elected Governor of Oklahoma in 1970 at the age of forty, Hall cut a handsome and imposing figure. A big man with a thick head of prematurely gray hair, he possessed a brilliant smile and a photographic memory for names, both of which helped propel his political ambition.

Whether attending a bean supper in Idabel or a formal dinner at Southern Hills Country Club in Tulsa, Hall knew which hands to shake and who to charm. He was intelligent and, without a doubt, had a capacity for great accomplishments. Unfortunately, he also possessed a fatal flaw that led him to use public office for personal gain. Though he quickly rose to the top of Oklahoma's political heap, he fell almost as fast, his political career ending in disgrace with a conviction for bribery and extortion in 1975.

How Hall went from a triumphant upset victory over an incumbent governor to a criminal conviction for abuse of high office is a story of greed and deception that includes a cast of unique and unpredict-able characters.

. . . . .

The product of a broken marriage between a mentally ill mother and a father who was married six times, Hall was the ultimate po-litical animal. At the age of thirteen, when his contemporaries were concerned with girls and sports, Hall set his sights on becoming the Governor of Oklahoma. His first political office was student council president of Taft Junior High School in Oklahoma City, and from then on his life was governed by a series of political decisions that led to the realization of his boyhood goal.

At Classen High School, determined again to become student council president, Hall went so far as to memorize the names of six-teen hundred of Classen's eighteen hundred students. He also earned a spot as the sixth man on Classen's 1948 State Championship Basket-ball Team. And, yes, he won the election for student council president.

After graduation he moved on to the University of Oklahoma in Norman, where he joined a fraternity, was selected chairman of the Union Activities Board, and excelled in Air Force ROTC.

His family was of modest means so Hall worked at a variety of jobs to finance his education, including driving a Pepsi Cola truck and working as a night guard for the *Daily Oklahoman*, a newspaper that would one day vilify him as a politician. He graduated from OU in 1952 after earning a Phi Beta Kappa Key for excellence in the liberal arts and sciences.

After college graduation, Hall was commissioned as a lieutenant in the U.S. Air Force and assigned to San Marcos Air Force Base in Texas where he served two years as a navigation instructor. While in the ser-vice, an Air Force buddy convinced Hall to apply for a scholarship to Harvard Law School. Hall did well on the entrance examination and was awarded a scholarship to begin in the fall of 1954. In later years when asked why he chose to go to law school, he replied, "Because it would be good for my political career."

After a year at Harvard, his grades were generally good, although a D in Property caused him to lose his scholarship. Unable to continue at Harvard without financial aid, Hall returned to Oklahoma and enrolled in the University of Tulsa College of Law where he made outstanding grades. While in law school, Hall met and married an attractive American Airlines stewardess named Jo Evans. The two remain married to this day and have three children and six grandchildren. While in law school, Hall also became active in Democratic politics, working in a number of local campaigns.

During his law school days, the always-industrious Hall worked as an insurance adjuster for State Farm Insurance Company and later found a good job in the land department of Shell Oil Company. His employment with Shell led to yet another career decision shaped by political ambition. As graduation from law school neared, Hall was offered a promotion and a raise by Shell, but to fill the position he would have to leave Oklahoma. Rather than committing to a life in the oil business, Hall chose to seek a much less lucrative job as an assistant county attorney in Tulsa County.

As luck would have it, County Attorney Howard Edmondson had just won election as Oklahoma's youngest governor and nearly his entire staff of assistants had moved on with him to the state capital. Ever the master politician, Hall used his connections with lawyers he had helped while an insurance adjuster and was hired by the new County Attorney Robert Simms before he had graduated or passed the Bar exam. Hall did go on to pass the Bar, and from 1959 to January 1962 worked at prosecuting criminal cases.

In January 1962, yet another piece of luck came Hall's way. Simms was appointed as a district judge in Tulsa County, leaving the post of county attorney vacant for the rest of his unexpired term. The Tulsa County commissioners would choose Simms's replacement, and that replacement would have the advantage of running for the office as an incumbent in November 1962. Simms was in a position to pick his successor, as the commissioners had made it clear they intended to affirm his recommendation. In an unusual move, Simms told his ten assistants they could decide on their new leader. Hall was an instant candidate, and when he out politicked another young assistant for the post, he made his next leap up the political ladder.

His appointment was followed by his election as county attorney in 1962, and again in 1964. As county attorney, Hall made a good name for himself with a high rate of convictions. At the same time, he worked tirelessly to advance his political influence, never missing a chance to make a headline or a public appearance.

CHAPTER THIRTEEN

Politics

IN 1965, HALL MADE A BOLD political move. He decided not to run for reelection as county attorney in 1966, but rather to take a shot at the governor's office. By his own admission, he was naïve about the requirements of a successful statewide campaign, particularly when it came to finances.

As the race for the Democratic nomination progressed, Hall learned that he did not have nearly the funds needed to finance a campaign for governor. Donations for a lightly regarded candidate were not forthcoming, and he possessed no personal wealth with which to bankroll his campaign. One publication dubbed Hall "The Credit Card Governor," a reference to the many times his campaign had been all but broke and a supporter kept things going by pulling out a personal credit card to pay the bills. This lack of funding laid the groundwork for his later troubles.

Despite his strained campaign coffers, Hall proved to be a tireless and imaginative campaigner. He tried to turn his lack of campaign donations into a plus with the voters, touting that it showed he was not beholden to special interests. Lacking money for television or radio advertising, he crisscrossed the state making personal appearances in small towns. Many a time he hitchhiked from Tulsa to Oklahoma City and back to Tulsa. In the end, Hall ran third in a field of thirteen candidates, just ten thousand votes behind a much better financed winner and a good showing for a first run at statewide office, especially an underfunded run. Hall was now a player in the Democratic Party, but he was also deeply in debt.

In November 1966, Dewey Bartlett, the Republican candidate, was elected governor. This gave Hall new hope for the 1970 race for the office, as he believed he could capture the Democratic nomination and then take a run at Bartlett. In order to support his family, Hall practiced law in Tulsa and taught at his law school alma mater. He never concentrated much on practicing law, preferring to continue politicking and organizing for another run at the governorship. This strategy would prove successful politically, but it also further eroded his personal finances.

As the 1970 gubernatorial election grew near, Hall faced an uphill battle. Governor Dewey Bartlett enjoyed the power of incumbency. As a business-friendly governor and an oilman himself, Bartlett was able to obtain all the financial support he needed. His record as governor was lackluster but noncontroversial, and, with plenty of money and connections, Bartlett was the heavy favorite.

Hall, however, perceived Bartlett's weaknesses. Originally from Ohio, educated at an eastern prep school and Princeton University, Bartlett came across as an aloof Yankee. His support was centered in the state's two largest cities of Tulsa and Oklahoma City; he did not play well in rural parts of the state, particularly the "Little Dixie" area of southeast Oklahoma.

Most importantly, Bartlett was complacent and over confident. He thought he could win solely on his record as governor with little personal effort. Bartlett's strategy was to run TV and radio ads across the state and do as little personal campaigning as possible. His approach was the exact opposite of Hall's grassroots, face-to-face, handshake-to-handshake-style of politics.

If anyone had asked him, Hall would have said he thought he had the formula for beating Bartlett, but first he had to win the Democratic primary. And that was no given. Hall was out of money before he had barely started the primary campaign. He eked out a campaign with small fund-raising events and minimal advertising. Against all odds, in a multiple candidate primary, he ran a solid first, but garnered only forty-eight percent of the vote, forcing a runoff with State Senator Bryce Baggett of Oklahoma City. Hall soundly trounced Baggett in the runoff by simply outworking his opponent, and then geared up to go after Bartlett.

Money remained an issue for the Hall campaign, but winning the Democratic nomination brought in donations from unions, trial lawyers, and other traditional Democratic supporters. And Hall continued as a tireless campaigner, eventually visiting 939 Oklahoma towns.

As Hall's campaign gained momentum, Bartlett stayed the course, never deviating from his own campaign strategy. In his defense, the governor was probably lulled by polls that showed him with a six percent or greater lead over Hall just a week before the election. Bartlett did seem poised and ready to coast to a win.

That's when two of Hall's staffers struck oil—not theirs, but Bartlett's. The staffers found a Bartlett-owned oil well near Shawnee leaking bubbling crude into a nearby creek. The last of Hall's campaign funds paid for a TV ad branding Bartlett as a major oil polluter.

This last-ditch ploy combined with Hall's rural strategy and intense ground game worked, but just barely. Hall defeated Bartlett by a margin of 2,187 votes out of more than 700,000 cast—the closest Oklahoma gubernatorial election of all time. Election Day didn't end the fight. Bartlett demanded a recount and every county had to be recounted. At the close of the recount, however, Hall remained the victor, and in January 1971, he was sworn into office.

CHAPTER FOURTEEN

Governor Hall

H ALL HAD NOW FULFILLED his boyhood dream, but the victory did not come without a cost. Hall's bank account and his campaign's had both been drained. Officially the campaign was in debt $1,000, but later grand jury testimony pegged the actual deficit at $300,000.

Hall himself was broke and owed personal bank loans and credit card debt of at least $30,000. At the time, the governor's salary was $35,000 per year, not nearly enough to support Hall's lifestyle or repay his personal obligations.

Even before he was sworn in, Oklahomans would later learn, Hall began to replenish his coffers by trafficking on the influence of his office. Much of the money he received went straight to his pocket and was never reported as either a campaign donation or personal income. Not only were the transgressions illegal, many of them were also ill disguised and traceable.

Hall's personal legal and financial problems would surface later. In his early days as Governor of the State of Oklahoma, it was his political actions that made news. He wasted no time in pressing an ambitious legislative agenda, promoting a bill that would raise the income tax rate on those with higher incomes and another bill that raised the tax on the production of oil and gas.

Having defeated a candidate backed by most of the business interests in the state, Hall now became those same businessmen's worst nightmare. He also drew the ire of the state's two biggest newspapers, the *Daily Oklahoman* and the *Tulsa World*. Both papers began a relentless attack on Hall and his populist political agenda. They blasted Hall daily, both personally and politically, for daring to attempt to raise taxes.

Hall's tax bills were presented in a House of Representatives in which seventy-eight members were Democrats and only twenty-one, Republicans—and a Senate in which Democrats outnumbered Republicans thirty-nine to nine. The numbers, however, did not reflect reality. The Democrats were widely divided amongst themselves on many issues, including taxes.

Many Democrats were fiscal conservatives who opposed the proposed tax increases and banded together with a united Republican minority to create a powerful barrier against passage of Hall's bills. The end result was a no-holds-barred legislative battle. When the final votes were taken Hall's tax increase bills narrowly passed, but he was left politically scarred and with many powerful enemies.

Throughout his term as governor, Hall pushed for more funding for education and higher pay for state employees. In any dispute between labor and management he landed on labor's side. That political stance generated an ongoing fight with a generally conservative legislature and infuriated a heavily right-wing state press.

The biggest crisis of Hall's tenure, however, came in the form of a riot at the state penitentiary in McAlester, in which prisoners took guards hostage and set fire to part of the prison. The riot had been provoked by a prison environment made dangerous by overcrowding and a serious lack of guards. Fortunately, it ended without harm coming to any of the hostages. Hall went to the prison to personally supervise the response, so when it ended without further incident or loss of life, he took the credit. In Hall's version, he persuaded the prisoners to release the hostages, saving their lives.

CHAPTER FIFTEEN

Kickbacks, Bribes, & The IRS

THE BACKSTORY TO HALL'S political achievements was, unfortunately, political corruption. Not long after he took office as governor, Hall became the focus of rumors. Whispers circulated that he'd been the recipient of kickbacks from people wanting to secure state contracts, particularly construction contractors.

Sometime in 1972, Attorney General Larry Derryberry was given information that suggested Hall had been paid a bribe in connection with a construction contract to build a tunnel between buildings at the state capitol complex. A friend and supporter of Hall's, Derryberry met with Hall and confronted him with the story. With convincing sincerity, Hall denied any wrongdoing. Derryberry believed his friend, and dismissed the allegations as political gossip.

As the rumors regarding corruption grew, however, the *Daily Oklahoman* assigned its best investigative reporter, Jack Taylor, to look into the Hall administration. Taylor proved relentless in his hunt to find dirt on the governor. The situation began to snowball, and by 1973, state grand juries had been convened in both Oklahoma and Tulsa counties to investigate corruption in state government. All of this threatened Hall politically and legally, but his real troubles started when the Internal Revenue Service got involved and began to assemble a tax evasion case against him.

The IRS believed that Hall had unreported income from monies he had supposedly raised for his campaign but had instead converted to personal use. In addition the IRS had information that Hall had received income from bribes in exchange for the awarding of various state contracts.

The IRS investigation became public in May 1973. As usual Hall denied any improprieties, but as the investigation went forward bits and pieces of allegations about the taking of bribes were disclosed in the press. Finally, in January 1974, a federal grand jury was convened to investigate Hall for bribery and extortion. All three grand jury proceedings were supposed to be secret, but in fact, they leaked like sieves. Evidence presented implicated Hall in a wide variety of criminal conspiracies, but much of the web of corruption led through two individuals, A.W. "Sunny" Jenkins and Carl Ballew.

Jenkins was a young, wheeler-dealer millionaire from Tulsa, who doubled as Hall's principal campaign fund-raiser and became his closest aide and confidant. Ballew was a paint contractor from south Oklahoma City, who was seduced by Hall's promises of payback from state construction contracts. Both men were believed to have helped collect money from contractors trying to buy favoritism on state contracts and then funneling the illegal funds to Hall.

The IRS focused on Ballew, and when confronted with the facts of the case, Ballew agreed to assist the government in exchange for immunity from federal prosecution.

In December 1973, Jenkins was charged with bribery by the Oklahoma County Grand Jury, but was then granted immunity from federal prosecution and cooperated fully with the federal grand jury. Another important witness against Hall was his personal secretary Dorothy Pike, who had dealt directly with Ballew and had kept her own records of what she believed were improper transactions in case she ever had to protect herself. Along with other evidence, the testimony of Ballew, Jenkins, and Pike established a laundry list of fraud and corruption infractions by Hall.

Many campaign contributions made to Hall had gone straight into his pocket rather than the campaign bank account. These funds were used for personal expenses, such as Hall's law office rent, monthly loan installment payments, and payments on Hall's home mortgage. Campaign funds raised from "Victory Dinners" were used to pay off Hall's $60,000 personal bank loan. An organization known as the "Governor's Club," a political fund-raising effort designed to attract $1,000 donors, led to a collection of another $60,000, which was funneled to Jenkins. Funds raised from architects, engineers, and other state contractors on a monthly basis went partly to Hall's personal expenses.

In the process of its investigation, the IRS learned that Ballew had been borrowing money in cash from a bank in south Oklahoma City. At Hall's direction, Dorothy Pike would meet Ballew at the bank with a list of Hall's personal debts that needed to be paid. Pike would purchase cashier's checks from the bank, using the cash provided by Ballew, and forward payment to Hall's creditors. This arrangement went on for eight or nine months, with the monthly payments reaching as high as $8,000 or $9,000 per month until Ballew exhausted his credit line of $50,000. Later the money was repaid to Ballew by Jenkins and then reimbursed to Jenkins by the Hall campaign from the Governor's Club monies.

Other serious charges revolved around the construction contracts for the tax and education buildings at the state capital complex and the construction of the Cimarron Turnpike. Hall reportedly guaranteed a Shawnee contractor, E. Allen Cowan, the contract to build the tax and education buildings. In return, Hall demanded payment of $122,000. Cowan borrowed the money at the American National Bank in Shawnee and delivered it to Jenkins in new twenty dollar bills, still bound in Federal Reserve wrappers. Jenkins called Ballew and told him to pick up the suitcase of money at the Habana Inn, a hotel in northwest Oklahoma City. Ballew, however, got cold feet and sent his secretary to make the pickup instead. Before making the drop, she took the suitcase home, where out of curiosity, she and her husband opened it to see what it contained. Faced with stacks and stacks of brand new bills, the secretary and her husband took a photograph of the contents to protect themselves in case of future trouble, before turning the cash over to Ballew.

Later, the IRS was furnished with the photographs the couple had taken, and after enlarging the photos, the IRS was able to trace the serial numbers on the bills back to the bank in Shawnee. The IRS agents complained later about getting the runaround from the bank and from Cowan as to their involvement, but the agents were confident that they could prove where the money came from and where it ultimately went. Evidence of this incident was presented to the Oklahoma County Grand Jury, which indicted Jenkins, Cowan, and three others in connection with the bribe.

Meanwhile, the construction of the Cimarron Turnpike had been generating bribes from its inception. Knowing the project was pending and that it would be financed with bonds in 1970, Hall had—prior to even taking office—sent Jenkins to Wall Street to solicit money from the bond firm of Loeb, Rhoades & Company. The carrot was to be the fees to be earned on the $74 million bond issue. Those fees would amount to approximately $2 million, and Hall had asked for a donation of $100,000 in return for delivering the contract to Loeb, Rhoades & Co.

Loeb Rhoades made a down payment of $25,000 and later, when the firm obtained the contract, kicked in the other $75,000. Hall sent the leading members of Loeb, Rhoades & Company letters thanking them for their "campaign contribution," backdating his thank-yous to a date prior to his election.

The Cimarron Turnpike was the gift that just kept giving. Next up: contracts to be awarded for engineering services. These contracts paid from $400,000 to $600,000. The work was divided into six separate sections, and Hall was able to control five of the contracts. Evidence would later show that he received kickbacks on each of the five in amounts ranging from $10,000 to $40,000, depending on the size of the contract.

CHAPTER SIXTEEN

Political Defeat

AS INFORMATION ABOUT such shady deals became public, both the *Tulsa World* and the *Daily Oklahoman* bombarded readers with stories about corruption in the governor's office. Hardly a day passed without an article—often on the front page, often above the fold—detailing allegations against Hall.

In April 1974, Derryberry, having become aware of the mass of evidence building against the governor and realizing that he had been most assuredly deceived by his friend, filed a report with the State House of Representatives asking it to pursue Hall's impeachment.

Derryberry felt this was his only viable move as attorney general. His office was poorly funded, and he had no investigators on his payroll to help build a case. He could not use the Oklahoma State Bureau of Investigation, because as part of the executive branch it worked under the governor and was obligated to report to Hall.

Derryberry went to the legislature hoping its leadership would pick up the ball and investigate the allegations involving the governor's office. What Derryberry hadn't reckoned with, however, was the partisan nature of the state legislature. Yes, a committee was appointed to investigate the governor's office by the House of Representatives, but the committee recommended against impeachment and the House voted accordingly not to proceed. The only thing the impeachment attempt did was generate even more unfavorable publicity against Hall.

While all this was hitting the news, Hall was faced with a reelection campaign. That reelection bid ended almost before it began when he finished a poor third in the Democratic primary behind Clem McSpadden and David Boren.

Boren went on to defeat first McSpadden in a runoff and then Republican James Inhofe in the general election to become the next Governor of Oklahoma. As a member of the state legislature himself, Boren had been able to take advantage of the adverse publicity against Hall in the primary by filing bills banning what had become a touchy word in the governor's mansion—"kickbacks." Boren's campaign theme was a "Clean Sweep" of government, with his supporters (the Boren Broom Brigade) carrying brooms and pledging to sweep corruption from the state capitol.

With the new governor chosen, Hall was not only a lame duck but also a duck in trouble with the law. In September, he was subpoenaed before the federal grand jury. On the advice of counsel, he took the Fifth Amendment, a prudent legal move, but a tactic that further destroyed his public credibility. Claiming the Fifth was especially demeaning to Hall, who treasured his public image and who had once fired the state director of the Department of Public Affairs for invoking Fifth Amendment rights on the grounds that public officials should be held to a higher standard than the general public.

Hall's abbreviated grand jury appearance brought him face to face with the man who would be the instrument of his doom. Bill Burkett, the U.S. district attorney for the Western District of Oklahoma, was running the federal grand jury. An experienced prosecutor, Burkett had practiced law in Woodward and served, like Hall, as a county attorney and then in the state legislature.

Burkett had also been state chairman of the Oklahoma Republican Party, a fact that led Hall to claim he was the subject of a Republican vendetta. Recommended for U.S. district attorney by U.S. Senator Henry Bellmon, Burkett had served in that capacity for five years at the time of the Hall incident. He loved his work and was dedicated to law enforcement. Serving as district attorney, was in his words, "the best damn job I ever had."

Burkett was convinced that he had a strong enough case to convict Hall on charges of bribery and extortion. Five construction contractors were ready to testify that they had delivered bribes to Hall or Hall's associates. But Burkett was also haunted by the unsuccessful public corruption trial of another state official, State Treasurer Leo Winters, who had been found not guilty at a recent jury trial. Burkett had promised himself that Hall would not be another Winters and so wanted to add a tax evasion charge, which he felt would sew up the prosecution against Hall. Such a charge required the approval of the IRS and the U.S. Justice Department in Washington. In the fall of 1974, Burkett made a request for approval of the tax evasion charges and was awaiting a response when a bombshell hit that opened up a whole new case against Hall.

. . . . .

On December 9, 1974, Burkett received a call from Derryberry, requesting a meeting with Burkett and the FBI. The meeting took place at the office of the FBI in Oklahoma City. Present at the meeting were Burkett, Derryberry, and Ted Rosack, the special agent in charge, as well as FBI Agent Paul Baresel, FBI electronics expert Jack De Witt, and Oklahoma Secretary of State John Rogers.

Rogers had a tale to tell about a meeting that had transpired with Hall on December 3. On that day Rogers had received a call from Hall summoning him to the Blue Room, a ceremonial meeting room adjacent to the governor's office.

Rogers and his father, who was the state auditor and inspector, were supporters of Hall and close friends of the governor. The invitation to a meeting came as no surprise, but the substance of the discussion did, as it pertained to Rogers's position as the chairman of the Board of Trustees of the Oklahoma Public Employees Retirement System.

The OPERS oversaw the investment of millions of dollars of state employee retirement funds. Hall told Rogers he wanted to discuss a proposal by Texas businessman W. "Doc" Taylor involving the Retirement Fund. It seems Taylor wanted to borrow $10 million from the Fund, add it to monies from other sources, and then have his company, Guaranteed Investments, loan the funds to minority and disadvantaged small business enterprises. The federal government under the auspices of the Small Business Administration would guarantee the loan. Hall said he had come to Rogers because the Retirement Board at a meeting in November had summarily rejected Taylor's proposal.

Hall wanted Rogers's help in getting the Board to approve the investment. He told his friend that Taylor had agreed to pay Hall $50,000 for the approval, which Hall would split with Rogers. Rogers was dumbfounded, but he let Hall leave their meeting thinking that he would consider the deal. Instead Rogers headed immediately to Derryberry's office, taking a circuitous route so that the governor would not see him.

Rogers told Derryberry about his conversation with Hall, and then suggested that he be wired and continue talking to Hall to obtain more evidence against the governor. Derryberry agreed in theory with Rogers's idea, but he lacked the resources to carry out such a plan. Instead, he turned to the FBI and the U.S. district attorney for help.

Rogers may have been an honest man, but he was an unlikely hero. Forty-six-years-old, Rogers was mustached, stocky, and had a reputation as a political loose canon. At the time of his tenure, Oklahoma's secretary of state was elected statewide. Rogers had been elected in 1966 and again in 1970 and 1974, largely due to the similarity of his name to that of Oklahoma's favorite son, Will Rogers. An article in the

Daily Oklahoman described Rogers as "an unpredictable character," and one legislator had publicly called him a "jackass" and a "nincompoop."

Rogers advocated his own brand of contradictory politics by calling himself a "Christian conservative," though he had backed candidates as diverse as George Wallace and Ted Kennedy in consecutive presidential elections. In the course of handling a liquor-by-the-drink initiative petition, Rogers's behavior had at times been so erratic that he was, at different points in the petition drive, accused of being a "puppet" for both sides of the issue. Rogers was also politically ambitious. He took a run at the U.S. Senate in 1972, finishing a distant fifth in the race for the Democratic nomination. At the time of the Hall overture, he still had his eye on a race for Congress, and his zeal to take part in a plan to convict Hall may have been partly motivated by a desire to parlay his involvement into political gain.

Meanwhile, Derryberry was anxious to catch and convict Hall, but given Rogers's reputation, harbored misgivings about the secretary of state's credibility. Before acting on Rogers's information, Derryberry suggested to Burkett that they should ask Rogers to take a lie detector test. Burkett agreed and so did Rogers, who passed the polygraph with flying colors.

CHAPTER SEVENTEEN

Wired

THE LAWMEN THEN DEVISED a plan to reel in Hall. The Retirement Board was composed of seven members: Rogers; Jim Cook, commissioner of charities and corrections; Leo Winters, state treasurer; L.P. Williams, state commissioner of labor; J.O. Spiller, director of state finance; Richard A. Ward, state highway director; and J.L. Merrell, a member of the Oklahoma Tax Commission.

The governor had indicated to Rogers that he had influence over several of the members having appointed them to their posts. Hall had claimed he could persuade those members to vote for Taylor's plan.

Taylor's proposal would have to win acceptance from the Board, as well as legal approval by the state attorney general and consent from the Retirement Fund's investment adviser, the First National Bank of Oklahoma City.

In order to collect evidence against the governor, the plan had to stay alive and under consideration. There was also a time element involved as Hall was leaving office in January, losing whatever influence he might have over the members of the board. Additionally, Taylor and his chief corporate representative, Kevin Mooney, would have to be convinced the proposal had a chance of success. Mooney, an attorney, was a law school friend of Hall's and had been part of the initial conversation regarding the bribe. Rogers was well aware of the delicate nature of the situation, and over the next few weeks he proved to be a consummate actor, playing to all parties involved to keep Hall's scheme alive. He also validated his reputation as he predictably had a hard time keeping his mouth shut.

It was important to the plan's success that as many conversations as possible be recorded, and a procedure was worked out to ensure the reliability of that evidence.

Baresel, who Burkett describes as a top-notch agent, was put in charge of the investigation. FBI agents were on call so that any time Rogers scheduled a personal conversation with Hall, Mooney, or Taylor, the agent could be there to place a recorder on Rogers's back, under his shirt and suit coat. Immediately following the taped conversation, the agent would retrieve the recorder for safekeeping. When it came to recording telephone calls, an agent was to be present with Rogers at the time of any calls.

Rogers would also collect evidence that wasn't recorded that he could testify to at a trial, but the more that could be documented on tape, the stronger would be the government's case. Given these rules to work with, Rogers set about to outwardly push Taylor's proposal with the Retirement Board.

Three days after his meeting with the FBI, Rogers had his first opportunity to tape a conversation. Mooney came to Oklahoma City and met with Rogers. Rogers managed to get Mooney on tape admitting that he was the contact man with Hall and that he knew about the $50,000 payoff. The deal that had originally been offered to the Retirement Board by Taylor pegged the interest rate on the notes at eight-and-a-quarter percent annual interest, but Mooney told Rogers if the board would accept eight percent they "would really be killing a fat cat."

On December 18, Mooney and Taylor came to Oklahoma City to discuss the proposal with the attorney general's office. They also met with Rogers who suggested a new deal. If Rogers could lower the interest rate on the bonds to eight percent he wanted an additional payment to be made by Taylor. It was agreed that if Rogers could get the bonds approved at the lower rate he would get another $12,500.

They also talked about how they could funnel the payoff funds to Rogers. Mooney suggested hiring Rogers as a consultant, and Rogers talked about Taylor finding a tenant for a vacant building owned by Rogers. That night Rogers called Hall, who was in California, and during their conversation described the deal to possibly receive another $12,500. Hall said he would call the trustees he had influence with and urge them to vote in favor of the investment including the lower interest rate. As it would turn out with many of the recordings made by Rogers, the tape of the phone call was of poor quality and hard to follow, but it did include some audible statements damaging to Hall.

On December 19, Rogers had a series of phone conversations with Hall who was still in California. In the last one, Hall told Rogers he had lined up his friends on the board and to call a meeting. Rogers did so for the next day. Leo Winters and Jim Cook did not attend, but a quorum was present and a vote taken on Taylor's proposal. The proposal failed to pass with Rogers and L.P. Williams voting for it, J.O. Spiller and J.L. Merrill voting against, and Richard Ward abstaining.

Ward's position came as a surprise as Hall had informed Rogers he had spoken with Ward and that he was ready to vote favorably. At the meeting, Spiller not only voted against the proposal, but stated, "This is crazy . . . a lame duck governor trying to put through a $10 million deal in the waning days of his administration—we don't know anything about this . . . I wouldn't vote for that for anything."

Burkett was informed of Spiller's remarks by Rogers and was concerned that Spiller might convince the other board members to kill the proposal, sidetracking the efforts to catch Hall. This was a touchy situation. Burkett did not want to disclose too much information about the investigation, but needed to keep the proposal alive. Burkett solved the problem by calling Spiller and without disclosing any details of the investigation asked him, as a personal favor, not to attend any more board meetings, to which Spiller agreed.

Another series of phone calls then transpired between Hall and Rogers ending in Hall asking Rogers to call yet another meeting of the board for December 23 to present the proposal at the original interest rate. As agreed Spiller did not attend, nor did Winters. The absence of Winters from all of the meetings could have been explained by his recent troubles with the federal government. Having been tried and acquitted for tax evasion, he might have sensed something fishy about the proposal and decided to stay clear of any involvement, or he may have even been tipped off by Hall, who was a friend. There is no known explanation for his absence, which also might have been coincidental.

At the meeting the proposal initially failed again, but then was passed when a provision was added requiring the further approval of the First National Bank and the attorney general.

Two different versions exist as to how this qualification came about. Derryberry remembers that it was added at his suggestion after a call from Cook, who had become concerned about the investment scheme. Derryberry asked Cook to approve it subject to approval by the attorney general's office; he assured Cook that no such approval would ever be granted and no retirement funds ever released.

Burkett's book *The Fall of David Hall* reports that Rogers added the provision on the suggestion of Hall, a suggestion received by phone during the meeting. Regardless of how it came about, the requirement was placed in the motion, and Rogers now had to play the game with these qualifications in place.

CHAPTER EIGHTEEN

The Sting

ROGERS HAD STARTED pressing Mooney and Taylor for payment, and he demanded the higher sum of $62,500 even though the interest rate was back at eight-and-a-quarter percent. From their side Mooney and Taylor pressed for a letter from the First National Bank approving the deal, which they needed to obtain their financing. At this point the wheels almost came off the track for the investigation. Rogers went to the First National Bank, and in an effort to obtain the letter, told two bank officers that he was working with the FBI to investigate Hall and demanded the letter. Baresel learned of Rogers's inept move at the bank, and along with Burkett met with the two bank officers, swore them to secrecy, and assured them that all dealings on the matter would be with the head of the bank trust department, William O. "Bill" Alexander. After Alexander was briefed he met with Mooney and Taylor and encouraged them, but never issued the letter.

As the investigation continued to unfold, a telling telephone conversation took place on December 26. Hall was in Utah skiing with his family when he and Rogers talked again by phone, a call Rogers recorded. Rogers tried to broach the matter of the payoff, saying, "I don't want those guys coming up here with the money." To which Hall tersely replied, "Don't talk about that on the telephone."

Shortly after this phone call a political consultant named Robert Sanders, who was a former resident of Oklahoma, passed through town. Sanders had many friends at the capital, including both Rogers and Hall. He dropped in on Rogers to say hello, and Rogers told Sanders the entire story about the $50,000 bribe and the FBI's involvement. After some thought, Sanders called Hall and tipped him off to what Rogers had said.

Incredibly, this didn't stop Hall or his plan. He simply began to handle Rogers differently—opting to talk directly to Taylor and Mooney, rather than using Rogers as a go-between.

Rogers, Mooney, and Taylor continued to deal with each other and on December 27, Rogers called Taylor from what he identified as "his girlfriend's house" (in reality it was Baresel's residence). Baresel was present throughout the conversation as Rogers pressed for payment of the money, always stressing that it should be paid to Hall and even going so far as to say, "At the same time you bring the money, and you don't pay me you pay David." Taylor affirmed responding, "Yeah, I understand."

Rogers also pinned down the amount of the first payment as $31,250, half of the $62,500, he claimed was owed. The second half was to be paid when the transaction actually closed.

Hall had begun to avoid some of Rogers's calls, but he did agree to meet at the governor's office on January 6, 1975. As the meeting began Hall wrote Rogers a message on a three-by-five-inch index card stating, "We are bugged."

"How do you know?" Rogers wrote back.

"We have a monitoring system," Hall wrote.

The rest of the conversation included Rogers talking and writing notes, with Hall's responses being entirely written. Hall ended the meeting with one last note that read, "Wait eight months." When the tape of the meeting was played in court it reflected an odd one-sided conversation.

On January 8, the Retirement Board had a regular meeting scheduled. Prior to the meeting Burkett recalls that Cook contacted Derryberry's office and asked about rescinding the board's approval of the proposal. At Burkett's request, Rogers delivered a note to Hall asking him to tell two of the trustees to stay away from the meeting so that a quorum would not exist. Only two trustees appeared at the meeting, and without a quorum the meeting was postponed.

After the meeting, Rogers saw Hall in the capitol parking lot and tried to talk. Hall motioned him to the governor's office. Rogers was quickly wired, then went to meet with Hall. The meeting was almost a repeat of their last, only this time all communication was done in writing. Once again Hall cautioned Rogers, "Wait eight months."

Then Hall gathered up the notes, set them on fire with a cigarette lighter, and flushed them down his private toilet. The sound of the toilet flushing was recorded on the tape.

CHAPTER NINETEEN

The Payoff

DERRYBERRY RECALLS THAT at some point in their meetings, Hall accused Rogers of being wired. According to Derryberry, Rogers fended off the accusation by responding that he didn't know if Hall was wired. Rogers then suggested they "go out in the country and get naked" so both could be sure the other wasn't wearing a wire or recording.

On January 10, Mooney came to Oklahoma City and again pressed Rogers for the commitment letter to close the deal. Rogers took Mooney to the attorney general's office where he obtained an approval letter that required only Rogers's signature to be valid.

That same day, Rogers ran into Hall in a corridor at the capitol. Rogers asked the governor if he could trust Mooney and Taylor, and Hall whispered in Rogers's ear, "Trust them." As far as their payoff, Hall also told Rogers, "I am as sure of that as I am that the sun will come up tomorrow."

Meanwhile, Mooney spent much of early January informing Rogers of calls between Hall and Mooney, or Hall and Taylor, and then telling Rogers what Hall wanted done. Time remained critical in carry-ing out the government's plan to catch Hall. January 13 was his last day in office, and Mooney and Taylor were pressing for the approval letter. Faced with these quickly deteriorating circumstances, Rogers took one last shot at getting an outright admission from Hall on tape.

The meeting was in the governor's office—just Rogers and Hall, but again Hall would only communicate in writing. "Trust me," Hall wrote. "You must give the letter before you lose control."

Rogers wrote back, "I need some money now. After I sign the letter they won't take a chance. They don't need to, they won't do it in a safe way."

"You can trust me," Hall wrote back. "If they don't, I will pay your part personally. Depend on me only." At this juncture the fact that Hall thought anyone would trust him shows the level of his arrogance.

After the meeting, Rogers tried yet again to talk to Hall, this time by phone, but Hall would not return his call. Rogers then called Taylor who was in Jackson, Mississippi. The two agreed Rogers would sign the approval letter, and Taylor would pay Mooney $31,250 for legal fees, which Mooney would pass along to Hall. Rogers insisted he needed $10,000 personally and immediately to which Taylor responded, "I can get this in a few days. This is routine for us."

The government was ready to make its final move. January 14, Mooney flew to Oklahoma City and came to Rogers's office. Rogers handed Mooney the letter and asked for the $31,250 check. Mooney didn't have the check. Nonetheless, along with the letter he had so cov-eted came his own arrest. He was collared by the FBI leaving Rogers's office. At the same time, Taylor was arrested in Jackson, Mississippi. Both men were booked and released on $25,000 bail.

Unbeknownst to the arresting officers, Taylor had a $31,250 check, payable to Mooney for "legal services," in his wallet at the time of his arrest. Taylor subsequently destroyed the check, but an incriminating check stub remained at Taylor's office in Dallas. So at Taylor's direction, his son-in-law, James Duckels, hurried to the office to change the check stub to show it was issued to the Small Business Administration and then voided. This bumbling attempt to alter evidence was thwarted by Taylor's attorney, Emmett Colvin. The ethical Colvin advised Taylor he could not alter evidence and sent Duckels back to Taylor's office to note on the stub that the check was originally written to Mooney for legal services.

CHAPTER TWENTY

Federal Charges

O
NE CAN ONLY SURMISE that by now Hall knew what was coming. Surely it was no surprise when on January 16, he was indicted in U.S. District Court on four counts, one count of attempting to extort $50,000 from Taylor, Mooney, and Guaranteed Investors Corporation in violation of the Hobb's Act; two counts of conspiracy with Taylor and Mooney to use interstate commerce to carry on an unlawful activity; and one count of attempting to bribe John Rogers and accepting a bribe in violation of the Federal Criminal Code.

Taylor and Mooney were indicted on the conspiracy charge and on two counts of attempting to bribe Hall and Rogers.

Surprised or not, Hall came out swinging. He denied all charges and demanded a speedy trial so that he could clear his name. Hall's bravado didn't last long. On January 21, he appeared in the U.S. District Court for formal arraignment, along with Taylor and Mooney. Hall and Taylor entered not guilty pleas, but Mooney pled guilty to the conspiracy count. The district attorney dismissed the other two counts against Mooney as part of a plea bargain. Further, Mooney admitted under oath that he had taken part in a scheme to bribe Hall for the sum of $50,000.

Ironically, one of Mooney's attorneys was Frank Keating, the state representative from Tulsa who had also authored the resolution calling for Hall's impeachment. Keating, who would later become Governor of Oklahoma himself in 1995, remembers that Hall was visibly shaken by Mooney's guilty plea. Hall now knew he would not only have to discredit Rogers, but also overcome direct testimony by Mooney. As an ex-prosecutor, Hall was well aware that he faced an uphill struggle to escape conviction.

Mooney's cooperation with the government caused other problems for Hall and Taylor. Mooney told Burkett that Taylor had shown him a check for $31,250, made payable to Mooney for legal services. Acting on that tip, Burkett sent FBI agents to Taylor's office where they found the check stub altered by Duckels. The stub later became evidence in the trial and corroborated both Rogers's and Mooney's testimony.

Hall's problems continued to multiply. Without truth on his side, he had to rely on obfuscation, misdirection, and trial court error to avoid conviction. The last was highly unlikely as he had drawn Judge Fred Daugherty as the trial judge. An ex-Army general and a combat veteran of both World War II and the Korean War, Daugherty ruled his courtroom with an iron hand. Possessed with superior intelligence and a wide command of the law, he peered imperiously down from the bench with a dark-eyed, hawk-like visage. Most importantly, Daugherty was known to make very few legal errors and was rarely reversed by appellate courts. Hall would certainly get a fair trial, but neither he nor his lawyer would get away with any foolishness in Daugherty's court.

As for Hall's lawyer, he had a good one. D.C. Thomas was an experienced criminal lawyer who had been an assistant county attorney in Oklahoma County. Possessed of an easygoing homespun-style that played well with juries, he knew how to defend criminal cases. Taylor was represented by James Linn. Another experienced criminal lawyer, used to high profile trials in federal court, Linn was something of a windbag, but handled himself well in jury trials. Both defendants were well represented. Jim Peters and O.B. Johnston III assisted Burkett in the trial. Bill Price and Drew Neville, young lawyers in Burkett's office, helped with preparation of the case and the briefing of legal issues.

The first order of business was the production of Rogers's tapes to the defendants and a decision on how to present them to a jury. The tapes were of very poor quality and in many places hard to understand. Burkett wanted the tapes transcribed and the written transcriptions made available for the jury to read while the tapes were played. Initially, the defendants agreed, but when they became aware of the incriminating contents of the recordings they changed their minds and objected to the transcription and to the introduction of the tapes.

The district attorney's office was faced with another problem anyway: it simply didn't have the manpower to transcribe the tapes before the February 24 trial date. But the tapes were deemed important enough to the proceedings that help was found. Secretaries from the FBI office and even the office of an appellate judge got to work, and the transcripts were finally completed just prior to the trial.

All that effort almost came to naught. Judge Daugherty, as usual sensitive to avoiding any chance of legal error, refused to allow the transcripts to be given to the jury to read along with the hearing of the tapes themselves. However, the transcripts were used by the lawyers and even the judge and, in Burkett's opinion, proved invaluable in both direct and cross-examination of witnesses.

Prior to the trial, the defense lawyers had pressed several other important motions. They moved for a change of venue based on the barrage of adverse pretrial publicity and tried to exclude the tapes from evidence as the fruit of an illegal wiretap. Judge Daugherty conducted an evidentiary hearing on their motions. With regard to their request for a change of venue, the defense made a weak case, calling two ill-informed political pals of Hall to support their position. The motion was denied.

In support of its motion to exclude the tapes from evidence, the defense called Rogers as a witness. Federal law requires a warrant for wire taping when neither party knew of the taping, but it allows the recording of any conversation when one party agrees.

The thrust of the defendants' motion was to prove that Rogers had only agreed to the taping under coercion from the government after being put under threat of criminal prosecution, making him less than a willing participant. Rogers had been a subject of both tax and SEC investigations at earlier dates and had received a non-prosecution letter from the district attorney before he undertook the recordings. The defense claimed this proved coercion, but Judge Daugherty did not agree and overruled the motion to exclude the tapes. He did, however, grant a motion to provide the defendants with the grand jury testimony of Rogers and two other witnesses.

CHAPTER TWENTY-ONE

The Trial

T HE TRIAL BEGAN AS scheduled on February 24, accompanied by intense local and national media coverage. In federal court, the judge, rather than the lawyers, usually does the questioning of the jury, or *voir dire*. Trial lawyers dislike this procedure, as *voir dire* is an important tool in introducing the jury to the theory of the case, the litigants, and the witnesses. In Hall's trial, Judge Daugherty conducted the *voir dire*, but he did ask some questions suggested by the defendants.

For the most part the qualifying of the jury went quickly. In only half a day, seven men and five women were chosen, along with two alternates. Burkett and Linn made opening statements, and Thomas reserved his opening statement until the beginning of Hall's case. The trial then moved forward to the prosecution's case in chief.

The government opened its case by calling Mooney. From the very start the case against Hall began to build momentum, as the facts piled up against him. Mooney testified that he had called Hall as a friend in October of 1974, and had inquired about the governor's plans after leaving office. Hall responded that along with practicing law, he was working on a real estate development in Palo Mesa, California; in fact, he was looking for financing for the project.

About a week later, Mooney testified Hall called him asking if he knew of anyone who might provide funding for his real estate deal. Mooney suggested Taylor and Taylor's company, Guaranteed Investors, as potential investors. Hall arranged to have Taylor and Mooney picked up in Fort Worth and flown to Oklahoma City in an Oklahoma Highway Patrol airplane. The governor then hosted the two for dinner at the governor's mansion where Hall pitched them his real estate project.

Nothing seemed out of line to Mooney until a subsequent meeting on December 2. On that date, on his return flight from a meeting in Houston, Hall had the state plane land at Fort Worth's Meacham Field where he met with Mooney and Taylor and again pitched the Palo Mesa project. Taylor had his own agenda for the meeting: he wanted to convince Hall to help with a bond proposal that had been rejected by the Retirement Fund.

After their meeting, as Hall and Mooney walked back to the plane together, Hall popped the question. The Oklahoma governor told Mooney he thought he could get Taylor's proposal approved, but that it would cost Taylor "one point" or $100,000, payable as a "finder's fee." Hall told Mooney he would split the fee with him, each of them to get $50,000. Hall wanted his money to be paid out $12,500 per year for four years. Mooney was surprised by the governor's request, but they parted amicably. Mooney testified that he then took the offer to Taylor, who told Mooney that finder's fees were normal on financial transactions of this kind and that the deal was okay with him. The final agreement was struck in a telephone conversation between Hall and Mooney. There was no doubt from Mooney's testimony that Hall had initiated the bribe.

Later, Hall advised Mooney that he had cut Rogers in on the deal for $25,000, and he expected Mooney to pay half of Rogers's payoff out of Mooney's fee. On Mooney's first visit with Rogers in Oklahoma City, Rogers confirmed this agreement. Mooney went on to pound more nails into Hall's coffin by confirming what would be Rogers's testimony on almost every point. He also testified that shortly before the two were arrested that Taylor had shown him a check for $31,250, setting the stage for the introduction of the altered check stub.

The defense attorneys tried to shake Mooney on cross-examination, but he held to his story, pinning the bribe on Hall and involving Taylor as a willing participant in the conspiracy. The prosecution had opened with a strong witness, but the star of the government's case was yet to come. After laying the groundwork for the introduction of the tapes, the government called Rogers to testify about his conversations with Hall, Mooney, and Taylor. It was time to present the tape recordings to the jury. And the prosecution was nervous.

Most of the tapes were of very poor quality, and in some cases it was difficult to even tell who was talking on them, much less what they were saying. Furthermore, some of the tapes were long and sometimes boring. One was more than an hour and thirty minutes in length. It wasn't ideal, but they had no alternative: there is nothing on par with hearing someone incriminate himself in his own words, even if one has to strain to hear it.

The prosecution, as directed by Judge Daugherty, had Rogers identify each conversation and then play the tape of that conversation if it had been taped. In some cases, meetings had not been taped, such as the initial conversation between Hall and Rogers in the capitol's Blue Room, and Rogers also testified about these events. Although Hall never made any direct admissions on the tapes, the cumulative effect of hearing the two men talk in taped meeting after meeting, along with Rogers's testimony, solidified the case against the governor.

Rogers's direct testimony took more than three days, and when it concluded, both Linn and Thomas subjected him to intense cross-examination. The defense lawyers sought to discredit Rogers on the basis of his prior problems with both the IRS and the Security and

Exchange Commission. They hammered on the non-prosecution letter Rogers had received from the government and tried to show that Rogers was the real culprit, not Hall or Taylor. As it developed Rogers was a good witness, he seemed to enjoy jousting with the defense lawyers and, in some cases, turned their questions against them by categorizing Hall as a "crook."

The prosecution also called Derryberry to corroborate Rogers's testimony. The defense lawyers tried to embarrass Derryberry over a campaign contribution he had received from State Treasurer Leo Winters that might have come from illegal funds, but the attack was collateral at best and was halted by Judge Daugherty with seemingly little effect on the merits of the case.

The prosecution also called four board members of the Retirement Fund—Williams, Cook, Ward, and Merrill—to testify that Hall had called them to urge that they vote for Taylor's proposal. Each member also verified that Hall had never before contacted him on any other Retirement Board matter.

Taylor's hapless son-in-law, Duckels, testified about his alteration of the $31,250 check stub and verbal admissions made to him by Taylor. During the course of the prosecution's case, other witnesses verified the details surrounding the meetings between Rogers, Hall, Mooney, and Taylor. The government's case took eight days to present, and when the prosecution rested, it was clear the defense would have a tough job to overcome the sheer volume of damning evidence presented against Hall and Taylor.

CHAPTER TWENTY-TWO

The Defense

HALL'S DEFENSE RELIED ON the governor's personal power of persuasion. This became evident from Thomas's unconventional opening statement at the beginning of the defense's case. It consisted of only one sentence: "If the Court please, ladies and gentlemen of the jury, the evidence of David Hall will show that he didn't do it."

True to form, Hall thought he could talk his way out of the mess. Testifying on his own behalf, Hall did his best to sell the jury that he was an innocent man, falsely accused, and everyone else was lying.

Burkett well remembers the staged delivery of Hall's direct testimony. Thomas would ask a question. Hall would then turn to the jury and, with what appeared to be the utmost sincerity, deliver his answer.

Throughout the questioning, Hall adamantly denied taking any bribe or committing any other unlawful conduct. He denied even meeting with Rogers in the Blue Room on December 3. As far as his other conversations with Mooney, Taylor, and Rogers, he tried to explain them away by giving them innocent connotations.

Hall consistently claimed that Rogers was trying to "frame" him. He testified that Rogers's behavior had sent up "red flags" on several occasions, making him believe that Rogers was corrupt and on the take. Hall claimed he never reported his suspicions because he did not trust the FBI, Burkett, or the grand jury.

Hall did his best to convince the jury that it was, in fact, he himself who was trying to ferret out corruption in state government by leading Rogers to expose the offer of a bribe. In Hall's improbable story, he planned to collect evidence against Rogers to support a criminal prosecution. The only problem with his story was that Hall was not working with any law enforcement agency and had not reported his alleged investigation to anyone except his personal lawyer, Frank McDivitt, a convenient claim since any conversations with his lawyer were privileged and confidential.

At one point Hall tried to sway the jury by making what amounted to a speech on his own behalf saying: "There was no amount of money that could have bought me. There is no amount of money for which I would have taken an official action or omitted an official action. Money has not been my concern. That's probably the reason I'm so far in debt and that's probably the reason you've heard testimony that I probably spend more money than I should. But my primary objective in life for the past twenty years has been to accomplish my goal of leaving a mark in history that was good for the people . . ."

It was a pretty speech, but under the circumstances, hardly persuasive. Hall's problem was that his story had to face cross-examination. As Burkett recalls, it was not any one question that undermined Hall's credibility, but rather there were just too many facts Hall could not explain. The cross-examination taken as a whole was more death by Chinese water torture than with an axe. Like most cross-examinations, particularly in criminal trials, the process was fact intensive and tedious. Nevertheless, it exposed the ludicrous nature of Hall's claim that he had realized he was being framed and had only continued to deal with Rogers to set Rogers up for prosecution.

In order to impeach Hall's testimony, Buckett led Hall through a series of questions highlighting all of the possible law enforcement personnel with whom Hall had had contact with and could have alerted who were not part of the alleged political conspiracy against him, including friends like Curtis Harris, the Oklahoma County district attorney, and his trusted employees who headed the Oklahoma Department of Public Safety and the OSBI.

In the end, Hall was forced to seize on the improbable story that he had instructed his lawyer to contact the special Watergate prosecutor. Such farfetched assertions revealed his testimony for what it was, a very tall tale.

Hall also had to admit that he had put pressure on the Retirement Board to approve Taylor's plan, even though he had never contacted its members on any other issue during his entire term as governor. He testified in this regard as follows:

> **Question.** "Governor, as a matter of fact, didn't you tell Mr. Rogers that the trouble with getting these board members to vote for this was that you were going out of office?"
> **Answer.** "That's true."
> **Q.** "Didn't you tell him that if you were still in office, you would call—you wouldn't cajole a J.O. Spiller, that you wouldn't cajole a Jim Cook, that you wouldn't cajole other board members—not Jim Cook because he's an elected official, but J.O. Spiller, didn't you tell Mr. Rogers that you would just call them on the phone and say, 'Boy, you vote that matter or you won't be here next week'?"
> **A.** "No. I think I referred to J.O. Spiller on that. If I had a budget director that would turn down a plan that would make this money for Oklahoma, I would fire him in a minute."

Q. "If he was, didn't you tell Mr. Rogers, if you were still going to be governor, that you would have said, 'You vote for that or you won't be here next week'?"
A. "In the case of Mr. Spiller, that is correct."

The exchange revealed a kind of heavy-handed approach to the Retirement Board that did Hall no favors with the jury. Hall didn't help his credibility any with a parade of prominent character witnesses, which included his old mentor Supreme Court Justice Robert Simms and State Senator E. Melvin Porter.

At another point in his testimony, Hall also floundered to explain his instruction to Rogers "not to talk about 'that' " on the phone. The Governor could give no coherent explanation as to what "that" was.

The sum of Hall's testimony, however, was to help disclose the truth. Rather than helping exonerate him, on this most important of occasions, Hall's silver-tongued oratory failed and he helped convict himself.

Taylor also testified in his own defense. He concocted a story about how he had led Rogers along to make Rogers think that he was cooperating with him. Taylor also tried to push any wrongdoing off on Mooney. During both direct and cross-examination, Taylor came down with an acute case of selective memory.

The defense also tried to discredit Rogers's account of that initial meeting with Hall by presenting a highway patrolman who had guarded the governor's office. The patrolman testified that he had not seen any such meeting take place on the date in question. As a rebuttal, the government called another patrolman who had also guarded the governor's office, and he testified that the officers often left their post for various reasons and that a meeting could have easily occurred when a guard was not present.

CHAPTER TWENTY-THREE

Guilty

CLOSING ARGUMENTS IN THE case were made on March 11. On March 12, Judge Daugherty delivered his instructions to the jury, and deliberations began at 11:30 a.m. The judge also determined that the jury should be sequestered during deliberations, and so arrangements were made for the jurors to stay at the Skirvin Hotel in downtown Oklahoma City. The jury continued its deliberation until 7:30 p.m. on March 12. On March 13, the jury deliberated again for six hours, ending deliberations at 4:30 p.m. because one juror did not feel well. This juror, a woman named Dell Meyer, became the source of another controversy.

At 5:25 a.m. on the morning of March 14, Ms. Meyer believed she was having a heart attack and was taken to the emergency room at Saint Anthony Hospital. When court convened that morning, Judge Daugherty suggested that the parties agree to excuse Ms. Meyer and proceed with eleven jurors. Rather than accept the judge's suggestion, the defense lawyers, no doubt by now fearing an adverse verdict, refused and asked for a mistrial.

Instead the judge contacted Ms. Meyer's doctors and was advised that she had not suffered a heart attack. In fact, the doctors believed Ms. Meyer was well enough to be able to take part in the deliberations. Based on this information, the jury deliberations resumed at 1:30 p.m. with Ms. Meyer present.

Desperate for an escape hatch for their clients, the defense lawyers now questioned whether Ms. Meyer was, in fact, able to mentally or physically continue since she had been given Dalmane, Valium, and ex-lax at the hospital that morning. This led to a hearing before the court on the defendants' new motion for mistrial. Ms. Meyer's two doctors were summoned and questioned by the lawyers and the judge. While this most unusual of hearings was taking place, the jury reached a verdict. The judge concluded the hearing on the defendants' motion for mistrial and overruled the motion.

The defense lawyers' apprehension proved justified. The jury found Hall guilty on all four counts against him and Taylor guilty on all three counts against him. Sentencing on the convictions was deferred to a future date.

In spite of the verdict and the weight of the evidence, Hall continued to publicly assert his innocence. He vowed to appeal the case and professed surprise in the verdict. Despite his protestations, Hall was done—the verdict finished him politically and professionally.

At his sentencing, Hall again professed his innocence to the court. His pleas went unheard. Judge Daugherty sentenced Hall to serve three years in federal prison. Taylor received a sentence of eighteen months. To add insult to injury, the Oklahoma Supreme Court disbarred Hall even before his appeal was complete.

CHAPTER TWENTY-FOUR

Pay Back & Denial

A S FOR ROGERS, HE WAS not greeted as a conquering hero for having sent a corrupt governor to jail. Instead he found himself reviled by Democratic state legislators who saw Rogers as a turncoat and a rat. Impeachment proceedings were brought against Rogers, and on June 5, 1975, the House of Representatives voted in favor of three articles of impeachment against Rogers: for incompetency, for soliciting funds during a liquor petition drive, and for failure to report a campaign contribution from Hall.

To avoid facing a trial before the state senate, Rogers resigned as secretary of state on June 27. It was the end of his tumultuous political career.

Hall and Taylor both appealed to the Tenth Circuit Court of Appeals. They alleged a number of legal errors by the court including failure to grant a mistrial due to juror Meyer's illness. Rejecting their arguments, the Tenth Circuit Court affirmed both the verdict and the sentences for both Hall and Taylor in May 1976. The U.S. Supreme Court denied a petition for *certiorari* in November 1976.

The government, however, declined to prosecute Hall on any other charges, although Hall would later settle an IRS income tax claim for $325,000.

On November 22, 1976, Hall began to serve his sentence at a federal minimum-security facility in Safford, Arizona, a small town in the southeast corner of the state. Hall served eighteen months in prison.

Ironically, one of his fellow inmates was John Ehrlichman, one of Nixon's White House aides who was serving time for crimes related to Watergate. Ehrlichman and Hall became friendly in spite of Hall's own belief that he was the political victim of a Republican conspiracy involving the U.S. Justice Department and the Nixon administration.

After his release from prison, Hall moved to the San Diego area where he still resides. Always the promoter, Hall has engaged in a variety of business ventures since his prison days, including a car rental company, a company investigating acid rain, and a Mexican furniture manufacturer. All of his businesses went broke, judgments were entered against him, and he bounced checks.

Hall managed to stay afloat, and he became chairman of San Diego's Senior Olympics. Under his leadership, the organization grew in participation and prominence, but his tenure ended badly. In 1995, he resigned under pressure, leaving the Senior Olympics $100,000 in debt. After 1995, Hall worked as a legal assistant at several law firms and then became involved with a wealthy investor with whom Hall worked as a "partner and adviser" for seven years.

In 2012, Hall published his memoir, *Twisted Justice*. In the book, he continues to assert his innocence and accuses everyone involved in his prosecution of lying. Once more he insisted that he was the subject of a political conspiracy that went as high as the Nixon White House. Totally devoid of any refutation of facts, the book is nothing more than a continued denial in the face of overwhelming evidence of his guilt.

Burkett calls the book "delusional."

The Girl Scout Murders

CHIEF
By Kent F. Frates

An Indian died today,
inside four walls,
not in those long green halls,
of forest boughs.

A criminal it's true,
but human through and through,
with all those faults,
that only humans have.

That big steel door
slammed shut on
just another con
that, they all called, "Chief"
or "Tonto," or such,
and he'll not roam the
woods because his heart
quit, broken maybe, and
whatever mysterious evil
he knew, or didn't, is buried
in a simple grave leaving
only a story with no
ending at all.

CHAPTER TWENTY-FIVE

The Crime

WE SHOULD BE GRATEFUL for the system of justice that we enjoy in this country. Regardless of the circumstances, regardless of one's background, the accused is entitled to a fair trial and the decision of an impartial jury that has heard all the evidence. A jury verdict fairly rendered is a proper conclusion to a criminal case, but in the forum of public opinion, not always the final word.

When a heinous crime occurs, and a suspect is charged and later found not guilty, public doubt always persists as to whether the defendant did or did not commit the crime. This is especially true when no other suspects emerge and no one else is ever charged with the crime. Such a case marks a failure by law enforcement. Either a guilty person was somehow acquitted, or the real perpetrator of the crime has not been found. In either event, the person who committed the crime goes free. It is this controversial result that marked the conclusion of what became known nationwide as "The Girl Scout Murders."

Gene Leroy Hart, a Cherokee from Oklahoma, was charged with the June 13, 1977, murders of three young Girl Scouts at Camp Scott near Locust Grove in northeastern Oklahoma. All three girls had been sexually molested and then killed. Hart proved a hard man to catch and an impossible one to convict. He was found not guilty at his trial, and no one else has ever been charged with the crime.

The debate over his guilt or innocence continues to this day. Perhaps the principal reason this particular case went unsolved can be traced to the state of scientific criminal investigation in the 1970s. Today we are all conditioned by television and movies to believe that criminal investigators, aided by scientific methods and state-of-the-art lab equipment, can solve almost any crime. At the time of the Hart case, this was certainly not true. There was no DNA identification available then, and the analysis of hair, semen, and skin was little more than educated guesswork. Twenty-twenty hindsight is always dangerous, but it would seem likely that DNA testing, had it been available, could have solved the Girl Scout Murders. In its absence, we must trust the verdict rendered by the jury after hearing the evidence.

. . . . .

The victims were eight-year-old Lori Lee Farmer, nine-year-old Michelle Heather Guse, and ten-year-old Doris Denise Milner. The three girls had arrived at Camp Scott on June 12 as part of a Girl Scout outing with a troop from the Tulsa area. The four-hundred-acre camp was located in a densely wooded area near State Highway 82 in Mayes County. Situated back in the trees, the campgrounds were divided into units named after Native American tribes.

Lori Lee, Michelle Heather, and Doris Denise were assigned to tent Number Eight in the Kiowa Unit. Their tent was situated the greatest distance from their counselors' tent. Like the others, it had a wooden floor and contained cots for four campers. Due to a scheduling mistake, however, only three girls were assigned to tent Number Eight.

At around 10 o'clock on the night of Sunday, June 12, a counselor checked the trio's tent and found nothing unusual. At about 1:30 a.m., another counselor, Carla Wilhite, who was sleeping in the counselors' tent, heard a strange sound coming from the woods near tent Number Eight. She went to investigate, shining her flashlight into the woods where she had heard the sound. Later Wilhite described the noise as being ". . . like a frog, a bullhorn, or something. It didn't sound human. It didn't sound animal. It was just different." The sound finally stopped and Wilhite returned to her tent.

Around 2:00 a.m., a girl sleeping in tent Number Seven saw a shadowy figure open the flap to her tent and shine a flashlight inside. Although she was frightened the young girl sounded no alarm and went back to sleep. Around 3:00 a.m. another camper several hundred yards away in another unit thought she had heard a scream, but uncertain she said and did nothing.

At six on the morning of June 13, Wilhite rose and went to take a shower. At the intersection of two trails about a hundred and fifty feet from tent Number Eight, she came across three sleeping bags sprawled on the ground. When she went to see why the bags had come to be outside, one of the sleeping bags was open and in it she saw Doris Milner's body. The girl's head had been severely beaten and she was nude from the waist down. Her hands were duck taped behind her back, and wrapped around her neck was a cord with a cylindrical piece of cloth attached.

The other two sleeping bags were zipped closed. All three bags were almost a hundred yards from tent Number Eight. A terrified and badly shaken Wilhite immediately summoned help, and Richard Day, husband of Camp Director Barbara Day, responded. When Day reached the scene, he lifted the bags to confirm that they contained bodies.

They did.

CHAPTER TWENTY-SIX

The Investigation

THE CAMP STAFF REPORTED the grisly discovery to the Oklahoma Highway Patrol. The first law enforcement officer to arrive at the scene was Highway Patrolman Harold Berry, who secured the crime scene. Mayes County Sheriff Glen "Pete" Weaver and his deputy, A.D. David, quickly followed. The OSBI entered the case, and later the FBI was called in to help. Sid Wise, the local district attorney, involved himself in the case as soon as he was informed. Weaver and Wise would both prove to be controversial characters that would greatly influence the conduct of the investigation and the outcome of the case.

Wise was politically ambitious and from the get-go he exploited the notoriety of the case. He appointed himself coordinator of the investigation and began operating from a command post set up at Camp Scott. He conducted news conferences several times a day. Unbeknownst to the other law enforcement personnel involved, Wise had made a deal with a Pryor newspaper reporter, Ronald Grimsley, promising to feed him confidential information in anticipation of the two men writing a book about the case together. This arrangement would ultimately backfire on Wise.

Weaver was the local sheriff, who in addition to his official duties owned "Pete's Drive In" in Pryor and ran cattle. He fancied himself an old time western lawman and always wore a signature cowboy hat. Weaver had already had a roller-coaster career as sheriff. First elected in 1968, he had failed to win reelection in 1970, but was elected again in 1972, and served until 1980. During his tenure as sheriff, Weaver had quarreled with the previous district attorney, Bob Vinzant, and the local bar association over the treatment of prisoners in the county jail. He had also been accused of public drunkenness. Weaver had been the subject of an OSBI investigation triggered by a citizen's petition accusing him of dereliction of office. The investigation did not result in any legal action against Weaver, but ironically some of the same OSBI agents who investigated Weaver also took part in the investigation of the Girl Scout Murders.

After Camp Scott was evacuated, law enforcement personnel took over, and the circumstances of the crime became clearer as clues were discovered.

Opening the other two sleeping bags had revealed the bodies of Lori Farmer and Michelle Guse. Michelle had been beaten around the head and face, possibly gagged, and her hands were tied to her sides. Lori had been killed by one massive blow to the head. Years later OSBI Agent Mike Wilkerson still appeared visibly moved as he recalled how "tiny, tiny, tiny" the three victims were.

The object attached to the cord found around Doris Milner's neck appeared to be a gag. A flashlight, a roll of duct tape, women's glasses, and an eyeglass case were also found near the girls' bodies. The lens of the flashlight had been covered with a piece of plastic pricked by a small hole to better limit the amount of light cast by the beam. The glasses and eyeglass case had been stolen from a counselor's tent. The wood floor of the girls' tent was covered with blood, though it appeared to have been partially mopped up with sheets from the victims' beds. One bloody footprint from a tennis shoe was found on the tent floor. Outside the tent, a boot print was found. The OSBI removed a portion of the tent's wood floor and sent it for analysis to the OSBI lab in Oklahoma City.

The evidence indicated Lori and Michelle had been killed in the tent while Doris was probably murdered just outside. Two purses containing a number of personal items had been stolen from one of the counselors' tents.

Two days after the murders, Jack Shroff reported a burglary at his farm near Camp Scott. A role of duct tape was among the items that had been stolen from the Shroff farm. Cords similar to the ones used to restrain the little girls were also discovered at Shroff's farm, and a boot print, similar to the one found in the vicinity of the girls' tent, was found near the Shroff home.

Initially, this was enough to make Shroff a possible suspect, but he agreed to take a lie detector test and was ruled out as a suspect by the OSBI.

On June 16, just days after the murders, two hunters stalking squirrels about two miles southwest of Camp Scott discovered a cave that appeared to have been recently inhabited. This would be the first of three caves to figure in the investigation. The cave came to be known as Cave Number One, or the "Cellar Cave." The latter was a reference to the cellar found near the cave—that cellar being all that remained of the house where Gene Leroy Hart had spent his childhood, though that wasn't known at the time.

The Oklahoma Highway Patrol searched the cave and found items that became crucial to the prosecution of the case, including two wrinkled photographs of well-dressed women, part of a Tulsa newspaper dated April 17, broken sunglasses, and a piece of green plastic with duct tape attached.

The plastic and duct tape were similar to what had been used on the flashlight found at the murder scene. The newspaper clipping was from the same edition as a newspaper page that had been found crumpled inside the flashlight at the murder scene, and the broken sunglasses were similar to a pair that had been stolen from the camp counselor.

Within days, tracking dogs were brought in from Pennsylvania. The team consisted of two German shepherds and a Rottweiler; the dogs were described as "Wonder Dogs" and were greeted with great fanfare by locals. The dogs confirmed the perpetrator had passed near the counselors' tent and tracked their way to a pond on the Shroff farm. The pond was dragged, but no evidence was discovered. The dog team also became a casualty of the crime. One dog was badly injured while tracking through the woods; another was killed when hit by a car. In the end, the dogs provided no great help in solving the crime.

The clues gathered from the scene, however, began to talk. Autopsies revealed Doris Milner had died from strangulation while the other two girls were beaten to death. All three of the victims had been sexually molested.

An OSBI forensic chemist concluded that a hair found stuck to tape used to bind Milner was of Mongoloid or Native American origin. A fingerprint was discovered on the flashlight.

During the early stages of the investigation, leaks and misinformation ran rampant. One minute, fingerprints had been found on the girls' bodies; the next, the murder weapon had been found and the tracking dogs had picked up the trail of the killer or killers. All of those reports proved false. One day, Wise told the press there were no suspects while Weaver was elsewhere stating they had a suspect. Meanwhile, the OSBI was reporting that three suspects existed.

In truth, besides Shroff, at least two other suspects would be held and questioned: one a drifter picked up in an adjacent county, the other a psychiatric patient. Authorities would clear both suspects.

Coincidentally, one of the victim's had family law enforcement ties. Doris's father, Walter, was a Tulsa police officer, and the Tulsa Fraternal Order of Police offered a $5,000 reward for information leading to the killer's capture. Other organizations pitched in funds, too, raising the reward to $14,000.

The media spotlight intensified with local and national TV, radio, and newspaper coverage. Governor David Boren offered the assistance of the Oklahoma National Guard. All of these factors put pressure on Weaver to solve the crime sooner rather than later.

CHAPTER TWENTY-SEVEN

Gene Leroy Hart

EARLY ON, WEAVER DECIDED that Gene Leroy Hart, an escaped convict, was the prime suspect. Hart had grown up in the Locust Grove area. His mother, Ella Mae Buckskin, lived within a mile of Camp Scott, and Hart was known to be familiar with the in and outs of the area.

Hart was an example of a good boy gone bad. He had played several positions on the football team at Locust Grove High School, where he also played basketball. Upon graduation from high school in 1963, Hart had married, had a child, and moved away to Tulsa where he worked in construction.

Three years after graduating Locust Grove High, Hart had abducted two young women, ages eighteen and nineteen, from the parking lot of the Fondalight Night Club in north Tulsa. Both women were in the early stages of pregnancy. He had forced them into the trunk of his car and headed to a remote part of Mayes County. During the trip he released the women from the trunk one at a time and raped them. After reaching his destination, Hart tied the women with friction tape and ropes, and left them in the woods. One of Hart's victims managed to free her hands, and the two women found their way back to a highway and reported the crime.

The victims were able to describe Hart and his car and remembered part of the license number. Hart was picked up the next day in Pryor and confessed to the crimes. He later pled guilty to the charges of first-degree rape and kidnapping, and was given three ten-year sentences to run concurrently.

After serving twenty-eight months in prison, including a stay in Granite Reformatory, Hart was released on parole in March 1969. By now, though, Hart had chosen a life of crime. He was again arrested on June 7, 1969, while unsuccessfully attempting to burglarize the apartment of a Tulsa policewoman. That arrest lead to Hart's arrest and conviction for four different burglaries. His new combined maximum prison sentences now totaled more than three hundred years.

While serving his sentences at the state prison in McAlester, Oklahoma, Hart was temporarily moved to the Mayes County Jail in connection with a post sentencing relief hearing. Along with another prisoner, Larry Dry, he proceeded to escape from the jail on May 20, 1973. After eleven days of hiding around Pryor, a friend convinced Hart to surrender, and he was returned to the Mayes County Jail.

Hart, however, proved allergic to jail, and on September 16, 1973, he escaped again—this time by sawing through his cell bars with a hacksaw smuggled to him by an unknown accomplice. Dry also accompanied Hart on this escape.

This time, Hart managed to stay free, hiding in the area with friends and relatives. A homeboy, he knew the territory and hid part of the time in the rural caves with which he was familiar from his childhood. He was aided by the fact that many of the Cherokees in the area did not trust the white man's law, nor Sheriff Weaver; some offered assistance to Hart, enabling him to avoid capture.

Whatever else Hart was or was not, he was clearly an embarrassment to Sheriff Weaver. From time to time, someone in Mayes County would spot Hart, and Weaver's inability to catch Hart became a running joke among the locals.

Hart's record and proximity to the crime made him a viable suspect, but to many, it started to seem like Weaver had prejudged Hart guilty and then set out to convict him, regardless of what the evidence had to say.

CHAPTER TWENTY-EIGHT

Manhunt

ON JUNE 21, A BURGLARY occurred at a rural grocery near Locust Grove; food and cigarettes were stolen. Two days later, another cave was discovered west of Camp Scott. This cave became known as Cave Number Two. A search of the cave yielded cans of food stolen from the same grocery that had been robbed on June 21. The search also turned up cigarettes that had been smoked by someone with Type O blood—Hart's blood type, yes, but also the most common blood type in the U.S. (forty-five percent of people in the U.S. have Type O blood). Another Mongoloid-type hair was also found in the cave. The cave was located on a ridge overlooking the house of Hart's mother.

Larry Dry who had been arrested again on other charges had identified the Cellar Cave as a hiding place used by Hart and Dry after their escape from the Mayes County Jail. Photographs found in the Cellar Cave were determined to have been taken at a wedding in southwest Oklahoma. Hart might have developed the photographs while he was working as a photographic assistant at the Granite Reformatory.

The Girl Scout Murders

On June 23, at Weaver's request, Wise had a first-degree murder warrant issued for Hart's arrest, and the manhunt was officially on.

Reacting to a report that a farmer had spotted a pair of legs in a cave or on a ledge north and west of the Girl Scout camp, tracking dogs and a search team were summoned. Several hundred volunteers, many of them equipped with citizen-band radios, formed a perimeter to contain the area searched by the dogs. The search went on for hours but proved futile. Not to be deterred, the volunteers again formed a huge line almost two miles long and swept an area near the camp looking for clues. Again, nothing of substance was discovered.

A reported sighting of a man, who was said to be carrying two weapons, running across a field not far from Camp Scott triggered another massive search of the wooded area near the camp. This time, four hundred volunteers and two hundred lawmen took part in the operation. Tracking dogs, helicopters, and heat-detection devices were also employed. Weaver warned the searchers that the man they were looking for could be armed and dangerous. Although cautioned not to carry weapons, many of the volunteers were armed, and a vigilante mentality prevailed.

In the end, what the posse discovered was not Hart, but the extreme nature of the wooded terrain of eastern Oklahoma. Dense undergrowth, intense heat, and snakes harassed the searchers. Ticks were everywhere and the chiggers were worse. Bug spray proved futile against the ornery critters. There are few things tougher or more irritating than an Oklahoma chigger, a minute flea-like insect that burrows into a person's skin and takes days or even weeks to die as it emits a toxic acid, driving its victim crazy in the process; ticks can also be dangerous, carrying Lyme disease and Rocky Mountain spotted fever. The brush was so dense where the search took place that Hart could have gone undetected, hidden within a few feet of any searcher. More likely, he was not in the area at all.

Given the harsh conditions, the search did not last long and was substantially abandoned within four days. The manhunt for Hart, however, continued. A group of U.S. Army veterans who had served in Vietnam, calling themselves the "Spooks," took a crack at finding Hart, but they also failed. As time passed, sightings and rumors surfaced now and again, but when pursued none led to Hart's arrest.

On August 1, authorities were led to a third cave by a Pryor jail inmate who alleged he had met Hart there after the murders. Known to the investigators as Cave Number Three, this cave was located south of the second cave. All three of the caves were within a few miles of Camp Scott and each other, which meant they were also fairly near the home of Hart's mother.

No evidence that would help apprehend Hart was found in the third cave, though someone had left a taunting message written on the cave wall:

The killer was here. Bye Bye fools. 77-6-17.

The message only added to the pressure to locate Hart.

CHAPTER TWENTY-NINE

Homeboy

PUBLIC OPINION ABOUT Hart and his role in the murders continued to polarize people. The Native American community along with many local whites believed Hart to be a scapegoat being framed by Sheriff Weaver. To these people, Hart was basically a "good boy" who was incapable of such a hideous crime. There is no doubt Hart's whereabouts were known to some Cherokees, and that some Cherokees aided him in hiding. Many of those who believed him not guilty of the murders would come to view Hart as an outlaw, wrongfully charged. Some of his supporters even believed that he was innocent of his previous rape and kidnapping convictions, in spite of his own guilty plea to those crimes.

As the manhunt dragged on, tension between law enforcement personnel and the Cherokees continued to grow. Hart's mother, Ella Mae Buckskin, contended that she had been repeatedly harassed by members of the sheriff's department and that FBI agents had drawn their guns on her six-year-old nephew. She enlisted the aid of the American Indian Movement, which quickly announced that its members were ready to stage a protest in Mayes County. An AIM spokesman accused the investigators of "acting as judge, jury, and executioner . . ." And that same spokesman reminded the public, "We don't want an innocent Indian around [here] to get hurt."

Local Cherokees and other Native Americans were particularly distrustful of Sheriff Weaver, whom they had long viewed as a racist. Weaver denied all of AIM's accusations and said its charges "didn't deserve an answer." But fear that Hart would be shot on sight, as well as distrust of white man's justice, persisted among some Cherokees. A proud and independent people, the Cherokees believed in their tribal customs and tribal sovereignty, the latter of which gave them the authority to govern themselves. The urge to protect one of their own was both instinctive and genuine, and, given their history with federal and local officials, understandable.

Meanwhile Sheriff Weaver continued to talk a tough game, vowing that he would apprehend Hart, though he did not appear to have a coherent plan for Hart's capture. The OSBI, on the other hand, was far more sophisticated. OSBI agents questioned members of the Cherokee community and even consulted with a Cherokee medicine man. Finally, OSBI Agent Larry Bowles was able to recruit an informant who was interested in the reward money.

The informant, who insisted on remaining anonymous to everyone except Bowles, began to feed the agent information. The informant reported that while attending a Cherokee religious ceremony, a medicine man, William Lee Smith, had told him that Hart was staying with an old Cherokee in the Cookson Hills. The rough and forested Cookson Hills have, over many years, been a hideout for many notorious outlaws from Belle Starr to "Pretty Boy" Floyd. They have also always been the home for many people who have little use for the law, including many Cherokees. To the OSBI, Hart's presence in this area seemed likely.

Later, the informant learned from the medicine man that Hart's protector was "an old man who sold firewood." Smith had expressed concern that hunters might spot Hart, as he had been hunting and fishing near where he was hiding. More information indicated that Hart's hideout might be close to Tahlequah.

Based on the new tips, agents scoured the countryside for a firewood salesman, but had no success in finding Hart's hideout.

Eventually, the informant advised Bowles that the person who was hiding Hart was actually related to Smith's wife, Eva. Mrs. Smith's maiden name was Pigeon, but the agents found pursuing Pigeons to be less than productive as the family name was common in eastern Oklahoma's Indian Country and Mrs. Smith had many relatives.

CHAPTER THIRTY

Captured

A S MONTHS WENT BY without Hart's capture, the pressure on the OSBI continued to grow. From the director on down the entire Bureau felt it would be an embarrassment if Sheriff Weaver, the FBI, the Highway Patrol, or some other law enforcement organization found Hart before the OSBI did. Three or more agents were assigned to work the case at all times, and in early April 1978, almost ten months after the crime, the pressure to succeed forced the agents to make a move.

Armed with the information furnished by the informant, the OSBI decided to confront Eva Smith and push for information about Hart's whereabouts. On April 6, agents Larry Bowles and Harvey Pratt presented Mrs. Smith with what they had learned.

The two agents told Eva they weren't interested in prosecuting her, but had to bring in the man they thought had killed the three girls. They pressed her hard to reveal Hart's whereabouts. Eva finally broke and agreed to show the agents where Hart was staying with Sam Pigeon, an old Cherokee, in rural Adair County. She led the agents to Pigeon's three-room, tar-paper shack located southeast of Tahlequah on a rough dirt road, some fifty miles from Camp Scott. Fearful that someone, including Eva herself, might alert Hart if there was any delay, the OSBI decided to go after him immediately. Eight heavily armed agents in two vehicles launched a raid on Pigeon's house about a quarter after four that same day. Mike Wilkerson, one of the agents involved in the raid, would later join with his brother, Dick, to write a book about the Girl Scout Murders.

The agents surrounded Pigeon's shack and struck quickly. Hart looked out the back door as if to run, but turned back inside where agents, who had rushed in from the front of the home, captured him. He was unarmed and did not put up a fight. At the time of his arrest Hart was wearing large frame eyeglasses, what appeared to be women's glasses, a tank top, and shorts. He was immediately handcuffed and led from the house. Excited by their success, the agents photographed themselves with Hart. The photographs later became a point of contention during Hart's trial.

The agents transported Hart to Tahlequah where he was fingerprinted and then escorted straight to the state prison in McAlester. Given his history of breaking out of the Mayes County Jail, no one wanted to risk holding him there even overnight.

Although, law enforcement officers were generally elated over Hart's capture, local residents held other views. On the date of Hart's arrest the *Daily Oklahoman* took a random telephone poll of fifteen Locust Grove residents, all of whom either thought Hart was innocent or at least questioned his guilt. Almost immediately, fund-raising efforts began to help finance Hart's defense.

While Hart headed to McAlester, a few agents stayed at the house to arrest Pigeon when he returned home from work. They also arrested Pigeon's brother, Freeman, when the two men returned. The Pigeons were questioned at length. Both men fully cooperated with the agents and were forthcoming with information, although Sam had trouble with English and was much more comfortable speaking Cherokee.

Sam told the agents that Hart had been staying with him since the previous summer. He had helped Hart, who he referred to as "Drum," at the request of Smith, the same medicine man who had talked to the informant. Sam said he knew Hart was in some kind of trouble, but only later asked Hart what it was.

According to Sam, Hart told him that he was accused of killing three girls, but he denied committing the crime. Pigeon believed him. A thorough search of Pigeon's house was conducted by the OSBI. The house was cluttered with numerous personal items. After examining them, it was concluded that nothing connecting Hart to the crime could be found.

William Smith was subsequently questioned by Agent Bowles. The medicine man proved evasive and untruthful and a warrant for harboring a fugitive was obtained for him.

Before Smith could be arrested, however, he left the state on business. Cherokee Chief Ross Swimmer learned of his departure and sent a private plane to Arkansas to bring Smith back to Pryor so he could surrender and make bail rather than risk being arrested on his return to Oklahoma. This would be one of several acts by Cherokee Nation officials expressing loyalty to Hart and any other tribal member involved in the case. Both Smith and Pigeon were charged with harboring a fugitive, but the State never pursued the prosecution of either case.

CHAPTER THIRTY-ONE

The Prosecution

THE SEARCH FOR HART was over, but the legal jousting had just begun. Hart could not afford a lawyer but was entitled to legal counsel. Had he not come up with a private attorney on his own, the judge would have appointed a member of the Mayes County Bar to represent him and his attorney would have been decided by the luck of the draw. Neither Hart nor the Cherokees wanted to take that kind of chance with his freedom and his life.

Fund raisers of all kinds—from chicken dinners to gospel sing-alongs—were held to raise money for Hart's defense. Before the case was over, contributions to the defense fund had come in from Native Americans and others from all over the country.

After being briefly represented by a Tulsa lawyer, Larry Oliver, and a locally appointed lawyer, David Poplin, Hart's defense was assumed by Garvin Isaacs of Oklahoma City and Gary Pitchlynn of Norman.

Isaacs was only thirty-four at the time and this would be his first murder trial. He was no stranger to the courtroom, however, having served as both an assistant district attorney and as an assistant public defender in Oklahoma County. Pitchlynn, fresh out of law school, was working at the Native American Center in Oklahoma City and was eager to help. Both Isaacs and Pitchlynn had Choctaw heritage. What both lawyers also possessed was enthusiasm and energy. They believed in Hart's innocence and were ready to ensure that his legal rights were protected and that he received a fair trial. Though underpaid and poorly financed, the defense was aggressive and combative.

Initially, the prosecution fell to Wise who, basking in his notoriety from the case, had filed for the office of state attorney general. A case of the magnitude of the Girl Scout Murders deserved the full attention of any lawyer, and running for a statewide office proved to be an unnecessary distraction for Wise.

Given this and Wise's questionable qualifications, the parents of the victims decided to seek help. With the full cooperation of Weaver and the OSBI, the parents approached Tulsa County District Attorney S.M. "Buddy" Fallis and requested that he join in the prosecution. Fallis agreed and, under heavy pressure, so did Wise. In order to save face, Wise announced that Fallis was joining the prosecution so there would be some continuity in the case if it continued beyond Wise's term as district attorney, which ended in January 1978.

An experienced and highly successful prosecutor with an excellent conviction record, Fallis had been the district attorney of Tulsa County since 1966, and before that an assistant county attorney and assistant district attorney. He knew how to handle a capital case and how to work with law enforcement to prepare a case for trial. Fallis's chief assistant, Ronald Shaffer, who joined in the prosecution, also had extensive trial experience.

In June, Grimsley ran an ad in a Tulsa newspaper seeking investors to finance a book about the case. An enterprising reporter called the telephone number listed in the ad. The number turned out to be that of Wise's campaign office where Grimsley was working as campaign manager. When asked if he was involved in the book deal, Wise denied any agreement with Grimsley.

CHAPTER THIRTY-TWO

Preliminary Hearing

A SPECIAL JUDGE FROM Claremore, Jess B. Clanton Jr., was assigned to the preliminary hearing, which was scheduled to begin in June. Emotions regarding the case and the defendant were running high, and extensive security measures were ordered for the hearing. Armed guards were posted at the courthouse, and spectators who entered the courtroom were subject to search by the sheriff's deputies. The courtroom only held about a hundred spectators, and in an unusual move, the Supreme Court, at the request of the *Tulsa Tribune* and KOTV of Tulsa, allowed closed circuit television coverage from the courthouse to an auditorium at Pryor City Hall.

Preliminary hearings in Oklahoma are usually perfunctory. The State is only required to prove that a crime has been committed and that there is probable cause to believe the defendant committed the crime. The determination of guilt or innocence is left for the trial. Routinely, the State puts on only the limited amount of evidence necessary to meet its burden of proof, and the defendant generally offers no evidence at all. But, this was clearly not a routine case. There was no doubt the crime of murder had been committed—not once but three times—but connecting Hart to the crime was more problematic.

Prior to the hearing, 176 witnesses were subpoenaed, fifty-six by the State and 120 by the defense. At the hearing, twenty-three witnesses were called by the State and seventy-five by the defendant. The hearing lasted four weeks. The prosecutors accused the defense of going on a "fishing expedition," and the *Daily Oklahoman* wrote an editorial criticizing the judge and defense lawyers for dragging the hearing out unnecessarily. In the end, Judge Clanton bound Hart over for trial on three counts of first-degree murder.

The evidence revealed at the hearing gave a preview of the trial. It was learned that the fingerprint found on the flashlight left near the girls' bodies was not Hart's. Likewise, the bloody footprint on the floor of the tent was left by a smaller foot than Hart's.

Hart, however, was implicated by the items found in the Cellar Cave, including the photographs he might have developed while a prisoner at Granite, as well as the eyeglasses, which were similar to a pair stolen from one of the camp counselors.

An OSBI agent also testified that the masking tape found in the cave matched that found near the victims' bodies. The Tulsa newspaper found in the cave was also from the same edition of the same date as the newspaper page that was wadded inside the flashlight found at the crime scene. One pathologist testified that he had found no evidence that any of the girls had been raped. Another pathologist testified that he had found evidence that two of the girls had been raped, including semen in their bodies.

The State also offered the testimony of Ann Reed, a forensic chemist for the OSBI. Ms. Reed testified that human hairs found on the tape binding the hands of Doris Milner and on her pajamas showed definite Mongoloid characteristics generally found in the hair of Native Americans. These were not the Milner girl's hairs, which displayed a blend of Caucasian and Negroid characteristics. There were no foreign hairs found on the bodies of the other two victims. Reed further testified that the hairs found on Doris had the "same microscopic characteristics" as samples of Hart's hair. This testimony was allowed by the judge in spite of the fact that the witness admitted, "I cannot identify a person by a hair comparison."

The real fireworks at the hearing were occasioned by the testimony of two convicts who had done time with Hart. Larry Dry, who escaped from the Mayes County Jail with Hart, tied the items in the Cellar Cave to Hart. Dry testified that he and Hart had hidden in the cave and that he had seen Hart with the photographs found in the cave. He also told of how on one occasion, he had restrained Hart from harming a thirteen-year-old girl by threatening him with a shotgun. Dry's testimony was placed in doubt when it was revealed that shortly after giving a statement to the OSBI, he was paroled by Governor David Boren. Also, at the time he appeared at the hearing, he was being held in the Delaware County Jail on burglary charges.

The most surprising testimony, however, came from another convict, Jimmy Don Bunch, who had served time with Hart in McAlester after Hart's arrest on the murder charges. Prior to the hearing, Bunch had met with both Isaacs and law enforcement officers. He had given the defense lawyers a recorded and signed statement asserting that he believed Hart was innocent. In the statement, Bunch also said that he had been offered parole by a prison guard if he would testify that Hart had admitted doing the murders when he testified. Instead of helping the defense, Bunch disclaimed the recorded statement, which he said was given under promises and pressure from Isaacs. Bunch then flipped his story and testified that when he asked Hart if he had committed the crime, Hart told him, "(He) really didn't know."

Bunch said Hart had confided to him that he had been "smoking reefers and drinking wine for three days. 'I woke up in the cave and had blood all over me.'"

An enraged Isaacs declared Bunch a hostile witness and set about trying to discredit the convict. In the end, Bunch's entire testimony was so unreliable that neither party later called him as a witness at the trial.

As if the case was not explosive enough, a bomb threat occurred on the last morning of the hearing. At around nine, while court was in session, an unidentified man telephoned the Mayes County court clerk's office and said a bomb was set to go off in the courthouse at 10:15 a.m. Judge Clanton cleared the courthouse and a search was conducted. Fortunately, no bomb was found, and the proceedings resumed.

Taking no chances, Sheriff Weaver immediately returned Hart to the state prison in McAlester. Wise expressed confidence in the State's case and said he would move for a trial within sixty days. Fallis was also convinced Hart was guilty, but he did admit to reporters that it would be hard to select a jury "because of the many opinions formulated in this community."

CHAPTER THIRTY-THREE

Newly Discovered Evidence

THE TRIAL JUDGE IN the case, District Judge William Whistler, was now presiding over the proceedings. Whistler— an experienced judge who had served for more than ten years as an associate district judge and then district judge for Craig, Rogers, and Mayes counties—set the case for trial in November and repeatedly refused to delay the date. The defense began to bombard the court with motions, mostly related to discovery and mostly overruled.

Regardless of the confidence and public pronouncements of the prosecution, it was clear that the evidence tying Hart to the murders was entirely circumstantial. Further, it was obvious that the defense was going to challenge every piece of evidence, and it would behoove the State to strengthen its case in any way possible.

Probably with this in mind, the OSBI decided to conduct another search of Sam Pigeon's home. With Pigeon's consent, agents once again scoured the place. In all, the agents would search the house a total of three times. Most of Hart's belongings had long since been removed and the place had been cleaned out to a great extent. This time the agents did find some items that might have been Hart's, including a corncob pipe and a decorative hand mirror. These items had not been found during the previous search, although one agent thought he remembered seeing them.

The agents then began to question counselors and campers' parents about ownership of the pipe and mirror. A counselor from Stillwater, Karen Mitchell, and her parents identified the pipe and mirror. Karen had taken the pipe to camp to use in play-acting sessions conducted with the young campers. The mirror also belonged to Karen. Pigeon confirmed that these items were not his, giving the prosecution further evidence to link Hart to Camp Scott.

On August 22, Wise finished last in a five-man contest for the Democratic nomination in the attorney general's race. He was now, among other things, a lame duck and anxious to have the case tried before he left office in January. On August 27, Sheriff Weaver suffered a heart attack but recovered and remained in office. Both Wise and Weaver continued to be the focus of intense animosity from the Cherokees. On October 16, Chief Swimmer announced the tribe was contributing $12,500 to Hart's defense fund. Swimmer said that the tribe was not expressing an opinion on Hart's guilt or innocence, but wanted to ensure that he received a fair trial.

OSBI Chemist Janice Davis took semen samples found in the body cavities of the victims and other samples obtained from Hart's underwear while in jail and presented them to a noted expert on reproductive medicine Dr. John McCleod, a Cornell University professor emeritus. This proved particularly interesting since at least one pathologist called by the State had testified at the preliminary hearing that no semen was found on the victims. McCleod reached an opinion that based on statistical computations, the sperm found on the victims was likely Hart's, although there was no way to scientifically verify it at that time.

Another case was filed with the Oklahoma Supreme Court by KOTV, this time asking to televise the trial for the public. The court ruled that the trial could be televised, but only if the defendant, the

State, and the judge agreed. Whistler indicated that he was inclined to allow the televising, but the defense objected, so there would be no TV cameras in the courtroom. Judge Whistler did allocate two rows of seats to the media and, in an unusual move, allowed one designated media person to be present during any proceedings that took place in chambers. Seats were also reserved for the families of the victims and Hart's family.

CHAPTER THIRTY-FOUR

The OSBI Reports

S HORTLY BEFORE THE TRIAL was set to begin, the Wise-Grimsley book deal became public. The partnership between Wise and Grimsley was exposed to the court and the public. After Wise's defeat for attorney general, Grimsley had approached the defense and agreed to work for it as an investigator, furnishing the defense with confidential OSBI reports for $895. Grimsley provided twenty-six pages of reports, which had been given to him by Wise, but could not produce any others.

The revelation of the book deal and the release of OSBI records to an unauthorized party were all the defense needed to serve a subpoena on the OSBI. The defense sought work papers and reports on the grounds that any legal client-attorney confidentiality had been breached when Wise furnished the twenty-six pages of documents to Grimsley.

On November 17, Judge Whistler held a hearing to determine whether the defense was entitled to the OSBI reports. Wise was called as a witness and admitted the book partnership, but denied giving the reports to Grimsley. He tried to explain away his earlier denial of the agreement with Grimsley by saying the contract had expired, but this was contrary to its written terms.

The defense produced an affidavit from Grimsley stating that he had obtained the reports with Wise's knowledge. The judge refused to consider the affidavit, but did issue a bench warrant for Grimsley, who had failed to respond to a subpoena and had left the state in order to avoid testifying.

Grimsley was located by the OSBI in Missouri and returned to appear in court. On November 21, Grimsley testified that Wise was present when he made copies of the reports. Judge Whistler denied the defendant's request for the reports as untimely, but chastised Wise saying, "I think Mr. Wise showed very poor judgment in allowing a stranger, an outsider, to handle, to read the work product belonging to the State."

The whole affair had also discredited Wise to the extent that he withdrew from the case. The newly elected district attorney, T. Jack Graves, replaced him, while Fallis, who had no part in releasing the OSBI reports, remained on as a prosecutor. The turmoil over the State's counsel caused the judge to continue the trial until March 1979.

The battle by the defense to obtain the OSBI reports raged on and would continue into the trial itself. The defense took the issue to the Court of Criminal Appeals, and on March 1, the appeals court ruled that the prosecution had to turn over any evidence that might tend to clear Hart. The court determined that Wise had forfeited the right of confidentiality when he furnished some of the reports to Grimsley. It remained unclear as to which reports the ruling covered, though, and Isaac moved for a continuance of the trial. The request was denied, and the trial was set to begin March 5.

During the run up to trial, the supporters of Hart increased their fund-raising efforts and enthusiastically sponsored a grassroots public relations campaign touting Hart's innocence. Bumper stickers with slogans like "Free Hart" and "In the Hart of Gene Country" popped up around the county. On the first day of trial and thereafter, supporters gathered near the courthouse brandishing signs and wearing T-shirts proclaiming their belief in Hart's innocence.

Strapped for funds, Hart's defense team rented a vacant building in Pryor for two hundred dollars a month. Dubbed the "Hart Hotel," they turned it into a combination office and living quarters for the lawyers and their support staff. Some Cherokees pitched in voluntarily to cook meals or donate food.

CHAPTER THIRTY-FIVE

The Trial

THE TRIAL COMMENCED on March 5 with jury selection. Judge Whistler had ruled each prospective juror could be questioned individually, and so the tedious process began. Two weeks later, after the questioning of 113 people, a jury of twelve was seated. Two more alternates were then picked after twenty-one more candidates were questioned.

The repetitious and lengthy questioning caused tempers to flare between the lawyers and the judge, and that further lengthened jury selection. In the end, the jury was comprised of six men and six women. Three housewives were joined on the panel by a pipefitter, a basketball coach, a utility foreman, a chemical plant manager, an inventory clerk, a grocery store employee, an airplane structure mechanic, a heavy equipment operator, and an apprentice electrician.

There were no Native Americans and no residents of Locust Grove on the jury. The judge ordered the jury to be sequestered at a local motel for the duration of the trial. The evidentiary portion of the trial began March 19, but not before Hart asked the court to allow him to give his own opening statement. Judge Whistler denied his request on the grounds that he could possibly make a legal error while delivering his statement. This was an obvious ploy by the defense. If Hart were never to take the stand during the remainder of the trial he could have told his story to the jury in an opening statement while not under oath or subject to cross-examination.

Denied the request, the defense announced that Hart would give a press conference the next day. The bizarre news conference consisted of Hart answering a series of written questions and a few closely monitored verbal questions. Nothing was revealed about the evidence to be presented, however, Hart did use the opportunity to state one of the themes that the defense would play upon throughout the trial when he said, "I am not a hero. I have no desire to be a hero. But maybe I represent fears and doubts that many people have about any system that has the means and the power to overwhelm each of us, each and every one of us."

The defense's theory was to cast Hart as a hometown underdog being railroaded by a runaway law enforcement team that needed to convict someone, whether the real murderer or not.

The prosecution presented the State's evidence in the same manner as it had at the preliminary hearing, except it was buttressed by the evidence connecting Hart to the crime with the newly discovered corncob pipe and hand mirror, as well as two expert witnesses who presented the scientific theory related to Hart's sperm.

The defense relentlessly attacked the reliability of the evidence and the State's witnesses, pursuing the theory that Weaver had prejudged Hart's guilt and that both Sheriff Weaver and the OSBI had planted evidence in an attempt to convict Hart of the murders.

All of the State's evidence was circumstantial, so it was crucial to connect the items found at the crime scene with the items found in the Cellar Cave and to connect Hart to the cave. OSBI agents, once again, identified the items found at the scene of the crime. As before, Larry Dry testified that he and Hart had hidden in the Cellar Cave after their jail escape. He also stated that they had rigged flashlights with plastic covers over the lens, in the same manner as the one found at the murder scene. He also said that he had seen Hart with the women's photographs found in the cave. This time, however, Dry's testimony about his other conversations with Hart was excluded from evidence.

Ann Reed once again testified that human hairs found on Doris Milner matched Hart's, but again admitted that a person could not be positively identified by hair analysis. The principal difference in the State's case came in two regards: Janice Davis, an OSBI forensic chemist, testified that blood samples found on the victims were Type O blood, which was Hart's blood type. She also pursued a theory related to sperm found in the body cavities of the victims. Her initial tests had not detected any sperm, but she testified that when she examined samples with a more powerful microscope, she was able to identify sperm. The samples of Hart's sperm had been obtained from the underwear he had worn while in jail and then all of the samples were taken to Dr. John McCleod for comparison.

McCleod testified to having conducted elaborate tests on the sperm samples, but he was only able to conclude that "it would not be unreasonable to infer" that the sperm found on the victims came from Hart.

"Conversely I did not find any evidence that would exclude Mr. Hart," McCleod testified. McCleod's conclusions were based on population statistics and probabilities rather than hard forensic evidence. His testimony was also questionable since Hart had undergone a vasectomy prior to the crime. On cross-examination, McCleod admitted that he could not confirm that it was Hart's sperm or that Hart had committed the crime. Under today's evidentiary requirements for the admission of "expert" testimony, it is unlikely either Reed's or McCleod's testimony regarding the sperm or hair samples would be admissible, but at the time, DNA testing did not exist and such inconclusive pseudo-science might well have seemed credible to the jurors.

Camp Counselor Karen Mitchell was called as a witness, and she identified the corncob pipe and mirror found on the second search of

Sam Pigeon's house as belonging to her. She had left them in a foot-locker at Camp Scott when the camp was evacuated. When the foot-locker was returned to her two weeks later in Tulsa, the items were missing. Mitchell had no knowledge as to where the footlocker had been located or how it was handled for those two weeks.

Near the end of the State's case, the jurors were taken to Camp Scott to view the murder scene. Nothing, however, was pointed out to them nor were any persons allowed to talk to them while they were at Camp Scott.

During the entire Hart case, the courtroom was packed with spectators, and the courthouse and vicinity were crowded with media and onlookers. Many of Hart's supporters were constantly on hand. The parents of Lori Farmer and Michelle Guse and the mother of Doris Milner attended every session of court, as did Ella Mae Buckskin and many other members of Hart's family.

The Pryor paper, the *Daily Times*, ran an article headlined "A Trial of Mothers" featuring Mrs. Farmer and Mrs. Buckskin. The article highlighted the intense opinions on both sides of the case. In the courtroom, Isaacs was contentious and aggressive, and Fallis never backed down from a fight. The two lawyers made numerous objections and quarreled constantly. The atmosphere both within the courtroom and around the courthouse was combative, tense, and electric.

Fallis, whose memory of the case remains crystal clear thirty years later, recalls two incidents that captured the mood of the trial for him. While standing at a urinal in the crowded bathroom, Fallis heard a voice say, "You're going to die." Fallis could not identify the voice, but reported it to Judge Whistler who let Fallis use his private restroom for the remainder of the trial.

Then when the trial was ready to begin, Fallis noticed that Walter Milner, Doris's father, was not present. He knew Milner, whom he referred to as Walt, from Milner's service as a Tulsa policeman. Fallis called Walt and suggested it would help their case if he were present in the courtroom with the other parents. Walt said he could not come, and Fallis, thinking Walt could not get off work, said that he would arrange things with the Tulsa police chief. Walt replied that it wasn't that he couldn't get off work, but that if he were to come to court, he would "kill that son-of-a-bitch." Fallis didn't ask again.

After the testimony by Karen Mitchell and McCleod, the State rested. The State had made some kind of a case against Hart, but as one reporter pointed out, it was "complex and difficult to understand."

CHAPTER THIRTY-SIX

The Defense

S OME OF HART'S MOST potent defenses had already been
brought out on cross-examination of the State's witnesses. It was
pointed out that there was a bloody footprint on the floor of the
girls' tent that was not Hart's. There was a fingerprint on the flashlight,
and it was also not Hart's. The corncob pipe and mirror were not found
in the first search of Pigeon's cabin, but only in a subsequent search
conducted after the preliminary hearing—and long after the murders.

These facts alone might have created reasonable doubt as to Hart's
guilt, but the defense still had more evidence for the jury to consider.

Two expert witnesses were called to refute the testimony of Ann
Reed and McCleod. John T. Wilson, chief chemist at the Regional
Crime Lab in Independence, Missouri, who had been employed by
the Kansas City Police Department, agreed that there was a presence of
sperm on the victims and Hart's underwear, but testified that "beyond
that I couldn't place any importance on it."

Wilson also testified that a person could not be identified by hair
comparison.

H.E. Maxey, a physicist/chemist and a former employee of the Oklahoma Health Department, criticized McCleod's assumptions and reiterated that sperm or hair comparisons could not identify a person.

In keeping with its emphasis on Weaver's bias and hatred for Hart, the defense called Tom Kite. Kite's testimony implied that Weaver wanted Hart killed on sight. Kite was one of the Vietnam veterans who searched for Hart after the murders. Weaver had told Kite that Hart's fingerprints were found at Schoff's burglarized house and that Hart was armed with a twelve-gauge shotgun and was dangerous. Hart's fingerprints were not found at Schoff's house, and he was never seen armed.

The defense also tried to establish an alternate suspect with the help of Okmulgee residents Joyce Payne and her son, Larry Short. Short testified that about a month before the murders he had loaned Bill Stevens, a convict now behind bars in Kansas, a flashlight similar to the one found at the crime scene. Both Payne and Short said that Stevens came to their home in Okmulgee the morning the girls were killed with scratches on his neck and arms and red stains on his boots. Stevens, however, later established an alibi, and both Payne and Short were tried for perjury. In their perjury case, the jury deadlocked on the question of guilt or innocence, unable to conclude whether Payne and Short's story regarding Stevens was intentionally false.

The evidence implicating Stevens also included testimony from a waitress who said a man resembling Stevens had come into the Choteau café where she worked on the morning of June 13, acting strangely and appearing to have blood on his boots. A young camper, Kimberly Lewis, who was at Camp Scott the night of the murders, also testified that the strange man she had seen at the camp was not Hart but did resemble Stevens.

Deputy Sheriff A.D. David was called to show that he had access to Karen Mitchell's footlocker, which was kept at the Locust Grove Police Station, but never inventoried, implying that the evidence found at Pigeon's cabin could have been removed from the footlocker and planted at Pigeon's cabin.

Also called by the defense was Allen Little, a former Mayes County jailer, who was at the time of the trial a dispatcher for the Jay Police Department. His testimony was supposed to bolster the defense's theory that Weaver had planted evidence to convict Hart.

Little testified that he had seen the wedding pictures found in the Cellar Cave in Sheriff Weaver's desk after Hart had escaped almost three years before the murders at Camp Scott. Little had taken part in the initial search for Hart, and he said that the word was out in the sheriff's department to shoot on sight and that "the man who brings him (Hart) in alive won't have a job." At the end of his testimony, Little said that he feared for his life and asked the judge for police protection.

Judge Whistler denied the request, and sarcastically told Little to "get Mr. Isaacs to escort you."

Sam Pigeon also testified through a Cherokee interpreter. The elderly Cherokee said he had never at any time seen the corncob pipe or mirror at his house. Pigeon said he only spoke two or three words of English, even though he had been interviewed by the OSBI in English.

In rebuttal, Weaver denied that the photographs of the women were ever in his desk. He identified the inventory of items Hart possessed when he was booked in the Mayes County Jail. According to the inventory, when Hart was originally booked in May, he had only a belt and nail clippers. After his escape, when re-jailed, Hart had no personal belongings on him.

Three Girl Scouts and two leaders, who had been at Camp Scott, testified that they had all been camping in the same tent with Kimberly Lewis and did not see a strange man. Ann Reed was recalled to the stand and stated that she had compared the hair samples found on Doris Milner to Stevens's. She concluded "the samples from Stevens's hair samples were not consistent in microscopic characteristics and did not have the same source as those from the victims."

The case concluded with the closing arguments of counsel.

The State emphasized the hideous nature of the crimes and the total weight of the many facts connecting Hart to the murders. The defense attacked the tenuous connections and assumptions required to tie Hart to the murders and insisted again that the evidence against Hart had been planted.

Fallis and Isaacs continued to wrangle, and at one point during Fallis's closing argument Isaacs yelled out, "Liar, liar." Judge Whistler remembers that he considered ordering a mistrial at the time but decided against it. He later held Isaacs in contempt for the liar remark but allowed him to purge the contempt with an apology.

In spite of television and movie theatrics to the contrary, closing arguments by the lawyers rarely decide any case. In the Hart case, however, remarks made by Isaacs in his closing statement may have had a profound influence on the outcome. Addressing the jury, Isaacs referred to the fact that Hart already had sentences of "three hundred and five years hanging over his head." Given this knowledge, the jury could assume that if it found Hart not guilty, he would still be in prison for the rest of his life. Knowing this, the consequences of a mistaken acquittal did not carry the same gravity it might have. To this day, Fallis believes this remark lead to the Hart verdict.

The jury began deliberating at about noon Thursday, March 29. After a dinner break and further deliberations, the jury requested to listen to a recording of the testimony of Karen Mitchell and OSBI Agent Cary Thurman. The jury ceased deliberating about 9:30 p.m. They reconvened at nine o'clock the next morning, and within thirty minutes announced that they had reached a verdict. The unanimous verdict of "not guilty" elicited screams of both joy and anguish from the spectators.

CHAPTER THIRTY-SEVEN

Controversy

LATER, JURORS WOULD SAY they had believed there was "manufactured evidence" and that "the investigation was a screwed-up mess." One juror believed Agent Bowles had lied on the stand. She also resented the photographs taken of the OSBI agents with Hart at the time of his arrest that portrayed Hart "like a big game trophy."

The same juror also stated that all of the jurors concluded that more than one person had committed the crime, however, she did also say, "I'm not saying he wasn't guilty."

Weaver and the OSBI both affirmed their belief in Hart's guilt in spite of the jury's decision. The OSBI agents were convinced in part by evidence that could not be admitted at trial—in particular, facts surrounding Hart's previous rape convictions. In that case, Hart had acted obsessed with the victims' eyeglasses, taking them off of the victims and repeatedly trying them on again. The agents related this behavior to the eyeglasses found at the scene, in the Cellar Cave near the murder scene, and those worn by Hart when he was arrested.

Judge Whistler, now deceased, recalled later what might have been an important piece of evidence that he had been forced to exclude from the trial. The State had wanted to introduce evidence that Hart had used a certain unique kind of knot to tie up the women that he raped in 1966, and that the same type of knot was used to tie up one of the Girl Scouts. The judge excluded this evidence because it would have improperly informed the jury of Hart's prior convictions. Whistler believed Hart was guilty but did not criticize the jury for determining that the State had not proved its case "beyond a reasonable doubt."

As for Fallis and Isaacs, they still believe in their respective case. Fallis is convinced Hart was guilty. Isaacs states with great conviction, "I don't just think Hart was innocent, I know he was innocent."

Isaacs is convinced Hart was in Tulsa at the time of the murders staying with his uncle, Groundhog Sulletemke. He notes that Hart worked one day as a temporary laborer while in Tulsa under a false name. Unfortunately for the defense, Hart's alibi witness, Sulletemke, died prior to the trial, and Hart's employment in Tulsa could never be verified.

Isaacs also points out testimony given at the trial by Floyd Cunningham, a funeral home owner in Pryor who was on the scene early the morning of June 13. When Cunningham arrived, the bodies had not yet been examined, but Weaver was already telling everyone emphatically that Hart's mother lived near the camp and that Hart had done the crime.

Pitchlynn also believes Hart was innocent: "Gene always said he was innocent. We were with him constantly for a year and never had any indication he committed the crimes."

Pitchlynn's belief in Hart's innocence was affirmed by his recollections that during the testimony of one OSBI agent at the preliminary hearing, it became obvious the OSBI had done a less than thorough job of searching Pigeon's shack. With Pigeon's consent, Pitchlynn and Isaacs had made a late night visit to Pigeon's residence. They looked for anything that might be Hart's that could tie him to the murders. They found nothing. Later at trial, the corncob pipe and mirror were offered by the OSBI as having been found at Pigeon's house after the preliminary hearing. Pitchlynn was convinced the items had been planted later, along with some pictures of young cheerleaders.

As to Fallis's assertion that Isaacs's closing remarks about Hart's prior prison time influenced the jury, Pitchlynn said, "I hesitate to think any jury would give a pass to a guilty person for such a heinous crime. If they thought he was guilty, they would have convicted him."

The case over and the verdict rendered, Hart was returned to the state prison in McAlester and placed in the general population. On June 4, Hart died of a massive heart attack.

Prior to his death he had been lifting weights and jogging, but an autopsy, conducted by Dr. A.J. Chapman of the Oklahoma State Medical Examiner's Office, concluded that Hart had died of "a plain simple heart attack." Chapman determined that Hart had previously suffered another heart attack, and that his condition was genetic.

In spite of the autopsy, many of Hart's friends and family still believe that he was poisoned, drugged, or otherwise murdered while in prison.

Just three days prior to his death, Hart, in apparent good health, gave a lengthy interview to the *Cherokee Advocate*, the newspaper of the Cherokee Nation. Ostensibly, he wanted to tell his story to "his people." In fact, the interview, which Isaacs and Pitchlynn also attended, was more like a pep rally for the defense. Hart continued to proclaim his innocence but refused to answer any questions relating to the case itself. Nothing of substance was presented in the interview that would have helped affirm his innocence.

In 1984, the new Mayes County Sheriff, Paul Smith, announced that he had reopened the investigation of the Girl Scout Murders and had three suspects. The suspects' identities were never revealed and nothing resulted from Smith's so-called investigation.

The parents of Lori Farmer and Doris Milner later filed a civil law suit for wrongful death against the Magic Empire Council of the Girl

Scouts and Hartford Insurance Company. The suit alleged negligence by the defendants in failing to provide proper security to protect the campers at Camp Scott. The case was tried in 1985, and resulted in a verdict for the defense. There was some evidence presented of strangers being seen around the camp prior to the murders, but nothing was brought out that could shed any real light on Hart's guilt or innocence.

As DNA tests became established as a credible source of scientific identification, at least three attempts were made to compare Hart's semen to samples taken from the victims and that found on a pillowcase in the tent. The first attempt by the FBI, some ten years after the crime, was inconclusive. The next attempt made by the OSBI in 2002 was also inconclusive. Likewise, when two private laboratories attempted a test in 2008, it also came back inconclusive. As time passed, serious questions began to surface about the chain of custody of the semen and the degradation of the samples.

Science could not solve this mystery.

The answers died with Gene Leroy Hart.

The Karen Silkwood Case

Plutonium
by Kent Frates

After the
mushroom cloud
what
will we do
with
this power
made by man
not by God
to blow
each other
to smithereens
or
Light the earth

It only matters
to the world

CHAPTER THIRTY-EIGHT

Unlikely Adversaries

KERR-MCGEE CORPORATION and Karen Silkwood were the most unlikely of adversaries. Yet this multibillion-dollar Oklahoma company and Silkwood, a mere wisp of a woman beset with a myriad of personal problems, squared off in a struggle with international ramifications.

In the end, Silkwood's influence on Kerr-McGee would prove to be more powerful after her death than during her life. But from the beginning, her story resonated with the public, and she was raised to heroic status by union activists, the National Organization for Women, and various anti-nuclear groups. Her life and death triggered investigations by Congress and the FBI, a lengthy contentious trial, and a public relations nightmare for Kerr-McGee and the entire nuclear energy industry. Her story would also go on to be immortalized in the hit motion picture, *Silkwood*.

To fully appreciate Silkwood's story requires a look at the culture of the early seventies. To paraphrase Bob Dylan's song, the times they were a changin'. The women's rights movement was just beginning to gain momentum and unions still had political clout. The nuclear power industry was in its infancy: on the one hand, hailed as the salvation to the country's energy problems; on the other, demonized as an environmental monster. Against this backdrop, Karen Silkwood's final days played out like some kind of predetermined Passion play.

The trial that rose out of her exposure to plutonium, a potentially dangerous and carcinogenic element, would not only be influenced by the mood of society at the time but also by extremely unpredictable and powerful current events, most significantly, the accident at the Three Mile Island Nuclear Plant and Hollywood's take on a possible nuclear disaster. These events came together to create a perfect storm that magnified the impact of the Silkwood trial.

· · · · ·

The association between Kerr-McGee and Silkwood began routinely in August 1972, when she was hired by Kerr-McGee Nuclear Corporation, a Kerr-McGee subsidiary, to work in its Cimarron plutonium plant near Crescent, Oklahoma. Silkwood was twenty-six years old and had moved to Oklahoma from the east Texas town of Nederland. A straight A student in high school, Silkwood studied medical technology at Lamar College in Beaumont, Texas, but dropped out after only one year to marry Bill Meadows. The couple had three children in what proved to be an unhappy marriage; in 1972, Silkwood walked away, leaving her children behind with Meadows.

Silkwood had always been interested in science, and signed on to work in the Kerr-McGee Metallography Laboratory, where plutonium pellets and reactor rods were tested. At the time the plant had only one customer, the Atomic Energy Commission. Kerr-McGee supplied the AEC with the plutonium pellets used to fire the Fast Flux Test Facility at Hanford, Washington. Managed by Westinghouse, that facility tested fuel cores in connection with nuclear plants the AEC hoped to build in the future.

The Karen Silkwood Case

A radioactive chemical element used for nuclear weapons and nuclear power, plutonium can be found in trace amounts in nature and fissionable quantities are produced from uranium. The element is principally used for making atomic bombs.

Plutonium emits alpha particles, beta particles, neutrons, gamma rays, and x-rays. It is without scientific doubt a carcinogenic and dangerous substance. Exposure to plutonium can be hazardous to a person's health if it is inhaled into the lungs or swallowed. External exposure is generally not serious. How much exposure is safe, however, was controversial in 1972 and remains controversial today.

The Kerr-McGee plant produced plutonium pellets from a plutonium nitrate solution shipped in from Hanford. The pellets, one-inch long and one-half-inch thick, were inserted into stainless steel rods that were then welded shut.

Silkwood's job was to test the pellets and rods to ensure their integrity. If she found faulty pellets, a large lot might be rejected. Likewise, rods with defective welds were also rejected. In testing rods, she conducted photomicrograph tests of the welds; the photos developed from the negatives were used to confirm the integrity of the welds.

Because of safety concerns, the radioactive material was placed in a sealed box outfitted with gloves so a worker could handle the pellets without being exposed to radioactivity. Workers, like Silkwood, also monitored themselves for contamination with devices supplied by the company. They were also tested before they left the plant each day.

In the event contamination was detected above a certain prescribed level, a worker would be immediately decontaminated, a process generally as simple as washing with soap and warm water (cold water can close pores and trap radioactive material; hot water causes pores to open and can enhance absorption of radioactive material through the skin). The contaminated employee would also be subjected to subsequent follow-up tests, including nasal swabs and urine and fecal analysis.

Rejecting pellets or rods cost the company time and money, and over the course of her employment Silkwood became convinced that

Kerr-McGee was falsifying quality control tests and shipping out defective products. She was unsure of the effect this would have at the Hanford reactor, but was concerned nonetheless.

Silkwood also observed practices at the plant that she believed to be unsafe. A large part of the work force was comprised of eighteen- or nineteen-year-old men and women who received little or no training (safety or otherwise)—many of whom did not seem to appreciate the dangers of plutonium.

The Texas native also believed the company failed to advise its workers about the carcinogenic nature of plutonium, both in company literature and communications between management and employees. The plant also suffered from problems with security, and it was easy for plutonium to be smuggled from the plant without detection, something both AEC examinations and worker testimony agreed upon.

Workers at the plant were represented by the Oil, Chemical, and Atomic Workers International Union. In November of 1972, the OCAW went out on strike. After two months the strike was broken, and the union signed a new two-year contract. Silkwood took part in the strike, which was her first introduction to union activities.

Through 1973 and into 1974, Silkwood also was dealing with a series of personal problems. She had started a relationship with another Kerr-McGee employee, Drew Stephens, and after their relationship ended, she attempted suicide by overdose in September 1973. Sometime in 1974, she began abusing the prescription drug Quaalude, which had originally been prescribed as a sleeping pill. She also smoked marijuana, drank heavily, and slept around. She maintained an off-and-on relationship with Stephens and went through several different roommates.

CHAPTER THIRTY-NINE

The Union

IN JULY 1974, SILKWOOD became contaminated while working in the laboratory. Her contamination was insignificant according to AEC standards, but Kerr-McGee technicians could not determine the source of the contamination. An investigation of the air filters in the laboratory led the Health Physics Director Wayne Norwood to suspect fraud, something that had previously occurred around the time of the 1972 strike.

In August 1974, motivated by her concern for worker safety at the plant, Silkwood ran and was elected as one of three OCAW bargaining agents to negotiate the next union contract.

From this time forward, events involving Silkwood at the plant began to accelerate. She started collecting evidence of contamination incidents and falsification of records, and kept a notebook documenting such incidents while also gathering information from other employees. Her objective was twofold: safety at the plant needed to be improved, and the information could be used as leverage in negotiating the next union contract.

The old union contract expired December 1, 1974, but before negotiations on the new contract had gotten anywhere, a group of workers filed a petition to decertify the OCAW. This move intensified union politics at the plant.

At the request of the OCAW, Silkwood—along with the other members of the bargaining committee, Jack Tice and Jerry Brewer—flew to Washington, D.C., on September 26 to meet with OCAW officials and then with the AEC. At the meeting with the AEC, the Kerr-McGee employees outlined thirty-nine examples of safety and security problems at the plant. The examples were furnished to support four allegations against Kerr-McGee including: "falsification of photomicrograph negatives of weld test samples; improper use of quality control sample analytical data by Kerr-McGee supervisors and employees; irregularity in pellet inspections; and falsification of computer input date." The AEC determined that it would investigate these allegations.

While in Washington the bargaining committee members also met with Anthony Mazzocchi, an OCAW official who would soon become vice president of the Union, and Steve Wodka, another union official. Mazzocchi unveiled a plan to combat the effort to decertify the Union at the Kerr-McGee plant: First, he would send two experts to Oklahoma to educate the plant workers on the danger of plutonium, which, without pointing fingers, would underscore Kerr-McGee's disregard for worker safety; secondly, he asked Silkwood to collect specific facts with regard to her allegations that quality control tests had been altered at the plant.

If Silkwood could collect evidence of such practices, Mazzocchi promised to use his connections to get a story in the *New York Times*, discrediting Kerr-McGee at a crucial time during the negotiations over the new contract. Mazzocchi warned Silkwood that her facts had to be ironclad for the *Times* to write a story. She assured him that she could produce credible evidence.

The union executed the first part of its plan by sending Dr. Dean Abrahamson and Donald Geesaman to Crescent. Dr. Abrahamson was a physician and a nuclear physicist. Geesaman was a biophysicist who had worked for the AEC's Lawrence Radiation Laboratory at Livermore, California, for thirteen years. The experts gave two lectures at the local American Legion Hall in Crescent, attended by about fifty people.

In their talks, both of the speakers underscored the toxic nature of plutonium. They told the crowd that plutonium caused cancer, especially when inhaled. They also contended that the so-called "safe" levels of contamination established by the AEC were not supported by scientific evidence and that even small amounts of plutonium ingested over time increased the likelihood of cancer in a person. The experts, who visited the plant, also made critical remarks about Kerr-McGee's training, safety, and security procedures.

On October 16, less than a month after the OCAW powwow in D.C., Kerr-McGee workers voted to retain the union. The bargaining sessions over the new contract then began in earnest, with OCAW at the table.

CHAPTER FORTY

Contamination

AFTER SILKWOOD'S return from Washington, her friends, family, and coworkers all noticed a marked deterioration in her health. She seemed increasingly dependent on Quaaludes and had lost almost twenty pounds. Her weight was down to a mere ninety-four pounds. She had threatened to quit her job, but had stayed on becoming more involved in the contract bargaining sessions. She also continued to compile evidence regarding the safety of the plant.

At 1:15 a.m. on October 31, just fifteen days after the OCAW vote, Silkwood had a one-car accident on Highway 33, about four miles outside of Guthrie. She was alone in her white Honda Civic and later said that she had swerved to avoid a cow. The car had spun, backed off a thirteen-foot embankment, and hit a fence post. Silkwood called a wrecker, which towed her car back onto the highway. Despite damage to the right quarter panel, the right tail light, and tag light, the car was drivable, and Silkwood did not report the incident to the police.

Five days later, on November 5, Silkwood became contaminated again while working in the Kerr-McGee lab.

The Karen Silkwood Case

The Atomic Energy Commission had established levels of contamination that its experts believed were safe in humans. The levels were measured in disintegrations per minute or d/m. Silkwood tested positive for contamination on her left hand, right wrist, upper arm, neck, face, and hair. She also had nasal contamination. The AEC safe standard was 500 d/m. Her skin contamination reached a level of 10,000 d/m. Her nasal congestion was 150 d/m.

Although under the presumed safe limit, the nasal contamination was particularly worrisome as plutonium is at its most dangerous when inhaled. The presence of contamination in her nasal passages meant Silkwood probably had plutonium in her lungs. Silkwood was decontaminated until all contamination sites were reduced below 500 d/m. She finished her shift and, after testing clean, left the plant. The health physics technician who investigated the incident afterwards could not find an explanation for the contamination.

As required by AEC regulations, Silkwood was given urine and fecal kits to take home to collect samples as a way to determine how much plutonium had invaded her body. Soluble plutonium can be detected by urine tests and insoluble plutonium by the fecal tests.

On November 6, Silkwood returned to work at the plant, where she spent the first hour working on paperwork in an office. She was scheduled to attend a union meeting, but upon monitoring herself found that she was again contaminated. She scrubbed with soap and water and was allowed to go to the meeting. After the meeting, she went to Norwood's office where it was determined that she had 5,000 d/m on her right forearm, neck, and face. Her right nostril was contaminated to 170 d/m, an even higher degree than the day before.

Norwood asked her where she thought the contamination was coming from, and Silkwood responded that it was "coming back out of my lungs." Norwood highly doubted this. Silkwood asked to have her locker and car tested, but the results from both came back negative. Silkwood left the plant and went home to her apartment. At the time she left the plant, she tested negative for contamination.

On November 7, when Silkwood reported for work at 7:50 a.m., she was again tested and the extent of her contamination had multiplied from the day before. She was highly contaminated, 45,015 d/m in her right nostril and 44,998 in her left nostril. Her hands, arms, neck, chest, and ear were also contaminated, as was her fecal sample. All this indicated that her contamination was occurring outside of the plant. Norwood decided it was time to check Silkwood's apartment for contamination. With Norwood standing by, Silkwood called her roommate, Sherri Ellis, and told her to "stay out of the bathroom and kitchen."

Norwood, Silkwood, and two Kerr-McGee health physicists went to Silkwood's apartment. Ellis was checked and found to have contamination on her hands and buttocks. Stephens, the sometime-boyfriend who had spent the night in the apartment, was checked and found to be clean. The kitchen and the stove were both found to be contaminated, but the most extreme contamination was found inside the refrigerator where a wrapper covering bologna and cheese registered 400,000 d/m. The bathroom was also highly contaminated; the toilet seat cover registered a reading of 100,000 d/m. This was likely the source of Ellis's contamination.

Norwood asked Silkwood where she thought the contamination had come from, and Silkwood attributed it to having spilled her urine sample in the bathroom. Afterwards she had picked up the bologna and cheese, which she returned to the refrigerator when she remembered having a sandwich left at work.

A test of Silkwood's November 7 urine sample contained insoluble plutonium that could not be passed through the body in urine. The urine sample had clearly been spiked. Although the urine kits were not kept in a secure place but rather where they were accessible to anyone at the plant, Norwood immediately concluded that Silkwood had spiked her own urine, presumably to discredit Kerr-McGee.

Jim Ikard, one of the attorneys who represented Silkwood's estate after her death, points out the unlikelihood of Silkwood spiking her own urine. He reasons that Silkwood knew enough about insoluble plutonium to know that it could not be passed in urine and that spiking her urine would do more to discredit herself than Kerr-McGee.

The next day Silkwood met with a union representative sent from Washington, D.C., and also with AEC investigators. The investigators found her clear of contamination. Norwood and Kerr-McGee technicians returned to her apartment. They wore respirators, galoshes, and gloves while they removed and disposed of all contaminated items in the apartment.

Two days after the discovery of the contaminated apartment, Silkwood met with the AEC's consulting physician, Dr. Neil Wall, and Kerr-McGee's consulting physician, Dr. Charles Stenhagen. The two doctors recommended Silkwood be sent to Los Alamos, New Mexico, for further contamination testing with more sophisticated equipment.

The next day, November 10, Silkwood, Ellis, and Stephens flew into Albuquerque, New Mexico, and then drove the ninety-eight miles north into the mountains to Los Alamos. At Los Alamos, all three were tested under the supervision of Dr. George Voelz. Dr. Voelz had been a physician for the AEC for twenty-two years and was considered an expert in radiation testing and radiation safety.

While at Los Alamos, Silkwood was also put through a number of tests, using highly sophisticated equipment designed to detect plutonium contamination in the lungs. In part, the tests detected americium. The amount of americium in a person's body indicates the amount of plutonium present. After two days of testing, Dr. Voelz gave her the preliminary results of the tests.

Based on the levels of americium found in her body, Silkwood probably had about eight nanocuries of plutonium in her lungs. Dr. Voelz told her that the results were only preliminary and that the contamination was less than the AEC's permissible limit of sixteen nanocuries.

There was one catch: the test could be off as much as three times in either direction. In an attempt to reassure Silkwood, Dr. Voelz told her that he had seen many Los Alamos workers with higher levels of contamination, who did not die or get cancer.

In spite of Dr. Voelz's reassurances, Silkwood continued to worry about her condition. Both Ellis and Stephens were found to have only insignificant traces of contamination.

CHAPTER FORTY-ONE

The Fatal Accident

THE THREE FRIENDS returned to Oklahoma City about eleven on the night of November 12. They went to Stephens's apartment where they drank Bloody Marys made with 190-proof alcohol until at least two the next morning.

November 13 was to be an important day for Silkwood. She planned to meet Wodka and the *New York Times* reporter, David Burnham, in Oklahoma City at 8:00 p.m. to disclose the evidence she had collected regarding Kerr-McGee's falsified tests.

Ellis woke Silkwood at seven the next morning. Silkwood went to the plant and spent the morning in contract negotiations. In the afternoon she met again with investigators from the AEC, who were still trying to determine the source of her contamination. During her interview with the investigators and depositions, Silkwood appeared emotionally disturbed. She cried and expressed fear for her health.

At 5:30 p.m., Silkwood went to a union meeting at the Hub Café in Crescent. At about seven, the meeting broke up. Both Brewer and another union member, Frank Murch, offered to drive Silkwood home.

Reports vary as to their comments on whether they were actually concerned about her ability to drive, but it seems they both felt she was "nervous" enough that driving might not be a good idea.

One of Silkwood's friends, Wanda Jean Jung, later signed an affidavit saying that Silkwood had a notebook and a folder with her when she left the Hub. Jung also swore that Silkwood had told her that she had proof concerning the falsification of records and was on her way to give the materials to a *New York Times* reporter. Jung assumed the folder contained the proof Silkwood had referred to, but Silkwood never showed Jung anything.

Silkwood left the Hub about ten minutes after seven and drove toward Oklahoma City on Highway 74. About 7.3 miles south of Crescent her 1973 hatchback left the road and crashed into a concrete culvert. Silkwood was killed.

. . . . .

At the point where the accident occurred, Highway 74 is a straight, flat, two-lane, asphalt highway. Silkwood's car crossed the oncoming northbound lane, and traveled approximately 255 feet on the east shoulder of the highway. The car then contacted the north wing wall of the culvert, went airborne, and crashed into the south wing wall. Her speed was estimated at fifty to fifty-five miles per hour, and there was no evidence Silkwood ever hit the brakes.

A passing trucker discovered the accident at about seven-thirty that same night. He reported it to the Guthrie police. A few minutes later, Oklahoma Highway Patrol Trooper Rick Fagan arrived at the scene. An ambulance came from Guthrie and transported Silkwood to the Logan County Hospital where she was pronounced dead on arrival.

Ted Sebring, a Crescent wrecker operator, was also called to the scene. Sebring was unable to remove the car from the culvert with his wrecker and had to call for assistance. A second wrecker driver, Harold Smith, came to the scene, and the two wreckers finally pulled the car out of the ditch. The Honda was then towed to Sebring's garage in Crescent.

Fagan stayed at the scene of the accident making measurements and examining the evidence. The trooper went home at around midnight, but shortly thereafter received a call telling him the AEC wanted to examine the car and needed his approval. Fagan drove to Sebring's garage where he was met by Norwood and three other men that he took to be AEC investigators. The men looked through the car and opened Silkwood's purse, which contained two rolled cigarettes, a pill, and half of another pill capsule. It was later confirmed that the cigarettes were marijuana and the pill, a Quaalude. The car was then locked and left at the garage.

The next day, Fagan returned to the accident scene and made a further investigation. He also went back to Sebring's garage and went through Silkwood's car again. In it, Fagan found a cigarette roller and a letter explaining how to roll "grass." Fagan put all of the personal effects he found in the Honda in an oil case and sealed it.

On November 14, Stephens, Burnham, and Wodka went to see Fagan. Fagan advised them that it appeared Silkwood had gone to sleep at the wheel and run off the road. He had found no evidence that another vehicle was involved.

The three men then went to Sebring's garage and claimed the car and Silkwood's personal effects. Included in her effects were a four-by-five-inch notebook and a number of other papers, but no folder similar to the one described by Jung.

On November 15, Fagan filed his official accident report. In it, he reported "witnesses interviewed stated that they had advised the driver was in no physical condition to operate a vehicle." He also added that Silkwood had been "under the influence of drugs" at the time of the accident. Silkwood's autopsy later showed that she had .35 milligrams of methaqualone, or Quaaludes, in her system, as well as a small amount of alcohol. The ordinary therapeutic level for this drug is between .20 and .30 milligrams.

Ikard has observed that because of her recreational use of Quaaludes, Silkwood would have built some immunity for the drug and that the level found would not necessarily have impaired her driving ability.

CHAPTER FORTY-TWO

Accident Reconstruction

THE OCAW DID NOT AGREE with Fagan's report and decided to conduct an independent investigation. It hired A.O. Pipkin Jr., an accident reconstruction expert from Dallas, Texas. Pipkin was an ex-Albuquerque policeman who was neither a college graduate nor an engineer. He did have extensive experience, however, investigating accidents, particularly truck accidents.

Pipkin arrived in Oklahoma on November 16. He met with Stephens, who now had custody of the Honda, and meticulously examined the entire car—going so far as to jack it up for a complete view of the under carriage. In addition to damage he credited to the fatal accident, Pipkin found a small dent in the left rear bumper—three-quarters of an inch by two inches—and a dent in the left rear fender near the bumper dent.

According to Stephens all of the damage from Silkwood's previous accident had been to the right side of her car. Pipkin also noted that the steering wheel was bent in from the sides. Typically if a body were slumped over the wheel, he would expect the wheel to be bent from the top. To him, this indicated the driver was clutching the wheel at impact and not asleep.

Pipkin also inspected the accident scene. He observed two things that again made him question whether Silkwood was asleep at the time the Honda left the highway. First the car had crossed to the opposite shoulder. Generally when a person falls asleep they drift to the right because of the crown of the road. At the accident scene, Highway 74 had a slight crown. Second, Pipkin's measurements indicated the car was already out of control before it left the highway, not simply drifting onto the shoulder.

On November 18, Pipkin contacted the OCAW office in Washington, and told Mazzocchi that there was evidence that Silkwood's car had been hit from behind by another car. Mazzocchi released this information to Burnham, who wrote an article in the *Times* about the accident. And all hell broke loose.

The press in Oklahoma was alerted to the story. Kerr-McGee hired the Pinkerton Detective Agency to investigate Pipkin, and the controversy over Silkwood's death began to play out in newspaper, TV, and radio reports across the country.

On November 21, Dr. A.J. Chapman, the state medical examiner, released information about Silkwood's autopsy. He stated she was under the influence of a "hypnotic" drug at the time of her fatal accident and that the amount of sedative in her system was enough to "unquestionably" impair her driving. The cause of Silkwood's death was attributed to multiple injuries, broken bones, and numerous cuts, scrapes, and bruises. Chapman certified the death as an accident, supporting the conclusion reached by Fagan.

Meanwhile, Pipkin was seeking a second opinion before preparing his written report. He engaged Dr. B.J. Harris, another accident reconstruction expert, to review his findings. Harris was an ex-University of Oklahoma professor and had credentials that Pipkin did not possess. Harris did not draw specific conclusions, but did generally conclude the theories promulgated by Pipkin were possible.

On December 15, Pipkin issued his written report in which he concluded: Based on all of the evidence present, along with the conclusions drawn by Dr. Harris, it is my opinion that there is enough circumstantial evidence present to indicate that V-1 (Silkwood's car) was struck from the rear by an unknown vehicle, causing it to go out of control, due to either the initial impact or the combined impact and driver overreaction.

Pipkin's opinion was theoretically possible, but there was no evidence to identify who might have caused the accident even if he was right. His opinion was also based in part on the existence of the dents in the rear bumper and fender, which could have been caused when the car was being towed from the ditch or sometime in the three days between the accident and Pipkin's examination.

The two wrecker drivers, Sebring and Smith, disagreed on this point. Sebring did not think the dent was caused after the accident, while Smith felt it was likely caused when the Honda was wrenched out of the ditch.

Pipkin's report inspired the Oklahoma Highway Patrol to reinvestigate the accident. The case was assigned to Lt. Larry Owen, director of the Oklahoma Highway Patrol Training Program. Along with two other accident specialists, Owen spent a week reviewing the evidence. On January 11, 1975, Owen and Public Safety Commissioner Roger Webb held a press conference refuting Pipkin's findings and affirming Fagan's conclusion that Silkwood's death was from a one-car accident caused by the driver falling asleep at the wheel.

Owen's investigation concluded that the dents in the car's rear bumper and fender were, in his opinion, caused when the car was pulled over the concrete wing wall of the culvert. He said that white paint flakes were found on the top of the wing wall and that the dents were consistent with gouging, not with contact with another vehicle.

The Oklahoma Highway Patrol investigators also disagreed with Pipkin's finding that the car had been out of control before it left the highway and further concluded that the Honda had drifted to the left because the wheels were out of line, probably from Silkwood's previous accident. Pipkin's and the Oklahoma Highway Patrol's findings have never been reconciled and the cause of the accident remains open to argument, although no evidence of the involvement of another vehicle exists other than Pipkin's theory.

CHAPTER FORTY-THREE

Headlines

SILKWOOD'S STORY—sparked by the original *New York Times* article—captured the attention of the national media. Articles over the next few months appeared in *Rolling Stone, Ms.*, and the *New York Times Magazine*, and daily coverage continued in the *New York Times*, other newspapers, and wire services. National Public Radio sent reporters to Oklahoma to cover the story, and the case was the subject of an episode on the popular ABC television show *The Reasnor Report*. Even publications in England and France picked up the story.

Kerr-McGee was caught off guard by the outcry over Silkwood's death. To Kerr-McGee management she was nothing more than a disgruntled employee—a pain in the ass, yes, but nothing serious.

Given the size and prestige of the company, this attitude was understandable. Robert S. Kerr and his brother-in-law (James Anderson) had started the oil company in 1929, naming it Anderson, Kerr. But the company didn't take off until 1937 when Anderson retired and Kerr hired Dean A. McGee away from Bartlesville's Phillips Petroleum Company where McGee had been the chief geologist.

Both Kerr and McGee were brilliant businessmen and each brought his own special skill set to the company. Kerr was the politician and front man for the company. Elected Oklahoma's governor in 1942 and U.S. senator in 1948, Kerr had also made an unsuccessful run at the presidency in 1952. He was a powerful force in the U.S. Senate and before his untimely death in 1962, was able to help Kerr-McGee not only win many government contracts but also expand into uranium mining and the nuclear industry.

McGee could find oil. He was one of those geologists with a nose for it. Possessed of an inquisitive mind, he also saw the profit in other materials, including helium, potash, and chemicals. A dour man respected for his forthright honesty, he managed the vast company from the inside out, while Kerr worked all the political angles from the outside in. By 1974, the two men had built Kerr-McGee into Oklahoma's biggest and most prestigious company. The sponsor of a nationally renowned youth swimming team and the benefactor of local charities, Kerr-McGee operated out of its own thirty-story office building in downtown Oklahoma City.

The vast majority of Kerr-McGee employees were content with good paying jobs and great benefits. To this day, retirees and ex-employees of the company, which sold to Anadarko Petroleum in 2006, remain loyal; they tend to view Silkwood as a malcontent who caused her own contamination and death. Some still castigate her for abandoning her children and using drugs. While the national media portrayed Kerr-McGee as a big heartless corporation, the company was widely popular and respected in Oklahoma.

The public heat generated by Silkwood's story, however, forced a number of investigations. While the AEC was investigating the circumstances of Silkwood's contamination prior to her death, its leaders announced that there would also be a further investigation into the OCAW's accusations that Kerr-McGee was falsifying records. The FBI also began an investigation on behalf of the U.S. Justice Department ostensibly to find out if any of Silkwood's rights had been violated, but also to see if any crimes such as the stealing of plutonium had occurred at the plant. Kerr-McGee had to protect itself and so it launched its own investigation.

December 18, the company closed the plant as a result of two new contamination incidents, both of which the company described as "contrived." Pending the reopening of the plant, Kerr-McGee announced that employees wishing to return to work would have to take a polygraph test to determine if they had been involved in any sabotage or illegal activities at the facility.

CHAPTER FORTY-FOUR

The AEC, the FBI, & Congress

THE PLANT REOPENED in January 1975, but before it did the AEC issued two reports. On December 19, the agency's investigation found that the allegations regarding the doctoring of photographic negatives were true, but confined to one or perhaps two employees and not sanctioned by management. On the other three allegations, the report was confusing and inconclusive. The union found the report weak and inadequate, basically a whitewash of the company.

The second report regarding Silkwood's contamination was released December 31. Although, fraught with bureaucratic doublespeak, that report determined Silkwood had been contaminated outside of the plant, had suffered internal contamination, and that the plutonium had been intentionally removed from the plant, although there was no evidence that Silkwood was the one who had removed it.

Also during December, it was disclosed that the AEC had forced the closure of the plant on two prior occasions because Kerr-McGee could not account for substantial amounts of missing plutonium. In each case, more than 1.8 kilograms was missing. It takes about 6 kilograms to make an atomic bomb. Both times the plant reopened after Kerr-McGee established that only an "insignificant" amount of plutonium was missing. The AEC also reported that it had held a prior meeting with Kerr-McGee management urging the company to improve the safety and security at the plant, and had been disappointed in management's lack of both cooperation and corrective action.

Silkwood, meanwhile, remained a controversial character. And rumors abounded. Some plant workers viewed her as a troublemaker responsible for the plant's shutdown, while others considered her to be an advocate fighting for their rights as workers. There was also speculation that the unaccounted for plutonium might have been smuggled from the plant and sold to foreign governments. Unanswered questions far exceeded concrete answers.

To further sensationalize the matter, Silkwood's roommate and former coworker, Sherri Ellis, showed up at the plant armed with a .22 caliber rifle, climbed the fence around the plant, and approached the plant yelling, "I want to be killed." A security guard and several employees disarmed Ellis only to discover the gun was unloaded. A search of her car turned up marijuana, and she was arrested by the Logan County sheriff.

The full extent of the FBI's probe into the Silkwood case and the operation of the plant has never been known. The FBI's records did become the source of intense controversy in a subsequent congressional hearing and a civil trial. The documents eventually revealed did not establish the source of Silkwood's contamination nor did they shed any new light on her fatal accident.

In 1976, Kerr-McGee closed the Crescent plant. The company attributed the action to purely financial reasons. After the plant's closure, information surfaced that as much as forty kilograms of plutonium might remain unaccounted for by the corporation. Kerr-McGee officials denied this, saying only a small amount was missing and it was most likely in the pipes in the plant. The plant has never reopened.

The Silkwood case also became a cause célèbre. It drew the attention of the National Organization for Women, and NOW actually adopted Silkwood as its own, presenting her contamination and death as an example of violence against women. NOW organized rallies around the country in which women marched carrying signs asking, "Who Killed Karen Silkwood?" Someone even placed a casket in front of the Kerr-McGee office building in downtown Oklahoma City during one of the many protests held there in Silkwood's name.

NOW also launched a campaign to force the FBI to reopen its investigation of the Silkwood case and tried to convince Congress to hold hearings on the matter. Using their combined political clout, NOW and the OCAW approached U.S. Congressman John Dingell, chairman of the House Subcommittee on Energy and Environment. Dingell was concerned about the allegations regarding health and safety at the Cimarron plant and the missing plutonium. He agreed to investigate those issues.

In preparation for the congressional hearings, however, the FBI refused to cooperate with Dingell and his staff, denying access to its files and records. Dingell's staff came to the opinion that the FBI had mishandled the investigation.

When the congressional hearing opened on April 26, 1976, Dingell began the proceedings by strongly reprimanding the FBI. Dr. Karl Z. Morgan, who had spent thirty years as the director of health and safety at the Oak Ridge National Laboratory in Tennessee and was a professor of nuclear engineering at Georgia Tech, also testified about conditions at the Kerr-McGee plant.

"I have never known of an operation in this industry that was so poorly operated from the standpoint of radiation protection as the Cimarron facility," he testified. "I consider this plant an example of how not to run the nuclear industry."

Testimony was also sought from a reporter for the *Nashville Tennessean*, Jacque Srouji. Srouji, a sometimes undercover informant for the FBI, had seen and copied some of the documents the Bureau refused to turn over to Dingell's committee. After Srouji's testimony, the FBI finally relented to some extent and allowed the committee staff to interview the agent who had conducted the Silkwood investigation. However, the battle to actually view the FBI files raged on when the Bureau still refused to release anything but the most superficial information.

The hearings dragged out over several months. Dingell was reelected in November 1976, and finally obtained the FBI files. He announced that the hearings would reconvene in December, but before that could occur, the House changed its rules, prohibiting a member from chairing two subcommittees. Dingell resigned his chairmanship of the Energy and Environment Subcommittee to retain a more powerful assignment, and without his leadership the congressional investigation died.

CHAPTER FORTY-FIVE

Silkwood v. Kerr McGee

GIVEN THE FACTS AND circumstances of Silkwood's contamination and death it was almost inevitable that litigation would occur. Sure enough, a few days before the two-year statute of limitations ran out, suit was filed by Karen's father, Bill Silkwood, as the administrator of her estate, for the benefit of her three minor children.

Filed in the U.S. District Court for the Western District of Oklahoma, the complaint cited negligence on the part of Kerr-McGee as the cause of Silkwood's contamination. The suit also contained allegations of a conspiracy to violate Silkwood's civil rights by twenty-three individual officers, directors, and employees of Kerr-McGee, including Dean A. McGee and Robert S. Kerr Jr., the senator's son.

The complaint accused the defendants of interfering with Silkwood's and other union members' right of free speech, as well as placing listening devices in private places and wiretaps on employees' telephones. The complaint also alleged that the FBI and two particular agents were engaged in the conspiracy. Srouji, the *Tennessean* reporter and FBI informant, was cited as a co-conspirator. The lawyer for the plaintiff was Daniel Sheehan of Washington, D.C. Sheehan had also enlisted the help of attorney Jim Ikard of Oklahoma City, who joined the case at the request of a mutual friend.

A product of the 1970s, Sheehan was a lawyer known for representing radical causes and controversial clients. A 1970 graduate of Harvard Law School, he worked briefly with a prestigious Wall Street law firm and noted criminal defense lawyer F. Lee Bailey, before teaming up with the American Civil Liberties Union in Denver.

At the time the Silkwood case was filed, Sheehan was associated with a Jesuit organization known as the Office of Social Ministries, which was involved in various political causes. Through the years, he had represented Black Panthers, members of the American Indian Movement, prison inmates, the comedian Dick Gregory, and the activist priest brothers Daniel and Phillip Berrigan. Along with the Trappist monk Thomas Merton, the Berrigan brothers had founded an interfaith coalition against the Vietnam War and later began the anti-nuclear weapons group, Plowshares.

Sheehan was a Yankee, fast-talking, abrasive, and prone to reckless statements and allegations, just the right kind of person to raise the hackles of the Kerr-McGee executives.

Ikard was an ambitious young lawyer who knew little about the Silkwood case when it was filed, but who would spend the next several years of his practice immersed in this litigation. "The number of hours I worked on that case," Ikard said, "and what I got paid—I could have made more money working at McDonald's."

Kerr-McGee had an extensive staff of in-house lawyers and legal assistants who worked on the case led by Associate General Counsel Bill Zimmerman. The company also hired what at the time was the state's largest law firm, Crowe & Dunlevy.

Bill Paul, a partner at Crowe & Dunlevy and a former president of the Oklahoma Bar Association (he would one day be president of the American Bar Association), would be the lead defense attorney on the

Silkwood case. He was assisted by L.E. Stringer and John J. Griffin Jr. Paul was an experienced litigator, particularly in federal court.

Kerr-McGee also had insurance coverage on some of the claims covered in the suit, so its insurance company later supplied a defense through Elliot Fenton of the Oklahoma City firm Fenton, Fenton, Smith, Reneau & Moon. Fenton had a lifetime of experience defending negligence claims in jury trials. He was assisted by Larry D. Ottaway, a young lawyer fresh out of law school.

From the very beginning of the case, the Kerr-McGee lawyers raised two powerful legal defenses: They asserted that the case actually belonged exclusively in Oklahoma's Workers' Compensation Court. And they argued that federal statutes relating to the AEC preempted the plaintiff's claim for damages. These defenses would be hotly contested throughout the trial.

The filing of the complaint ignited a contentious legal battle; both sides quickly began to sling motions, briefs, and discovery requests at each other. A conspiracy is hard to prove under the best of circumstances, even if it really occurred, so Sheehan's style was to press the defendants for every scrap of information that might have even the most remote bearing on the case. Meanwhile, the FBI, through the U.S. Justice Department, fought to maintain the confidentiality of its records, while the Kerr-McGee defendants focused their efforts on getting the case dismissed without a trial.

The first judge assigned to the case was Luther Eubanks, a plainspoken country lawyer who had little regard for Sheehan or his lawsuit. At one of the early hearings, Eubanks declared Sheehan "was running off at both ends" and that his case "did not amount to a hill of beans."

Sheehan moved to recuse Eubanks for his remarks, but Eubanks beat him to it, by reassigning the case to Judge Luther Bohanon. Judge Bohanon was even less impressed with the plaintiff's case than Judge Eubanks. Bohanon quashed the plaintiff's request to take depositions of law enforcement officers and otherwise blocked discovery. It was common knowledge that Bohanon owed his judgeship to Senator Robert

S. Kerr and using this leverage, Sheehan asked the Tenth Circuit Court of Appeals to remove Bohanon. The court sustained Sheehan's request and appointed U.S. District Judge Frank Theis of Wichita, Kansas, to preside over the case.

During the pretrial jousting, the plaintiff made a move that would greatly influence the outcome of the case. Sheehan prevailed on Gerry Spence to enter the case and conduct the trial on behalf of the plaintiff. Spence was a noted personal injury lawyer from Jackson Hole, Wyoming, renowned for his colorful personality and ability to win big verdicts against corporations and insurance companies.

Spence was also a successful criminal defense lawyer. Over the course of his career he had defended, among others, Randy Weaver over the shootout at Ruby Ridge in Idaho and former First Lady of the Philippines Imelda Marcos on corruption and racketeering charges. He had also won a judgment for "Miss Wyoming" against *Penthouse* magazine, and successfully defended a number of high profile murder cases. Spence liked to play the role of a gunslinger, and he dressed the part, wearing a ten-gallon cowboy hat and leather western jacket. His ego was as big as his hat, but he had the record to backup his high opinion of himself. He was flamboyant, artful, and knew how to persuade a jury, making him a formidable opponent for Kerr-McGee.

Arthur Angel, another young lawyer, also entered the case for the plaintiff. Ikard and Angel did the hard, grunt work of preparing witnesses, briefing the law, and arguing motions.

Meanwhile, Judge Theis took control of the case. He helped the parties wade through discovery and pretrial motions and scheduled a trial. Sheehan was given wide latitude to try to develop his conspiracy theories, but that proved impossible as no proof existed or surfaced to support such allegations.

In fact, prior to trial, Judge Theis dismissed the conspiracy suit against all of the individual defendants holding that there was no evidence of any conspiracy. Thus, the case was set to proceed only against Kerr-McGee and solely on the negligence claim.

The plaintiff proceeded under the theory of strict liability based on the ultrahazardous nature of plutonium. Under this legal theory, the plaintiff did not have to prove any specific acts of negligence by Kerr-McGee or even how the plutonium got out of the plant and into Silkwood's apartment. The only proof needed was to show that it was Kerr-McGee's plutonium and that it had contaminated Silkwood, causing her injury.

If the plaintiff was able to establish this, then the burden would shift to Kerr-McGee to show that it was not at fault for Silkwood's contamination. However, if the plaintiff wanted punitive damages, it would also have to prove gross negligence by Kerr-McGee. Going into the trial, the plaintiff asked for $1.5 million in personal injury damages, $5,000 in property damages, and $10 million in punitive damages. During the trial the demand for punitive damages was increased to $70 million.

The claim for property damages seemed insignificant, but it later took on disproportionate importance from a legal standpoint. There really was no doubt that the plutonium found on Silkwood had come from the Kerr-McGee plant, so the battle became whether plutonium was ultrahazardous in the quantities involved and whether, as Kerr-McGee asserted, Silkwood had removed it from the plant and contaminated herself to discredit the company.

To frame the issues, Judge Theis made two significant evidentiary rulings: The plaintiff could not put on evidence regarding the facts of Silkwood's fatal car accident. And the defendant could not introduce evidence of Silkwood's suicide attempt, drug problems, and sex life.

The trial was to be limited to the negligence case.

In another important pretrial legal maneuver, Kerr-McGee refused to admit that plutonium was a hazardous substance, a key element of strict liability. This decision allowed the plaintiffs to put on wide-ranging evidence of the extreme dangers of plutonium, which reached far beyond any issues regarding the Kerr-McGee plant, but certainly had an impact on the jury.

CHAPTER FORTY-SIX

The Trial

THE TRIAL FINALLY BEGAN March 6, 1979. It would not end until May 18, lasting more than two months, the longest civil trial in Oklahoma history at the time. In federal court, civil cases are tried by a six-person jury. In this case the jury was comprised of four men and two women: a telephone repairman, a retired schoolteacher, an electrical engineer, a utility company foreman, a clerk-typist, and a housewife. There were also four alternates.

Like all good trial lawyers, Spence sought to develop a simple theme and narrative for the case that was supported by the evidence, which in this case would involve complicated science. In his opening statement, he referred to the "fiendish power of plutonium," which he called a "substance of the devil." He also likened plutonium to a "lion." Arguing in favor of the theory of strict liability, Spence told the jury that if a "lion" escapes and hurts an innocent person, the owner is liable regardless of how the lion had escaped.

During trial Spence could repeatedly be heard to say, "If the lion gets away, Kerr-McGee must pay," drumming the mantra into the jury.

Spence also developed another theme referring to the Kerr-McGee attorneys as "the gentlemen in gray." Spence was good at turning his client into the underdog, a simple small-town gal fighting against a big bad corporation. His reference to the attorneys reinforced that.

In his opening statement, Paul planted the seeds for the Kerr-McGee defense. He stated that Silkwood was not actually damaged by her level of contamination and that she was responsible for her own contamination. He said she had "both motive and intent" to contaminate herself. Paul also emphasized that the plant was operated within safety standards set by the AEC and was repeatedly monitored by AEC investigators.

At the time of their opening statements, neither Spence nor Paul could anticipate the powerful forces outside of the courtroom that would come along to influence the outcome of the trial. But that's exactly what happened.

On March 16, the movie *China Syndrome* was released in theaters all across the country. Featuring Jack Lemmon, Michael Douglas, and anti-nuclear activist Jane Fonda, the movie portrayed the story of a valiant whistleblower (Lemmon) fighting against a powerful corporation to reveal dangerous conditions at a nuclear power plant. The plot even included the falsification of welds related to the construction of the plant.

The release of *China Syndrome* was a bad break for Kerr-McGee, but matters got even worse. On March 28, 1979, the worst nuclear accident in the history of the U.S. nuclear industry took place at the Three Mile Island Nuclear Generating Station in Pennsylvania. Radioactive gasses were released into the atmosphere after mechanical and human errors at the nuclear power plant. As a result, the plant was allowed to dump radioactive wastewater directly into the Susquehanna River. The accident was reported nationwide, and the resulting panic led to the evacuation of thousands of pregnant women and preschool children in the area and fueled a waive of national hysteria against both nuclear reactors and the nuclear industry.

The Karen Silkwood Case

After the Three Mile Island accident, Kerr-McGee asked for a mistrial. Judge Theis overruled the motion, but did instruct the jury that the Three Mile Island incident should have no bearing on the Silkwood case. However, it begs credulity that the movie and the national uproar over Three Mile Island didn't register in some way with the jurors, no matter how conscientious they were.

CHAPTER FORTY-SEVEN

The Plaintiff's Case

A CCOUNTS OF THE PLAINTIFF'S case over the years have cited Spence's dominance as a lawyer and credited him for the outcome. It is true that he did a masterful job. Lawyers, however, don't make cases—cases make lawyers.

What actually proved most critical to the final verdict was the credibility of the plaintiff's witnesses. Spence's team was able to call three extremely well qualified and believable experts, including Dr. John Gofman, Dr. Edward Martell, and Dr. Karl Morgan. Most notably, all of these experts agreed to testify free, otherwise the plaintiff could not have afforded their normal fees.

Gofman was perhaps the foremost expert on the effects of radiation in the world at the time. With a doctorate in both nuclear and physical chemistry, he was also a physician. Gofman worked on the Manhattan Project, which produced the first atomic bombs in World War II, and shared patents on the fissionability of uranium 233. He was sometimes referred to as the "Father of Plutonium."

Most importantly, Gofman was one of the few scientists who had studied in depth the health effects of low-level exposure to radiation, including the potential for cancer. Gofman was a dynamite opening witness for the plaintiff. He pointed out the danger of exposure to plutonium in even infinitesimal amounts, and discredited the so-called "safe" level of contamination set by the AEC.

In regard to Silkwood's contamination, Gofman testified that she had "1.3 times as much plutonium as was required to give her lung cancer." He also memorably said she was "unequivocally married to cancer," a quote that appeared in newspaper stories around the country.

Gofman savaged Kerr-McGee over its employee training and its training materials, or lack of them. In reference to the Cimarron plant, he said, "Such a plant should never have been allowed to open."

The plaintiff's next witness also possessed impressive credentials. Dr. Edward Martell was a radiochemist for the National Center for Atmospheric Research in Denver. A West Point graduate and retired Lt. Colonel, he had taken part in nuclear tests and studied the effects of plutonium on the environment. Martell also debunked the AEC standards for contamination as baseless and unscientific. He agreed with Gofman that Silkwood's contamination would likely have caused cancer had she lived.

Dr. Karl Morgan was the third powerful witness. He reiterated the testimony he had given before Dingell's congressional committee. In reference to the Cimarron plant, he said, "I felt this was one of the worst operations I have ever studied."

Morgan went on to say that Kerr-McGee's treatment of its employees was "inexcusable and irresponsible," and that the corporation was "callous." Of course, Paul and Fenton vigorously cross-examined all of these witnesses, but, as the verdict would reflect, their efforts did not resonate with the jury.

By this time the trial had taken on a certain character. It was clear that Spence was playing fast and loose with the rules of evidence. More of a showman than a craftsman, he seemed to ask any question that came into his head, no matter how legally improper. This forced Paul and Fenton to have to repeatedly object, which often resulted in trial delays for bench conferences and meetings in chambers to argue legal points.

Although, the defense attorneys really had no choice in some instances, the overall strategy played in to the plaintiff's hands, making Kerr-McGee look like it was hiding facts from the jury and causing tedious delays for the jurors. Spence did run the risk of a mistrial or reversal on appeal, but by dint of personality and pure *chutzpa* he managed to bait the Kerr-McGee lawyers while not offending the jury or inciting the wrath of Judge Theis.

Theis proved an even-tempered judge with a sense of humor. He cracked jokes and was a bit of a courtroom entertainer himself. He had settled into the case and seemed to enjoy most of Spence's courtroom antics. A consummate actor, Spence was also known to smirk at the jury to indicate disbelief in a witness's testimony, and was not above feigning sleep during more tedious parts of the defendant's case.

Spence also repeatedly agitated and aggravated the defense lawyers outside the presence of the judge or jury by insulting them and adopting generally rude and obscene behavior toward them. Paul particularly remembers introducing Spence to Fenton when Fenton joined the defense team, shortly before trial. Spence's response to Paul's proffered courtesy was "fuck you." Paul and Fenton, both experienced trial lawyers, were unaffected by Spence's tactics themselves, but they were concerned about the latitude given to Spence in the courtroom.

One of the defense lawyers, Larry Ottaway, remembers another strategy employed by the plaintiff. Even though the trial had commenced, the plaintiff's attorneys made an almost daily request for more discovery of Kerr-McGee documents, including hard-to-find records. Repeatedly the defense team was ordered to respond to the requests, causing its members to spend nights and weekends scrambling to pull together what they often considered irrelevant information.

· · · · ·

The plaintiff's first three witnesses had been used to establish the ultrahazardous nature of plutonium, but they had also been persuasive in expressing their opinions as to the poorly run nature of the Cimarron plant. The next barrage of plaintiff's witnesses would reaffirm the lack of safety, training, and overall security that seemed to characterize Kerr-McGee's plutonium operation.

James Smith was a production supervisor who had worked at the plant since it went online. A twenty-six-year veteran of the nuclear industry, he had worked at various uranium plants, including the Rocky Flats Nuclear Weapons plant near Denver.

"The [Cimarron] plant was deplorable," he testified. "I never saw anything so filthy in my life as that uranium plant, and I have worked in uranium plants."

Smith criticized everything from the design of the plant to the working conditions. He was particularly critical of the company for repeatedly forcing employees to work long hours in respirators meant only for short periods of use in emergencies.

His most devastating testimony, however, came when he confirmed that forty pounds of plutonium had gone missing at the Cimarron plant and that the missing plutonium was not contained in the plant's pipes, as Kerr-McGee officials had claimed. He also testified that the lack of security could have easily allowed plutonium to be smuggled out of the plant. His was a firsthand workingman's account of the serious problems at the plant, and it seemed to ring true with the jury.

Smith's testimony was followed by a number of plant workers'. The workers uniformly denied receiving any meaningful training for their jobs and pointed out that no one ever warned them of the actual dangers of working around plutonium, particularly the risks of cancer. One witness was unaware of any risk at all associated with plutonium exposure until just days before he testified.

The next phase of the case was for the Silkwood team to convince the jury of the extent of Silkwood's damages. To maximize the damages, Silkwood had to be presented in the best possible light. Her plight had to elicit the sympathy of the jury, and her mental pain and suffering had to come across as real and substantial.

To portray Silkwood's last days, Spence called Steve Wodka, the union representative who had worked with Silkwood and who had been waiting to meet with her and Burnham on the night of her death. Wodka described how Silkwood had cried and told him that she believed she was going to die from her contamination.

Silkwood's father, mother, and sister also testified. They described Silkwood as a loving person who was "hysterical and upset" over her condition and who thought she only had five years to live. With this sympathetic evidence, the plaintiff rested.

From the Archives

George "Machine Gun" Kelly, handcuffed and shackled, is led under heavy guard from the Shelby County Jail in Memphis after his capture on September 26, 1933. (Courtesy of AllPhotosMaps)

© The Oklahoman

Kelly was pistol-whipped by a U.S. marshal in the federal courthouse in Oklahoma City during his trial for the Urschel kidnapping.

Kathryn Kelly, the woman credited with creating the Machine Gun Kelly mystique, circa 1933. (Courtesy of the Oklahoma Historical Society)

© The Oklahoman

From left to right, Tom Slick Jr., son of Tom Slick "The King of the Wildcatters" and Urschel's stepson, with Arthur Seeligson (Urschel's brother-in-law and executor of Tom Slick's multimillion dollar estate), Charles Urschel, and E.E. Kirkpatrick. Kirkpatrick was Urschel's longtime friend and business associate, and it fell to him to deliver the ransom money to the kidnappers).

© The Oklahoman

From left to right, Herbert Hyde, U.S. district attorney for the Western District of Oklahoma and the youngest U.S. district attorney in the country at the time; Joseph B. Keenan, special prosecutor for the U.S. Justice Department and the man assigned to major criminal cases; and Charles Urschel.

From left to right, George Kelly, lawyer James Mather, and Kathryn Kelly. (Courtesy of the Oklahoma Historical Society)

This picture was taken at a hunting camp in South Texas five years after the Kelly trial. Charles Urschel is kneeling in the center, to his left is U.S. District Judge Edgar S. Vaught, the judge in the Kelly trial. To Urschel's right is C.L. Frates, Urschel's brother in law (the author's father). On the far right is J.A. Frates, the author's grandfather. (Author's collection)

© The Oklahoman

David Hall leads a campaign parade down the streets of Tulsa while stumping for the Oklahoma governorship in 1970.

Larry Derryberry, left, and David Hall, right, in April 1974—by this time Derryberry had become convinced that Hall was involved in bribery and kickbacks, and had asked the state legislature to investigate and impeach Hall. As a result, Hall branded Derryberry a "traitor." (Courtesy of the Oklahoma Historical Society)

John Rogers, left, and David Hall, right, December 1974. The governor had a habit of bear-hugging his friends, and Rogers had to keep him at arm's length for fear Hall would discover the tape recorder wired to Roger's back. (Courtesy of Larry Derryberry)

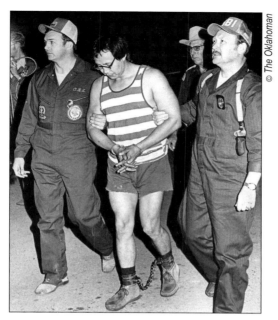

© The Oklahoman

Gene Leroy Hart on the day of his capture,
flanked by OSBI agents Larry Bowles, left, and Bud
Ousley. Bowles was able to find Hart through the
use of a Cherokee informant.

© The Oklahoman

Della Barnes, left, and Mary Jo Potts, right, hold a sign supporting
Gene Leroy Hart. Many Cherokees and other residents of the Locust
Grove area rallied behind Hart and raised money for his defense because
they believed he was a scapegoat for the local sheriff.

Photos of three young victims graced the Tulsa World *on June 14, 1977.
(Courtesy of the Oklahoma Historical Society)*

*Led by Mayes County Sheriff Pete Weaver, highway patrolmen and deputy
sheriffs escort Gene Leroy Hart into the courthouse at Pryor for his trial.*

Karen Silkwood, circa 1974.
(Courtesy of the Oklahoma Historical Society)

Karen Silkwood's 1973 Honda hatchback, which she was driving at the time of her
fatal accident. (Courtesy of the Oklahoma Historical Society)

© Bettman/Corbis/AP Images

Gerry Spence talks to the press outside the federal courthouse during the Silkwood trial.

© Kent Frates

Jim Ikard, one of the lawyers for the Silkwood Estate, holds an exhibit which Gerry Spence used as part of his closing statement to the jury. Throughout the trial, Spence repeatedly said, "If the lion gets away, Kerr-McGee has to pay," a reference to Kerr-McGee's strict liability for the release of the plutonium.

Five years after Karen Silkwood's death, an anti-nuclear protester hangs a picture of Silkwood facing what was then Kerr-McGee's corporate headquarters in downtown Oklahoma City. (Courtesy of the Oklahoma Historical Society)

*One of the many faces
of Roger Dale Stafford.*

*Stafford with his attorney, J. Malone Brewer,
during the Sirloin Stockade trial.*

*Verna Stafford testifies against Roger Dale Stafford.
Verna holds a gun that was used in both the Sirloin Stockade
and Lorenz murders. She remains in prison at Mabel Bassett
Correctional Center near McCloud, Oklahoma.*

© The Oklahoman

OSBI Forensic Artist Harvey Pratt displays the composite drawings he created based on a description by a witness. The release of the drawings attracted an anonymous phone call—a call that Roger Dale Stafford later admitted making. That call eventually led to Stafford's capture and conviction.

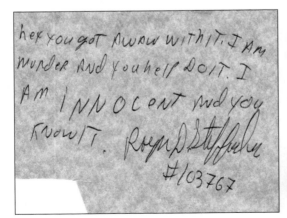

A few days after Roger Dale Stafford's execution, OSBI Agent Arthur Linville received a letter from the killer. Enclosed was a gift certificate from the Sirloin Stockade in McAlester, Oklahoma, on the back was a note signed by Stafford. (Courtesy of Larry Floyd)

Timothy McVeigh on the date of his capture for the Oklahoma City bombing, April 21, 1995; he was arrested for traffic violations and jailed the day of the bombing near Perry. (Courtesy of the Oklahoma Historical Society).

Terry Nichols, wearing an armored vest, is led from the federal courthouse in Wichita on April 22, 1995. (Courtesy of the Oklahoma Historical Society)

The Alfred P. Murrah Federal Building, April 19, 1995. (Courtesy of the Oklahoma Historical Society)

Manuel Hurtado / Shutterstock.com

The Oklahoma City National Memorial, Oklahoma City, Oklahoma. The one hundred and sixty-eight chairs at left represent the lives taken on April 19, 1995.

Darlene Tompkins / Shutterstock.com

The Survivor Tree at the Oklahoma City National Memorial, Oklahoma City, Oklahoma.

CHAPTER FORTY-EIGHT

The Defense

IT WAS NOW Kerr-McGee's chance to put on its case. The plaintiff had been persuasive, but Kerr-McGee was not without defenses. There were three things that could help its case: First, if it could prove that the plant was operated in a safe manner; second, if it could prove that Silkwood had not been injured by her contamination; third, if it could prove that Silkwood had contaminated herself.

Kerr-McGee intended to sell its first defense by proving that the Cimarron plant operated within AEC guidelines and, therefore, was safe. It intended to prove its second theory by explaining that historically Silkwood's level of contamination was not known to cause cancer—basically that she was not contaminated beyond a "safe" level.

It was its third defense that was most controversial. Circumstantial evidence existed to prove self-contamination, but no conclusive proof. Silkwood had access to the plutonium. She, along with Ellis and Stephens, were the only known people with access to her apartment. Her urine samples were undeniably spiked, and she had a motive to discredit the company, since she saw it as the bitter enemy of the union and the employees. The big problem for Kerr-McGee was trying to overcome the obvious logic that someone who knew and feared contamination would surely never intentionally harm herself.

The defense team began its case by calling Wayne Norwood. Norwood, who had been the defendant's representative throughout the trial, was a conscientious man who made a good witness for the defendant. The plant's health physics director sincerely believed that the plant was safe because it operated within the AEC guidelines. And he was credible up to a point.

The problem with Norwood was his credentials. His college degree was in poultry husbandry. He was a man who tried hard, but didn't have the proper education, work experience, or professional expertise to handle the job he held. In addition to Norwood, Kerr-McGee called several other loyal employees. They all brought with them the bias of working for the company without the gravitas of the plaintiff's experts.

Two representatives of the AEC, Gerald Phillip and James Keppler, were also called as witnesses. They affirmed Kerr-McGee's position that the company had, for the most part, conformed to AEC rules and regulations. However, on cross-examination, both men conceded the dangerous nature of plutonium, and they admitted Silkwood's level of contamination had at some point exceeded the AEC's safe standard. They also admitted that the AEC had found violations of safety standards at the plant and that the agency had criticized Kerr-McGee management for this in various memos.

The last line of defense for Kerr-McGee was to prove that Silkwood had not been damaged by her contamination. The company had saved its two best witnesses for last. Dr. Richard Bottomley was an oncologist, a professor at the University of Oklahoma Medical School, and a cancer researcher. Bottomley testified that Silkwood did not have cancer and had suffered no acute injury at the time of her death.

The last witness for Kerr-McGee was Dr. George Voelz, the doctor who had conducted the tests on Silkwood at Los Alamos following her contamination. Voelz possessed credentials as impressive as the plaintiff's experts. His career spanned almost thirty years devoted to the health and safety of the employees at Los Alamos. He had also conducted a study of 224 workers who had been exposed to low levels of contamination from plutonium. Voelz defended the AEC "safe" guidelines, and he testified that Silkwood's level of contamination was well within those standards.

When it was his time to question Voelz, however, Spence effectively attacked his study for its limited number of participants. Still, all in all, Voelz put the outcome of the plaintiff's case in doubt going to the jury.

The closing arguments by the lawyers took four hours on each side. Spence pursued his image of the "lion" escaping and called upon the humanity and sympathy of the jury. Paul and Fenton took a more analytical approach, attempting to persuade the jurors to reach the conclusion that Silkwood had stolen the plutonium from the plant to discredit Kerr-McGee and had either intentionally or accidently contaminated herself.

Judge Theis gave the jury lengthy instructions, including instructing them that plutonium was an ultrahazardous substance, thus supporting the plaintiff's theory of strict liability and placing the burden on Kerr-McGee to show that Silkwood had removed the plutonium from the plant and contaminated herself.

The jury was sequestered after the jurors began deliberations on May 15. It took them more than three days to reach a verdict.

While the jury deliberated, Spence was busy outside fighting with representatives of NOW who wanted to hold what he considered to be a premature press conference blasting Kerr-McGee and the entire nuclear industry. After all of his hard work on behalf of Silkwood, he rightfully did not want to risk a mistrial over some chance inflammatory statements by a group with its own agenda.

Finally on May 19, the jury announced its verdict. They rendered judgment for the plaintiff in the sum of $10,505,000: $500,000 for personal injuries, $5,000 for property damage, and $10,000,000 as punitive damages.

In spite of the way the trial had unfolded, Paul, no doubt, was telling the truth when he said upon hearing the verdict: "I'm disappointed. More than that, shocked and dismayed."

The Kerr-McGee executives were even more surprised and vowed to appeal the case.

CHAPTER FORTY-NINE

Appeals, Reversal, & Settlement

O N BEHALF OF THE plaintiff, Spence stated: "The jury cut through all the government red tape and saved the people. The nuclear industry has been found wanting, and they condemned it." As usual, the far more intemperate Sheehan bugled: The verdict indicates "clearly that people think they've been lied to by industry, government agencies, and scientists that this stuff isn't going to hurt them." The jurors actually had quite a different view of the verdict.

Juror Robert Guyer of Edmond, when asked if he felt it was a landmark case for the nuclear industry, said: "We never really thought about it that way. We discussed the case. We didn't really discuss nuclear power. It was a damage suit; that's all." Another juror who chose to remain unidentified said, "Just like a car wreck suit. Somebody did something wrong. Somebody got hurt, and somebody had to pay." Yet their statements were not consistent with the punitive damage award.

In a personal interview in 2012, Paul probably best summarized an overview of the trial from Kerr-McGee's perspective when he said, "It was a perfect storm. There was antinuclear power sentiment through-out the country. Not only did the *China Syndrome* film come out, but Jane Fonda was interviewed on national TV specifically mentioning Silkwood and criticizing Kerr-McGee. Then Three Mile Island oc-curred, which was the most publicized event of the decade. There was also a huge antinuclear march in Washington. All of this happened during the trial."

Paul added, "I thought that Kerr-McGee should win the case on the facts and the law, but the trial ended up being about the nuclear industry, not the merits of the case."

After Judge Theis overruled the defendant's barrage of post-trial motions, Kerr-McGee made good on its promise to appeal.

The case was next considered by the Tenth Circuit Court of Appeals in Denver. A three-judge panel accepted Kerr-McGee's legal defenses. In a two to one decision, the Circuit Court ruled that Silkwood's claim for personal injuries was within the exclusive jurisdiction of the Okla-homa Workers' Compensation Court.

As to the punitive damages, the court found that federal statutes preempted an action brought under a state law negligence theory, and thus, reversed the award of punitive damages as well. The court did let the five thousand dollar property damage award stand. Round One had gone to the plaintiff, but the defendant was clearly the winner in Round Two. But, the fight was far from over.

The plaintiff appealed to the U.S. Supreme Court, and the Su-preme Court agreed to hear the appeal. In 1984 the Supreme Court issued its opinion. The plaintiff had not appealed the ruling on the actual damages so the issue before the Supreme Court was the punitive damage award.

Once again the legal outcome proved close. The justices ruled five to four as follows: "We conclude that the award of punitive damages in this case is not preempted by federal law. On remand, Kerr-Mc-Gee is free to reassert any claims it made before the Court of Appeals, which were not addressed by that court or by this opinion, including its contention that the jury's findings with respect to punitive damages were not supported by sufficient evidence and its argument that the amount of the punitive damages awarded was excessive. The judgment of the Court of Appeals with respect to punitive damages is therefore reversed, and the case is remanded to that court for proceedings consistent with this opinion."

In 1983, while the case was pending before the Supreme Court, public interest was revived in the case by the release of the movie *Silkwood*. Starring Meryl Streep, Kurt Russell, and Cher, the film was sympathetic to Silkwood and exaggerated many of the facts about her contamination. In the final scene of the movie a set of mysterious headlights appear behind Silkwood's car and close in on her as she is driving to Oklahoma City. The movie was a hit and received five Oscar nominations.

Back in the world outside Hollywood, the Supreme Court's decision stood in favor of Silkwood, but it had left Kerr-McGee the right to make further arguments before the Tenth Circuit regarding the amount of punitive damages and the conduct of the original trial. So in 1985, the Circuit Court issued another lengthy opinion. Again ruling two to one, the case was remanded to the trial court for a new trial on punitive damages with the direction that the punitive damages should be based only on the $5,000 property damage claim since the personal injury damages were confined to Workers' Compensation Court.

The case thus returned to the trial court for retrial, five years after the original verdict.

By now, the Cimarron plant was closed and Kerr-McGee was out of the plutonium-processing business. The plaintiffs were war weary, and the lawyers had not been paid for their years of work. Silkwood's children were growing up and had yet to receive any compensation.

The insurance company was now faced with the expense of a retrial, a trial that would most likely also produce more bad publicity for Kerr-McGee. Such factors finally forced a settlement. In August 1986, Kerr-McGee agreed to pay $1.38 million for a settlement of all of the plaintiff's claims. Silkwood's children received $500,000. Spence was paid $250,000, and Angel and Ikard received $160,000 each. Bill Silkwood was paid $70,000 as administrator of Silkwood's estate. Ernest L. Massad, who acted as *guard ad Litem* for the children and was instrumental in the settlement, received $30,000. The remaining funds went to repay the expenses of the case and the individuals who helped finance the expenses.

. . . . .

No construction has begun on a new nuclear power plant in the U.S. since 1977, although recently four nuclear reactors have been constructed at existing plants. Certainly forces far more powerful than the Silkwood case were instrumental in this. The Three Mile Island accident caused serious doubts about the safety of nuclear power, and these concerns multiplied after the 1986 disastrous meltdown at Chernobyl, Ukraine, in the former Soviet Union and, more recently, the 2011 nuclear accident at Fukushima in Japan.

Possibly more importantly, the low price of natural gas has made gas-fired plants an attractive economic alternative to nuclear.

All of these factors have greatly influenced the nuclear industry, yet it is impossible to ignore the impact of one obscure Oklahoma worker on the nuclear power story both here and abroad.

Perhaps this can be attributed to the underdog nature of the Silkwood case or the mysterious circumstances surrounding Silkwood's contamination and death. Whatever the reason, the case of *Silkwood vs. Kerr-McGee* remains an undeniable part of both Oklahoma's history and the history of the nuclear industry in this country, and a tale to be resurrected whenever the expansion of nuclear power is considered.

The Sirloin Stockade Murders

"Who knows what evil lurks in the hearts of men?"

—*The Shadow*,
Radio show 1930-1954

CHAPTER FIFTY

The Crime

SOME CRIMES ARE SO random and senseless that they are almost impossible to solve. What came to be known as "The Sirloin Stockade Murders" was just such a crime. The perpetrators robbed a Sirloin Stockade restaurant in south Oklahoma City and killed six employees.

There was no evidence to indicate the victims had resisted the robbers. No rational motive existed for the killings, and no obvious suspects could be identified. Solving the murders had to be accomplished the old fashioned way, by intense and thorough police work. The officers involved deserve credit for cracking the case, though the big break came compliments of the bizarre personality of the killer, Roger Dale Stafford.

. . . . .

The robbery and killing spree happened on Sunday, July 16, 1978, at the Sirloin Stockade, a freestanding restaurant in the Southern Hills

Shopping Center at Seventy-Fourth Street and South Pennsylvania in south Oklahoma City. The restaurant was near Interstate 44, with easy access to and from the highway.

Before all hell broke loose, the night had been moving toward its normal end. About a quarter after ten, Carlos Joy arrived at the restaurant to pick up his girlfriend, Terri Horst, who worked there as a waitress. It was just after closing time. Joy went into the restaurant and spoke to Terri, who was still helping clean up. Joy returned to his car, waited for a few minutes, and then, to pass time, drove around the shopping center.

Upon his return to the Sirloin Stockade, he noticed an older green Oldsmobile Vista Cruiser station wagon with wood-paneled sides parked behind the restaurant with the motor running. After some time passed, Joy grew tired of waiting and entered the restaurant again, yelling for Terri. Receiving no response, he decided the employees must be in a meeting in the back and returned to his car, where he played with his citizens-band radio and waited some more.

After another fifteen minutes or so, Joy became concerned that something was wrong and decided to check on Terri. His CB unit was attached to a public-address system, and as he drove toward the restaurant he spoke into the CB, saying, "The building is surrounded. This is the police." His words were projected and amplified by the PA system; it was Joy's attempt to scare off anyone who didn't belong in the restaurant.

Joy then left his car and headed into the restaurant; once again he did not see or run into anyone inside. He was headed for the back of the restaurant, where he still thought Terri might be in an employee meeting, when Mike Click, the restaurant manager, entered the restaurant through the front door. Click was there because the assistant manager in charge had not followed the normal routine and called in the week's receipts.

Click went to the rear of the restaurant and noticed the freezer door standing open. When he started into the freezer to investigate, he was met with a horrific scene of bloody carnage: All six of the restaurant employees lay covered with blood on the floor of the walk-in. They had all been shot. Five of the victims were dead; one, Joy's girlfriend, was alive, but just barely. Joy called the police and then for an ambulance. Both arrived quickly.

Laboring for breath and critically hurt, Terri Horst was taken to Hillcrest Hospital in south Oklahoma City and then to Children's Hospital where she died shortly after arrival. In the end, the Sirloin Stockade victims—six in all—included Horst, David Salsman, Louis Zacarias, David Lindsey, Isaac Freeman, and Anthony Tew.

Four of the victims were just young high school students. Terri Horst was fifteen years old and a student at Moore High School where she played on the basketball team. She had been working to save money for a trip to Hawaii with a friend's family, and her plan called for her to quit her job in two days.

David Salsman would have turned sixteen in a few days. He had been working as a busboy to pay for the customizing of an old truck his parents had purchased for him. The other busboy, Anthony Tew, was seventeen and a resident of Cape Charles, Virginia; he was in town for only a few months while his father attended a class at the local Federal Aviation Administration Academy. David Lindsey had moved to Oklahoma from California in January; the seventeen-year-old was a straight A student at Moore High, where he was attending summer school while working part time as a cook.

The two adult murder victims were Louis Zacarias and Isaac Freeman. A native of Mexico, Zacarias was the assistant manager of the restaurant. Forty-three-years-old, he was survived by a wife and three teenage daughters. Until the month before his death, he had worked at a Sirloin Stockade in Yukon.

Fifty-six-year-old Isaac Freeman was the pastor of the Church of God Church on Northeast Sixteenth Street. The owner of a janitorial service that serviced the restaurant, Freeman was filling in for an employee who was on vacation the night of the murders.

When the crime scene was processed, police would note that eleven shots were fired and there were eleven hits. Three of the victims were killed with one shot to the head and had no defensive wounds, indicating the entire attack had lasted only a matter of seconds.

All of the victims had been shot in the freezer, which was only slightly larger than a walk-in closet. The door to the safe in the manager's office was open, and $1,290 in receipts was missing. There was no sign of forced entry.

CHAPTER FIFTY-ONE

The Investigation Begins

TWENTY-ONE DETECTIVES were assigned to the case by the Oklahoma City Police Department, which mustered all of its resources to hunt down the killers. The lead detective was Les McCaleb, an aggressive, hard-charging veteran. One contemporary described McCaleb's style of interrogation as "getting in front of a witness and yelling at him until his face melted down in his shirt."

Right from the start, clues were scarce, and the detectives began work with only two real leads: The green Oldsmobile station wagon sighted behind the restaurant by Joy, which became the focus of an all-out search, and Zacarias's missing watch, presumably stolen that night.

Larry Koonce was one of the robbery/homicide detectives assigned to the case. He was new to the division having previously served as a patrolman and an undercover narcotics detective. "Every officer grabbed their favorite maggot and shook him for information," Koonce recalled. Unfortunately, nobody's maggot knew anything about the crime.

The detectives believed at least two and probably three people were involved in the murders. Based on this theory, Oklahoma City Police

Chief Tom Heggy gave the press an open letter to the unidentified accomplice offering a $50,000 reward for identification of the killer or killers. The letter admonished the accomplice:

> . . . you are in danger! These men have killed at least six times, coldly and without feeling. They will not hesitate to kill again, because they must remain free and undetected. The penalty they face is monumental. If you know them and what they did, you will almost certainly be their next victim, if only to insure your silence.

In addition to the reward Heggy also promised, "Your safety will be insured."

The letter was unsuccessful in establishing contact with a witness to the crime, drawing only a dozen responses, mostly crank calls.

CHAPTER FIFTY-TWO

The Lorenz Case

EARLY IN THE INVESTIGATION, some of the detectives working the case developed a theory that the murders were related to another crime. Just a few weeks prior on June 22, 1978, the bodies of a man and a woman had been discovered shot to death about two miles south of Purcell, Oklahoma. A passing motorist had spotted the bodies in the grass, not far from the shoulder of the northbound lanes of Interstate 35.

The man had been shot twice and the woman three times. Neither victim had any identification on them, but a magazine mailing label found at the scene led to the identification of Air Force Tech Sgt. Melvin Lorenz, age thirty-eight, and his wife, Staff Sgt. Linda Lorenz, age thirty-one.

The Lorenzes, who were stationed at Lackland Air Force Base in San Antonio, Texas, had left San Antonio at around five the evening of June 21. They were traveling to Fargo, North Dakota, to attend the funeral of Melvin Lorenz's mother. Traveling with the couple was their twelve-year-old son, Richard Lorenz.

The Lorenz family had been driving a blue 1975 Ford pickup with a white camper shell and a North Dakota license plate. It was believed the family had also been accompanied by two dogs and that they had three guns with them: a Colt .357 magnum pistol, a .22 caliber pistol, and a .22 caliber rifle.

An immediate search was begun for Richard Lorenz, who had serious health issues. A nationwide bulletin was issued describing the truck, while lawmen on foot and in a helicopter searched the area for Richard. On June 23, Richard's body was sighted from the helicopter in a field less than a mile north of where his mother and father had been found. Richard had also been shot to death. Five .38 shell casings and one live round were found in the vicinity of his body.

On June 26, the Lorenz pickup was found abandoned in the parking lot of the Sheraton Airport Inn near Will Rogers World Airport in Oklahoma City. Attention had been drawn to the truck after the Lorenzes' two dogs scratched their way through a screen on the back of the camper and began to wander around the motel parking lot. An employee recognized the truck from news reports and contacted the police. There was blood in the truck and two bloody handprints on the truck tailgate.

. . . . .

Meanwhile, on June 22, the same day the Lorenz bodies were found, a Stillwater businessman, E. Ray Tackett, had stopped by a local convenience store at about seven in the morning. As he parked, he noticed a blue pickup with a white camper parked at an angle in front of the store. The two men occupying the vehicle struck Tackett as suspicious; he noted the truck's North Dakota license plate and a hole torn in the camper's screen.

A little later that same morning, Tackett dropped in for a cup of coffee at Sambo's Restaurant, where he again saw the two men, this time accompanied by a woman. Later that day, Tackett heard a news report about the murders of Melvin and Linda Lorenz. The next day he heard that the body of Richard Lorenz had been found. Two days later, Tackett reported what he had seen to the Payne County Sheriff's Office.

When the OSBI learned of Tackett's sighting, they sent OSBI Forensic Artist Harvey Pratt to meet with him. Using Tackett's descriptions, Pratt created composite drawings of the two men Tackett had seen in the truck.

Pratt had joined the OSBI in 1972, and he still works for the bureau as a forensic artist. Over the years he has become nationally recognized for his skill in rendering composite drawings of suspects, witnesses, and victims. The Sirloin Stockade Murders was one of Pratt's first high profile cases and his drawings of the two men would prove to be remarkably accurate.

Pratt's drawings were filed with the OSBI and furnished to the Oklahoma City Police Department, but they were not circulated to the public.

CHAPTER FIFTY-THREE

The Guns

ON AUGUST 3, THE Oklahoma City police chief, along with Detective Division Commander Major Robert Wilder and Robbery Homicide Commander Lt. Dennis Bergland, gave a press briefing to update the media on the progress of the Sirloin Stockade investigation. Heggy announced he had assigned an additional ten detectives from the Oklahoma City Police Department's Organized Crime Unit to assist in the investigation.

Heggy also reported that officers had already conducted 423 interviews, given twenty-six polygraph examinations, and made out 340 reports. Six witnesses had undergone hypnosis. And police had checked 10,000 criminal records, 30,000 fingerprints, and 400 possible suspect vehicles (mostly green Oldsmobile Vista Cruiser station wagons with wood paneling) with 638 more vehicles remaining to be investigated. One hundred and forty-one individual police officers had been involved in the investigation, as well as agents from the Federal Bureau of Investigation; Bureau of Alcohol, Tobacco and Firearms; the OSBI; and the Oklahoma County Sheriff's Office.

In spite of this all-out effort, no concrete suspects had been identified; it went without saying that as time passed, the chances of finding the killers diminished. The detectives continued to investigate known criminals in the area and similar crimes in other states, but none of their efforts proved fruitful.

Finally in September the investigators got a break. Ten-year-old Greg Martin and some friends had been playing in an empty field in far northeast Oklahoma City when they found a sack containing three handguns: a .38 caliber Taurus, a .357 Colt revolver, and a .22 caliber Steger pistol. The boys also found an antifreeze can containing bullets.

Greg took the sack to his father, Frank Martin, and showed him the contents. His dad noticed that the serial numbers had been filed off of the guns and he contacted the police, who came by and picked up the weapons.

The guns stayed in the evidence locker of the Oklahoma City Police Department for more than a week before someone thought to see if they were connected to the Sirloin Stockade murders.

Upon examination, one of the guns, the .38, proved to have been used in the Lorenz killings. The gun had been stolen from a Purcell pawnshop the day before the murders. Further, the .357 and the .22 were identified as the guns stolen from the Lorenz family. Ballistic tests confirmed that the .357 and probably the .38 had been used in the Sirloin Stockade murders.

The two crimes were now linked.

CHAPTER FIFTY-FOUR

Getting a Break

IN THE MEANTIME, NEITHER the green Oldsmobile station wagon nor Zacarias's watch had been found, and the investigation once again stalled for a lack of leads. In December someone at OSBI remembered the composite drawings of the suspicious-looking people seen in Stillwater with the Lorenz truck. The sighting of a woman with the two men was also recalled, and Pratt was sent back to Stillwater to prepare a composite of the woman from what Tackett could still remember. Pratt's drawings now depicted three young Caucasians.

This time, it was determined the drawings of the three suspects should be released right after the first of the year in January 1979. Arthur Linville, the OSBI agent who was supervising the Lorenz investigation, points out that this decision had its risks. The composites might help create an alibi if, for instance, the real killers turned out to be African-American or Hispanic or looked nothing like the drawings.

When the drawings were released on television, more than two hundred calls offering information about the suspects came into the OSBI. And that created its own kind of problem: All of the tips given by the callers had to be checked out and pursued or discarded, creating another time-consuming task. There were, in fact, so many calls that the calls had to be prioritized and divvied up among the investigators. Linville had the agents rate the leads as to their likelihood of success. The top third were then pursued over the next few months.

Among the possible leads was an anonymous caller who had identified himself only as a truck driver. He reported that two men and a woman had approached him in an Oklahoma City restaurant. One of the men and the woman had asked for a ride to Tulsa. The other man left to hitchhike to Panama City, Florida. After arriving in Tulsa, the truck driver and his wife partied with the two strangers. The strangers identified themselves as Harold Stafford and Verna Stafford. The truck driver said he recognized them from the composite drawings.

"I am damn positive that they are the same people," he said, but he refused to give his name or any contact information.

Later on the same night, the truck driver called back. Once again he refused to give any contact or personal information: instead he asked for the name of an OSBI agent that he could speak with the next day. He was given the name of Arthur Linville, but never made another call to the OSBI.

As part of the follow up to the calls, investigators began to look for Harold Stafford and Verna Stafford. The Staffords had been living in Tulsa around the time of the murders, and the investigators learned that Harold had died in a motorcycle accident six days afterwards. Finding Verna presented a challenge.

Married to Roger Dale Stafford, Verna was a drifter who moved frequently and had lived all over the country. But the detectives did have a lead. A woman calling herself "Fay" had appeared at the funeral home in Tulsa to view Harold's body, and she had identified herself as Harold's widow.

The woman, who became known to the detectives as "Crazy Fay," was later found in a mental institution in Arkansas. Fay had known Harold as "Charlie" and also met his friend "Jimmy Wayne." She said Charlie had admitted being involved in the Lorenz murders but pinned the shooting of Richard Lorenz on Jimmy Wayne. She was able to identify a picture of Harold, and she also identified "Jimmy Wayne" as Roger Dale Stafford, Harold's brother.

Meanwhile, Harold Stafford's real wife, Mary, was in Chicago. In a series of telephone calls with her, Linville was able to extract that she, Harold, Roger Dale, and Roger Dale's wife, Verna, had been living in Tulsa at the time of both the Lorenz and Sirloin Stockade murders.

On March 6, McCaleb, Greg Schultz, and Linville found Verna in Chicago with her children. She had separated from Roger Dale some months before. After some heavy questioning and pressure, she agreed to return to Oklahoma City and cooperate with the police.

Although willing to talk, Verna initially lied, giving conflicting stories to the police. After extensive questioning over several days' time, she finally gave what the detectives believed was a mostly true account of both the Sirloin Stockade killings and the Lorenz murders.

Her story implicated herself and identified Roger Dale as the killer of the Lorenz family, and Roger Dale and Harold as the shooters at the Sirloin Stockade.

Based on Verna's statement, arrest warrants for nine murders were issued for Roger Dale Stafford on March 10, 1979, and a nationwide manhunt for him began, which included the FBI.

On March 14, Roger Dale was arrested by officers from the Chicago Police Department and Illinois State Police at a YMCA in Chicago, where he had been staying. McCaleb and Linville then flew to Chicago from Oklahoma City. Bill Cook and Phil Stinett, members of the OCPD-OSBI task force, also arrived there from Nashville, where they had been tracking leads on Stafford.

The four officers brought Stafford to Oklahoma City by plane.

CHAPTER FIFTY-FIVE

Roger Dale Stafford

W HO WAS ROGER DALE STAFFORD? Koonce has described him as a "sewer rat that would do anything to anyone to survive." His own younger brother called him a "bum who lies a lot."

At the time of his arrest, Roger Dale was twenty-seven years old and Verna was twenty-six. Roger Dale and Verna had married in 1972 and had three children ages four, three, and two. The children were put in foster care when Verna was arrested.

One of ten children, Roger Dale was born in Alabama but in 1956 at the age of four moved to Chicago. His father was generally unemployed and his mother was a housekeeper. He dropped out of school in the ninth grade and after several problems with the law was sent to the Illinois State School for Delinquents at Joliet.

In 1968, Roger Dale joined the U.S. Marines but was medically discharged after only twenty-eight days. From that time until his 1979 arrest he had led the life of a drifter, thief, conman, and, almost surely, murderer. Typically he traveled the country accompanied by Harold and Harold's wife and children; he never lived in any one place for long or held a job for more than a few months. Sometimes Roger Dale would identify himself as being from Staffordshire, England, and he was known to affect a phony British accent.

Oklahoma City Police Lt. Dennis Berglan placed Roger Dale in cities around the country at the time of twenty-two unsolved murders, including the multiple killings of restaurant workers associated with robberies in Indiana, Virginia, and Florida.

While in custody, Roger Dale was charged with murder in connection with the 1974 killing of Jimmy Earl Berry. An employee of a McDonald's in Muscle Shoals, Alabama, the twenty-year-old Berry was shot to death during a robbery which netted his killer $1,400. Muscle Shoals is near Roger Dale's hometown of Sheffield, and he and Harold had been living in a mobile home park about a mile from the restaurant at the time of the crime. Roger Dale left town on a motorcycle two or three weeks after the murder. Police picked him up in Tennessee, at which time authorities confiscated a .22 Ruger pistol he was carrying. A similar weapon was used in the Berry murder.

After the Sirloin Stockade killings, Stafford traveled to Arkansas, Mississippi, Tennessee, Alabama, New York, Florida, and England. In one instance he met a woman in Florida and conned her into driving him to New York and paying for a ticket to London for him. Koonce believed Roger Dale was likely in Chicago to kill Verna, which would have eliminated the only living eyewitness to both the Sirloin Stockade and Lorenz murders.

After Roger Dale arrived in Oklahoma City and was read his Miranda rights, he was questioned by McCaleb and Linville. Later, he was questioned again by Cook and Linville. During both interviews, Stafford never admitted to any crime, but made some statements that helped establish his guilt. He revealed to a flabbergasted Linville that he was, in fact, the "truck driver" who had called the OSBI not once but twice, identifying Verna and Harold as the subjects of the composite drawings in the process. It seems Roger Dale had been drunk in an

Oklahoma City motel when he saw the drawings on TV. (Coincidentally Linville had stopped at that very same motel to speak with the OSBI dispatcher on the night of Roger Dale's call.)

At the time of his calls, Roger Dale and Verna had separated and Harold was dead. The drunken calls were his hapless attempt to pin the crime on Verna, which obviously backfired, as without the calls to the OSBI the crime might never have been solved at all. Fittingly, Roger Dale was the instrument of his own demise.

At one point during his questioning, Roger Dale asked Linville a pointedly, whether "Verna is for or against me?" Linville told Roger Dale that Verna had been cooperating with the authorities.

"But she can't testify against me, she's my wife," Roger Dale responded.

When Linville advised Roger Dale that she could indeed testify against him, Roger Dale was visibly shaken.

"Man, I can't think. I've got to think. All I can see is the gas chamber," he said.

Roger Dale would later say his concern at the time was not because he was guilty, but because he believed Verna was out to get him since he had caught her fooling around and left her.

Linville's questioning of Roger Dale went on for some time, but at one point Roger Dale turned the tables with a question of his own.

"I hear screams and see blood in my dreams. Do you think that means anything?" he asked Linville.

Although not admissions per se, such statements helped to confirm Roger Dale's guilt. All in all, he was a talker who couldn't stop talking, because, as he later testified, he could talk his way out of anything.

CHAPTER FIFTY-SIX

Lawyered Up

A T THE TIME OF Roger Dale's arrest Andrew M. Coats was the district attorney of Oklahoma County. Elected in 1976, Coats was an experienced and persuasive trial lawyer. In 1980, he would make an unsuccessful run for the U.S. Senate. Later, he served as mayor of Oklahoma City and the dean of the University of Oklahoma College of Law in Norman.

By coincidence, at the time of Roger Dale's arrest, Coats was having dinner at the Kentucky Club in Oklahoma City with Buck Revell, the FBI's resident agent in charge for Oklahoma City. This was before cell phones, so Revell carried a pager. He was summoned from dinner to accept a telephone call.

When he returned and said a suspect in the Sirloin Stockade case had been arrested, Coats says his first thought was "Oh my God, I hope they have the right person who can be convicted." Coats's concern was well founded. Verna's testimony would end up being the single most important part of the prosecution's case, and Roger Dale's staunch belief that his wife could not testify against him proved almost correct.

Prior to October 1, 1978, Oklahoma statutes had contained a prohibition preventing one spouse from testifying against the other. The legislature had modified this privilege in 1978, and under the prosecution's theory of the new law, Verna would be able to testify to anything she had actually seen or any conversations she had with Roger Dale in the presence of a third party.

Since Harold and Verna were generally present when the crimes were planned and carried out, her testimony would indeed be admissible. Verna was in a position to cook Roger Dale's goose. However, the law was new to Oklahoma and its interpretation was still in doubt. The uncertainty over the admissibility of Verna's testimony and the need to corroborate it drove the detectives to search for more evidence.

Their digging turned up a new lead. Roger Dale, Verna, Harold, and his wife, "Fat Mary," had lived on and off at a Holiday Inn in Tulsa, and, even while residing elsewhere in town, had access to rooms at the motel because Verna also worked there as a housekeeper.

The detectives tried to locate other people who were living or working at the motel at the same time as the Staffords. This search took McCaleb to Enid, Oklahoma, where he hoped to find Linda Louise Lewis, a woman who had worked at the motel at that time. The search at first proved futile; McCaleb was about to give up and leave town when a random conversation with a gas-station attendant led him to Lewis's house.

When the door opened and McCaleb identified himself, Lewis's husband told her, "I knew they would find you."

Lewis then helped McCaleb locate two other women who had been residents of the Holiday Inn. All three had information that could help convict Roger Dale.

. . . . .

The opportunity to question Roger Dale before he obtained a lawyer didn't last long. On March 16, Gary Dean, an attorney from Pryor,

Oklahoma, obtained a writ of *habeas corpus* and forced the police to bring Roger Dale before District Judge Raymond Naifeh for arraignment that same day. Roger Dale was arraigned on one count of murder for the killing of Terri Horst.

Roger Dale's brother-in-law had asked Dean to represent Roger Dale on the advice of a Tulsa newspaper reporter. Dean, though not yet employed by Roger Dale, was already claiming he had been denied access to his client.

At the arraignment hearing Assistant District Attorney James McKinney at one point told the police to remove Roger Dale from the courtroom. Lt. Bergland mistakenly thought McKinney was asking for the removal of Dean, and tempers flared when Bergland grabbed the lawyer's arm to do just that. "Arrest me or get your hands off of me," Dean snarled at Bergland.

The question of Dean's representation of Roger Dale was only settled after a meeting in Judge Naifeh's chambers in which Roger Dale officially named Dean as his lawyer in the case.

The pretrial skirmishing then began in earnest.

Dean quickly fired off a barrage of discovery motions and requests, including that Roger Dale receive a mental examination to determine his competency and medical condition. On March 23 with the agreement of the prosecution, District Judge Carmon Harris ordered that Roger Dale be transported to Eastern State Hospital in Vinita, Oklahoma, for comprehensive mental and physical examinations. He was returned to the Oklahoma County Jail after twenty-four days, having been found to be sane and able to stand trial. The level of his through and through meanness was not medically quantifiable.

After vigorously representing Roger Dale, Dean asked to withdraw from the case on June 15. Stafford's family had not been able to raise the fees and expenses promised to Dean, and he alleged that Roger Dale was indigent. Dean's request was granted on June 20.

Oklahoma City Attorney Garvin Isaacs entered an appearance next, but withdrew only fourteen days later when Stafford's family again failed to raise promised attorney's fees. Harris then appointed T. Hurley Jordan, a public defender, to represent Roger Dale.

Jordan was able to get a continuance of Roger Dale's preliminary hearing moved from the scheduled date of July 16 to August 2. On July 24, the lawyers who would eventually try the case—J. Malone Brewer and John T. Hall—took up Roger Dale's defense. Brewer was a young, burly ex-Marine with a criminal practice in Oklahoma City. It was thought that he had accepted the case in return for the book and movie rights. Brewer again attempted to continue the preliminary hearing, but Special Judge Leonard Geb, the hearing judge, denied his request. Finally the preliminary hearing took place on August 2.

By then, additional murder charges had been filed against Roger Dale for the killing of the other victims. At the hearing Coats put on the barebones of the State's case, calling only Verna, McCaleb, and an assistant medical examiner as witnesses. Verna testified she had seen Roger Dale and Harold commit the crime. Based on her testimony, Judge Geb ordered a trial for Roger Dale on all six murder counts. Meanwhile Kay Huff, county attorney for Cleveland and McClain counties, announced she would withhold filing charges for the Lorenz murders pending the outcome of the Oklahoma County trial.

The admissibility of Verna's testimony at trial continued to remain in doubt. Brewer adamantly argued against its admissibility. In the end, the question revolved around whether the change in the Oklahoma law was procedural or substantive, a fine point of law, but crucial to the outcome of the case.

If the change was *substantive* then the privilege to bar Verna's testimony, which existed at the time the killings were committed, still remained and Verna could not testify. If the change was *procedural*, the path was open to the interpretation of the new law. Ultimately, Judge Geb allowed Verna's testimony, but the fight over this pivotal issue was far from over. Along with other motions, the defense would raise this issue again with District Judge Charles Owens, who was assigned to hear all pretrial motions and try the case.

The first African-American district judge in Oklahoma, Judge Owens was appointed to his post in 1968, and had experience in trying both civil and criminal cases. In the Stafford case, Judge Owens faced a number of evidentiary issues. The judge's first important ruling came on September 24, when he ruled that Verna's testimony, as to what she had actually witnessed and as to her conversations with Roger Dale in which a third party was present, was admissible.

Prior to trial it was also determined, by the agreement of both parties, that the trial would be televised. Only one camera was used, and it was placed in the back of the courtroom facing the judge and the witnesses. For the most part only the backs of the lawyers were shown. The trial would be televised on commercial stations and also on closed circuit to another room in the courthouse so that the press could watch the trial from that location. It was the first trial in Oklahoma to be broadcast on television.

At first, Coats had been reluctant to agree to televising the trial, but before it was all over he would be pleased the media was not present in the courtroom, as it helped to diminish the circus-like atmosphere that inevitably comes with a high profile case.

During the trial, each witness was asked if he objected to being shown on television, but none objected.

CHAPTER FIFTY-SEVEN

The Trial

THE TRIAL BEGAN on October 8. Jury selection took two days, and thirty-five potential jurors were excused before a jury of seven women and five men were seated. Brewer, who had previously attempted to change the venue of the trial due to pretrial publicity, said that he was "surprised" more jurors had not prejudged the case. Judge Owens, however, did decide to sequester the jury for the remainder of the trial.

The prosecution opened the State's case by setting the scene found at the restaurant on the night of the murders. Carlos Joy and Mike Click told of finding the victims. Richard Klein, one of the first ambulance attendants to arrive, described the bloody scene in the freezer room and the attempts to save Terri Horst's life.

Over the defendant's objection, pictures of the bodies were entered into evidence. Several police officers also testified about the grizzly nature of the crime scene. One of Judge Owens's most vivid recollections of the trial was his realization of the impact seeing all those bloody bodies had had on hardened police officers. The sight of the six maimed corpses crammed into the small freezer had caused one officer to leave the building and vomit. Dr. Fred Jordan, the associate chief medical examiner who had performed the autopsies, testified Isaac Freeman, Louis Zacarias, and Anthony Tew had all been killed by a single shot to the head. The absence of any defensive wounds indicated they had been shot instantly before they even had a chance to react.

David Salsman had been shot three times in the face, neck, and left arm. David Lindsey had been shot in the right hand, chest, and head, while Terri Horst had bullet wounds to her right leg, right arm, and two shots to her head. The hand and arm wounds to these three victims were likely defensive wounds, although it appeared that all of the killings took place in a matter of seconds.

Ten-year-old Greg Martin and his father, Frank D. Martin, testified about the boys finding the three guns in a field in northeast Oklahoma City. A number of police officers established the chain of custody for the weapons, laying the foundation for the expert testimony of Thomas D. Jordan, an OSBI firearms and tool mark examiner.

A ballistic expert, Jordan described the tests he had conducted on the .38 Taurus and the .357 Colt revolver, as well as comparisons made to bullets found at the crime scene. He concluded one of the bullets had been fired by the .357 and that the five other bullets were consistent with bullets fired from the .38, but they could not be conclusively attributed to that specific weapon. The .22 pistol was not tested as no bullets of that caliber were found at the murder scene.

Linville took the stand and recounted his conversations with Roger Dale after Roger Dale's arrest. In particular, he told the jury how Roger had admitted that he was the "truck driver" who had called in to tip off the OSBI about Verna and Harold.

. . . . .

All of the State's testimony had been an effort to set the stage for Verna's testimony. Verna was the State's star witness. Since arriving in

Oklahoma City, she had been held in protective custody and extensively interviewed and coached by the police and prosecutors. She would testify as to all of the details of the crime.

On the stand during questioning, Verna described how prior to the murders she and Roger Dale, Harold, Fat Mary, and their children had been living in Tulsa at the Holiday Inn where she worked cleaning rooms. They had then moved to a nearby house, though they retained access to rooms at the hotel because of Verna's job. Fat Mary was along mostly as a babysitter, Roger Dale was working some, and Harold was unemployed. All of the Staffords were short of money and, as usual, Roger Dale's solution was to rob somebody.

Roger Dale told Harold and Verna he knew of a good target, a restaurant in Oklahoma City that was near the interstate and easy to get in and out of quickly. Although they would be armed, Roger Dale assured them "no one was supposed to get hurt." Whether Verna believed him—given the previous murders of the Lorenz family—would seem doubtful.

At the time, the Staffords were driving an old blue '63 Ford, but Harold borrowed a 1965 green Oldsmobile station wagon for the job. This was the car Carlos Joy saw parked behind the restaurant the night of the murders. The trio arrived at the Sirloin Stockade shortly after closing time. All three were armed: Roger Dale with the .357 Colt, Harold with the .38 Taurus, and Verna with the .22. They knocked on the back door and were greeted by Zacarias, who they presumed was the manager. They forced Zacarias to the cash register at gunpoint. According to Verna, Zacarias remarked "that he couldn't understand why people had to take other people's money, why they couldn't work for themselves." Given Zacarias's experience and his apparent cooperation in every other way with the robbers, some of the detectives questioned whether such a statement was ever made, but it was consistently part of Verna's story.

Zacarias called all of the employees to join him at the cash register, and when they arrived he told them that they were being robbed and they should cooperate with the robbers. Finding no money in the cash register, Roger Dale took Zacarias into the manager's office where $1,290 was placed in a sack. Harold and Verna forced the other five employees into the small freezer room. The employees "were told to sit down, that no one was going to get hurt."

Roger Dale returned with the manager who was still telling Roger Dale he couldn't understand "why people couldn't work with their own money and why people had to take other peoples' money." According to Verna, this made Roger Dale "a little furious."

Harold reminded everyone that "no one was supposed to get hurt," but Roger Dale responded, "They are going to get what they deserve."

With that, Roger Dale told Harold, "Don't be a chicken shit and a coward," and he shot the "black man," Isaac Freeman.

That first shot acted like the blast of a starter pistol, and Roger Dale and Harold unleashed a volley of shots into the freezer room. The .38 had a defect and fired only five of six shells in the gun. Verna said she turned away, trying not to watch. Roger Dale, however, told her it was time for her to help, put a gun in her hand, pointed it into the freezer, and helped her pull the trigger.

Verna ran from the restaurant. Just outside, she picked up three empty boxes with the Sirloin Stockade name on them and put them in the back of the station wagon. Roger Dale and Harold jumped in the car next, and with Roger Dale at the wheel they sped out of the parking lot and up onto the highway, nearly colliding with another car in the process.

After stopping at a convenience store to get drinks, Roger Dale determined that they should dispose of the guns. He drove around northeast Oklahoma City until he found a wooded vacant lot that suited him. He and Harold put the guns in a sack from the convenience store and hid them on the lot. The killers then returned to Tulsa.

The next day, the threesome met up at the Holiday Inn where Verna worked and went to a vacant room to count their spoils. While they were divvying up the money, a maid, with whom they were familiar, walked in and asked where they had gotten all the cash. Verna told her they had borrowed it. Before they finished, Roger Dale discovered the Sirloin Stockade boxes. The discovery angered him, and he ordered Verna to get rid of them. He later personally asked one of the maids at the hotel to burn the boxes.

Despite Verna's coherent recount of what had happened on the stand, both Linville and Oklahoma City Police Detective Bill Cook believed it was actually Verna, not Harold, who was the second shooter that night. They based this on statements she had given them while in custody. Verna's version, however, is the one memorialized in a recorded statement prior to trial and in her testimony at the preliminary hearing, and it was the one she stuck with under oath.

Anticipating Brewer's cross-examination, however, Coats established that Verna had originally given the detectives two different versions of her story, at one point denying she had anything at all to do with the crime.

Brewer extensively questioned Verna in his cross-examination trying to highlight inconsistencies in her story. He also suggested that she had made a nice deal for herself with the prosecution in exchange for her testimony, an accusation that she denied.

In an attempt to shift the blame away from Roger Dale, Brewer also introduced a new name, Danny Kerr, the name of an acquaintance of the Staffords. Brewer implied that it was Kerr who had accompanied Harold and Verna to the restaurant and committed the murders. Detectives, however, had already eliminated Kerr as a suspect after their investigation placed him in Tulsa, not Oklahoma City, at the time of the crime.

Despite Brewer's laborious and detailed cross-examination, Verna stuck to her story, making a persuasive, but unsympathetic witness.

CHAPTER FIFTY-EIGHT

Roger Dale Takes the Stand

AFTER VERNA'S TESTIMONY the prosecution set about offering evidence to corroborate her story and further pin Roger Dale to the murders. Pamela Ann Lynch testified that she had been driving near the Sirloin Stockade restaurant at around ten-thirty on the night of the crime when a green station wagon came careening out of the shopping center and almost ran into her. She was able to identify Roger Dale as the driver.

To underscore how scary it was for witnesses like Lynch to come forward and testify against someone like Roger Dale, Coats recalls that while Lynch was outside the courtroom waiting to testify, Roger Dale walked past, caught her eye, and pretended to slit his throat with his finger. The young woman was not deterred by the unspoken threat.

The State also called Linda Louise Lewis as a witness. Lewis, who had been staying at the Tulsa Holiday Inn on the day after the Sirloin Stockade murders, recalled hearing a loud argument outside her room. When she opened the door, she saw Roger Dale hit Verna.

"I'm calling the police," Verna cried.

"Go ahead! You would be in as much trouble as I would," Roger Dale retorted.

"I didn't kill them Roger—you did."

"You were there and you were with us," said Roger Dale.

And the witnesses for the State kept coming.

Terecia Darlene Bennett cleaned rooms at the Holiday Inn and knew the Staffords. On the day of the murders she said she saw Roger Dale and Harold drive away in the green station wagon. After the crime she saw the Sirloin Stockade boxes and also a pair of blood-splattered jeans in the hotel dumpster. She had jokingly asked Roger Dale if he had heard about the Sirloin Stockade killings.

"You're probably the one who killed them," she said.

To which Roger Dale answered, "Yes I did."

According to Bennett, his reply was dead serious.

Rose Anna Marie Collins was the Holiday Inn housekeeper who had walked in on the Staffords as they were dividing up the cash only to be told by Verna that it was a loan from a friend in Oklahoma City. Collins also testified that later Roger Dale asked her to burn the Sirloin Stockade boxes.

Terecia Bennett had also told Collins about her conversation with Roger Dale regarding the murders. Later Collins said she had asked Roger Dale about them, too.

"You didn't really kill them did you, Roger?"

"Yes, I did," Roger Dale said. "It was just like shooting a balloon in a bag of water . . . shooting a person is just like shooting a fence post."

When Collins said she was going to turn him in, she said Roger Dale told her, "If I did, I wouldn't live long enough to testify."

Collins believed him.

. . . . .

After the prosecution rested, it was the defense's turn. Roger Dale's only hope was to convince the jury that he wasn't even at the crime scene. By his own admission, Roger Dale believed he could talk his way out of anything, even murder. But given the case against him, eloquence might not be enough. Putting Roger Dale on the stand was also a risky move for the defense. However, given his personality and ego, it was probably inevitable that Roger Dale would insist on testifying on his own behalf.

On the stand, Roger Dale described himself as a conman but denied being a thief: "Why should I steal when I'm blessed with this gift of gab, as some would say?" He demonstrated his fake British accent and described some of his exploits with gullible women who had given him money in the past.

Repeatedly he denied any involvement in the crimes.

"I'm innocent of these crimes. I didn't commit them," he said.

In another outburst, he declared: "I'll take a lie detector right now. Right here, right in front of the camera, in front of the jury, in front of your Honor."

Judge Owens describes Roger Dale as "cocky" and eager to testify. In order to explain his whereabouts at the time of the murders, Roger Dale told a tale about the night in question. He claimed to have begun drinking the afternoon of July 16 with Danny Kerr, with whom he proceeded to another establishment where they continued to imbibe with "three black gentlemen." Roger Dale testified he "found it strange" the "black gentlemen couldn't be found" to corroborate his story.

About six that night, Verna left—not to return to the motel until two the next morning. Between ten and eleven, when the murders took place, Roger Dale said he "was drunk as I could be on the hood [long pause] . . . on the hood of a Chevrolet in front of my house on Troust Street," a reference to where he was living at the time in Tulsa.

Roger Dale did admit he was the "truck driver" who had called the OSBI and tipped them off to Verna and Harold. He had opinions, too, about the three composite drawings by Harvey Pratt.

"One of them was a dead ringer of my brother, Harold," he testified, "and the other was absolutely my wife."

As to the third drawing, he would only say that "it was a fellow [pause] . . . he had with glasses and didn't have a mustache and had brown hair [pause] . . . " Roger Dale testified that he never wore glasses and always had a mustache.

The main contention of the defense was that Verna was lying. In Roger Dale's version of the truth, Verna was out to get him because he had caught her "playing around" three times, once with a "black gentleman."

In order to accept Roger Dale's testimony as the truth, however, the jury would have to believe that all of the State's witnesses were lying. Coats took advantage of this on his cross-examination of Roger Dale, who he led through a litany of questions—each showing in its own way that, according to Roger Dale, Roger Dale was the only honest person in the world.

On cross-examination, Roger Dale denied ever owning any guns or showing guns to anyone. This was a classic set up by the prosecution, as it then called two coworkers as rebuttal witnesses who testified Roger Dale had not only bragged about the guns he owned, but had also shown them the guns.

The other witnesses for the defense proved ineffective. Roger Dale's work supervisor established Roger Dale had reported for work at 3:15 p.m. on July 17, which in no way precluded his participation in the murders on the night of July 16. A social worker's testimony regarding Roger Dale was largely irrelevant.

During rebuttal, the prosecution also employed the dubious tactic of calling a jailhouse snitch, Ronald Watkins, a convicted felon who had served time with Roger Dale while awaiting trial. Watkins claimed Roger Dale had told him about the night in question.

"Well, he said that, you know, like he was there, but he didn't participate in any shooting. He said that his wife and his brother, Harold, did the shooting," Watkins testified.

Additionally, Watkins said Roger Dale had told him about filing the serial numbers off of the guns and disposing of them.

CHAPTER FIFTY-NINE

The Death Penalty

THE JUDGE ALLOWED the defense further rebuttal, and Brewer called Kenneth Thomas, another convicted felon who had been in jail with Roger Dale. Thomas must have convinced Brewer he could prove that Ronald Watkins was lying; instead, Thomas's testimony further torpedoed Roger Dale's defense. Thomas testified he had heard Roger Dale refer to the restaurant employees as "suckers or they wouldn't have been working there anyway." According to Thomas, Roger Dale claimed "the only mistake he made was not leaving Verna in the freezer."

Roger Dale took the stand again to testify that both Watkins and Thomas were lying.

On October 17, counsel presented closing arguments, the judge instructed the jury, and deliberations began.

Addressing the jurors, Coats proceeded to describe Roger Dale as "a little man who wants to be a big shot." As for the evidence, Coats told them it "paints a picture—paints a puzzle. When you get [that] puzzle all put together you see the face of Roger Stafford."

In his closing argument, Brewer tried his best to discredit Verna, pointing out every discrepancy in her testimony and emphasizing her first statements to the police, which she later admitted were lies.

"Here is a confessed murderer at the Sirloin Stockade, walking the streets of our country right now, walking among us with the blessing of the State," Brewer said of Verna.

Brewer also attacked the motive of the three witnesses from the Holiday Inn—Linda Lewis, Rose Collins, and Terecia Bennett—observing, "There's a large reward in this case" and suggesting the three not only wanted it but had collaborated on their testimony to get it.

Regardless of the arguments, by this time, the jurors had made up their minds. The jury needed only twenty-seven minutes to return a guilty verdict on all six counts. The case then moved to the punishment phase. The defense called no witnesses on Roger Dale's behalf but Brewer implored the jury not to execute his client.

"If we're going to administer this law equally, are we going to execute this man and let Verna Stafford walk away?" he asked the jury.

Brewer also argued Roger Dale had acted under Verna's influence.

In his argument for the death penalty, Coats asked the jurors to put themselves in the place of the victims that night. "Can you imagine the sheer terror in the hearts and minds of those young people when he shot Freeman and Zacarias? It was so pitiless, so terribly pitiless. He had no feeling for anything he did. He thought no more of killing those people than stepping on an insect," he said.

Once again the jury had no trouble cutting to the heart of the matter. After fifty-three minutes of deliberation, it recommended the death penalty on all six counts. The man who had thought he could talk himself out of anything had learned that cold-blooded murder was the exception. As Roger Dale left the courtroom, he couldn't resist one last sally: "Unless someone comes forward and tells the truth I'll die an innocent man."

From the bench, Judge Owens told the jury, "I do sincerely believe justice was done."

CHAPTER SIXTY

The Lorenz Trial

A S IF THINGS WERE NOT BAD enough for Roger Dale, McClain County District Attorney Kay Huff announced that she would be filing murder charges against him for the murders of the Lorenz family. Once again, Verna's testimony would be crucial for a conviction, and once again the defense would challenge her right to testify against her spouse.

In the McClain County case, Brewer also raised another unique issue, claiming that Verna's testimony should be barred because she had been hypnotized. The State countered by saying that an attempt to place Verna under hypnosis after she was arrested had actually failed. Judge J. Kenneth Love, the associate district judge in McClain County, overruled the defense's motions, and Verna once again would tell her story.

Judge Love also overruled yet another imaginative defense motion seeking to have Roger Dale administered sodium pentothal in an attempt to illicit information helpful to his defense. Judge Love ruled that any information so obtained would be inadmissible at trial.

This time going into the trial, Roger Dale at least appeared to have mustered more of a defense, revealing that he had alibi witnesses to prove that he could not have been at the crime scene at the time of the murders. Whether or not this would persuade a jury, it was at least better than his story in the Sirloin Stockade trial of being drunk with three unidentifiable "black gentlemen."

Verna testified at Roger Dale's preliminary hearing in December 1979. She detailed the facts of the Lorenz killings that she would later repeat at the trial. Her testimony along with that of just two other witnesses was enough for McClain County Special Judge Sam Goodwin to order Roger Dale bound over for trial.

The Lorenz trial began Monday, February 25, 1980. By noon the next day, a jury of seven men and five women had been selected, and, as in the Sirloin Stockade trial, the jury was sequestered for the duration of the trial.

After opening statements were made, testimony began Wednesday, February 28. Huff leapt full speed into the guts of the case, putting Verna on as her first witness. Once again Verna's testimony proved devastating to Roger Dale. It also, this time, deeply implicated her in the crime. According to Verna, the deadly trio that included Roger Dale and Harold stole the .38 Taurus pistol from a pawnshop in Purcell, Oklahoma. They first planned to rob a motel in the Pauls Valley area but discarded that idea for another target.

In the early morning hours of June 22, the Staffords parked their car on the shoulder of Interstate 35, south of Purcell. Verna stood by the vehicle pretending to have car trouble while Roger Dale and Harold hid behind it. After about an hour the Lorenz family stopped their pickup, and Melvin went to the aid of what he believed was a troubled motorist.

When Melvin, after looking under the hood of the car at the engine, announced, "I can't find anything wrong," Roger Dale and Harold appeared. Holding Melvin at gunpoint, Roger Dale demanded his money.

Melvin responded by saying he would give up some of his money but couldn't give it all. His response upset Roger Dale, who promptly shot Melvin twice, once in the neck and again in the chest. Linda Lorenz rushed to her husband's aid and attacked Verna. Verna pushed Linda away, and Roger Dale shot Linda three times. The bullets penetrated both of Linda's lungs and her aorta.

Roger Dale, Harold, and Verna then dragged the bodies of their two victims away from the highway, but their killing spree was not yet over. As Roger Dale drove the Lorenzes' truck north on Interstate 35, following Verna and Harold in Stafford's car, he heard sounds coming from behind him. That's when he discovered Richard and the dogs inside the camper. Both vehicles pulled over, stopped, and Roger Dale explained the problem to the other two.

As Verna told it, Harold saw "no sense in hurting the little boy because he couldn't identify us." Roger Dale disagreed, saying It wasn't right to leave anybody around who could testify to anything.

With that, Roger Dale tore a hole in the camper's screen and fired into the back of the pickup, wounding young Richard. With Harold's help, Roger Dale then dragged the badly bleeding boy into the field, where his body would eventually be found, and fired at him again with the .38 Taurus. In all, Richard was shot three times, in the hand, neck, and shoulder.

Dr. Fred Jordan later testified that none of the boy's wounds would have killed him instantly, and that he was probably alive when left to die by the Staffords. Linville, who dissected the crime scene and autopsy reports, believes Verna may actually have fired the fatal shots that killed Melvin and Linda Lorenz. The angle of Melvin's wounds were consistent with the shots having been fired while he was leaning in under the hood of the car, and Linda's attack was aimed at Verna, not Roger Dale.

In any event, the prosecution adopted Verna's version of the murders. And Brewer once again went after Verna on cross-examination, pointing out that she had lied repeatedly to the police about what had happened that day. "You've told so many lies," Brewer told Verna. "You don't know what the truth is. Isn't that correct?"

"I do know what the truth is," Verna said.

Brewer also pounded on the fact that Verna had not been charged with any crime and that she was simply lying to save herself from the death penalty.

. . . . .

After Verna testified, a number of investigators were called to set up the chain of evidence on the murder weapon and the guns stolen from the Lorenz family. Melvin Lorenz's brother identified the two guns stolen from the Lorenzes and pictures of the bodies. Jerry Potter, owner of the Purcell pawnshop, identified the murder weapon as being stolen from his shop. The serial number had been ground off, but the gun was still unique. It had a malfunction that caused a misfire one out of six chambers, making Potter certain it was the stolen gun. Potter's testimony about the gun was also consistent with the crime scene where five shell casings and one live round were found near Richard's body.

The prosecution also called the same three coworkers who had testified against Roger Dale in the Sirloin Stockade case. Each reiterated conversations with Roger Dale in which he bragged about the guns he owned and, in the case of one witness, Michael Jones, had actually shown him the .38 Taurus used to murder the Lorenz family.

Some of the most controversial testimony came from Ray Tackett, the Stillwater businessman who had first sighted the Staffords the day of the Lorenz murders, and Harvey Pratt, the OSBI forensic artist who had drafted the composite drawings based on Tackett's description from that morning.

Brewer tried hard to shake Tackett, accusing him of only being interested in the reward attached to solving the Sirloin Stockade murders. Tackett correctly pointed out that he had been unaware of any reward when he reported his observations to the Payne County sheriff after the

Lorenz crime which was before the Sirloin Stockade murders had even taken place.

"Mr. Brewer, the worse thing in the world would be to convict an innocent man," Tackett testified. ". . . But the next worse thing would be to turn someone loose who was guilty."

Despite Brewer's best efforts, Tackett never wavered. Throughout his testimony Tackett insisted Roger Dale was the man he had seen that day in Stillwater. Pratt then threw the defense a curve. He not only identified the original composite drawings, but also produced a series of sketches in which he had dropped the glasses, added a mustache, and lengthened the hair on the Roger Dale look-alike. His revised drawings were admitted over Brewer's objection that he had been tricked and "shanghaied" by the State. Brewer made it clear to Pratt what he thought of his efforts when the forensic artist took the stand.

"What Kay Huff wanted you to do was to make it look like Roger Stafford," Brewer said.

Pratt simply shrugged. "It looks like him to me," Pratt said.

Huff later asked Pratt: "If you added those characteristics to a composite of Mr. Brewer, would it look like Roger Dale Stafford?"

Pratt replied "No."

Linville also testified again, naming Roger Dale as the anonymous "trucker" whose call to the OSBI first identified Verna and Harold.

. . . . .

After the State rested, the defense took its best shot. Roger Dale, being Roger Dale, had to testify. Undeterred by the Sirloin Stockade verdict, he still thought he could talk his way out of another conviction and a death sentence. On the stand, he denied any involvement in the crime and placed the blame on Verna, whom he said was out to get him because "I caught her with another gentleman."

This time his story was that he had come home from work June 21 to find Verna gone. He then watched television until midnight when he went to bed. The next day he was at work at his job at Baird Manufacturing in Tulsa at 6:30 a.m.

The big difference from the Sirloin Stockade case was that this time, Roger Dale actually had corroborating witnesses to support his alibi claim. Calvin Mendenhall, a social worker at the Emergency Housing Center in Tulsa where the Staffords were living at the time, testified that he remembered seeing Stafford watching television the night in question because Roger Dale made a special request to leave the television on after the midnight curfew. He further stated he had told OSBI investigators about seeing Stafford that night. This testimony was later rebutted by OSBI Agent Phil Stinett.

Other witnesses also bolstered Roger Dale's alibi defense. Three officers and two employees of Roger Dale's Tulsa employer testified that Roger Dale was at work the morning of June 22, just hours after the Lorenz family was shot and killed. None of the witnesses could say he had specifically seen Roger Dale at work that morning, but they claimed his absence would have been noticed and that time cards and payroll records indicated that he was at work.

On rebuttal by the State, Ted Ballinger, who serviced the time clocks at Baird Manufacturing Company, demonstrated how easily the time clock could be manipulated to falsify a time card. Buck Rudd, a supervisor at the Emergency Housing Center, also attacked Mendenhall's testimony, saying Mendenhall had never raised the issue before and that the former counselor "tells untruths."

Huff also decided to call Kenneth Dan Thomas, the same notorious jailhouse snitch who had testified in the Sirloin Stockade case. In spite of Thomas's dubious credibility, the evidence he offered was damaging to Roger Dale.

Thomas stated that Roger Dale had told him, "He always killed the most dangerous ones first" and "He said it doesn't make any difference if they're two or eighty-two, they grow up to be just the same." Thomas further said Roger Dale was not worried about a conviction because some coworkers would punch him in at work.

245

Brewer effectively cross-examined Thomas, pointing out how a large number of theft-related cases had been dropped against him in return for his cooperation with the prosecution, and he noted that Thomas had testified for the prosecution in other cases in exchange for leniency. Thomas admitted he was a thief but stuck to his story regarding Stafford.

The attorneys made their closing arguments, and the judge instructed the jury on March 7.

Huff argued that the Lorenz family had been "killed for kindness," referring to their willingness to help a stranded motorist. She reminded the jury that Roger Dale described himself as "a survivor. . . . Whatever it takes." She said the photographs of the bodies of the Lorenz family showed Roger Dale's philosophy of life: ". . . survival for himself and death for others."

Brewer's closing argument featured one last attack on Verna. He also referenced Roger Dale's alibi. "If the clock card is correct Roger Stafford was not out there on that road killing people," he told the jury.

The jury, however, wasn't buying what Roger Dale and his lawyer were selling. It took just one hour and twenty-four minutes to find Roger Dale guilty on all three counts. After hearing further arguments from counsel, the jury returned its verdict in favor of the death penalty on all three counts.

As the news came in, Roger Dale appeared nonchalant. Asked his reaction as he left the courtroom, he simply flung his arms wide and shrugged. Apparently three more death sentences didn't bother him much. The State could only kill him once.

. . . . .

Roger Dale would go on to file a lengthy series of appeals, first to the Oklahoma Court of Criminal Appeals then to the U.S. Supreme Court, and after that in both U.S. and Oklahoma courts, none of which overturned either the verdict or his death sentence.

Finally, on July 1, 1995, some seventeen years after the crime, he was put to death at McAlester. While he had awaited execution, he had grown fat and married twice. And, even in death, the big talking criminal had to have the last word.

A few days after Roger Dale's execution, Linville received a letter. Inside was a five-dollar gift certificate from a Sirloin Stockade in McAlester. On the back was written:

> Hey, you got away with it. I am murder (sic) and you help (sic) do it. I am innocent and you know it.

The certificate was signed Roger Dale Stafford 103767.

An assistant attorney general, Sandy Howard, who represented the State in opposing many of Roger Dale's appeals, received a similar gift certificate.

CHAPTER SIXTY-ONE

Verna

THE QUESTION NOW WAS what to do with Verna. Deciding her fate fell to Coats and Huff. Clearly, Verna had cooperated with the State, and without her testimony Roger Dale might have gone free, likely to kill again.

On the other hand, she was at the least a willing accomplice in all of the murders. She had to pay. The result was a plea bargain negotiated between Coats, Huff, and Verna's attorney, Raymond Burger.

Verna pled guilty to two counts of second-degree murder: one for the killing of Linda Lorenz, the other for the killing of Terri Horst. Just a few days after the Lorenz trial, Judge Owens sentenced her to an indeterminate prison term of ten years to life.

Verna's only response to her sentence was surprisingly matter of fact: "All I can say is they did what they had to do." No doubt Verna had been hoping she would be released from custody in ten years give or take a few years, but that never happened thanks to another twist in the law. In 1989, while Roger Dale was still alive, sitting on death row and continuing to fight off execution, Verna made a bid for freedom.

In an unrelated case, the Oklahoma Court of Criminal Appeals had ruled that a court could not set an indeterminate sentence in which a life sentence was the maximum imposed. Based on this decision, Verna moved to set aside her sentence and be resentenced to ten years, which, given time served, would have allowed her to go free immediately.

Her resentencing hearing was assigned to Oklahoma County District Judge Richard Freeman. The judge correctly set aside Verna's original sentence but then proceeded to conduct a hearing in which both parties offered evidence.

In that hearing, Verna played up her cooperation with the prosecution and even called former District Attorney Coats to testify in her behalf. The current district attorney, Bob Macy, offered evidence from the two trials detailing the grizzly nature of the murders and pointing out Verna's involvement in them. Both Linville and Oklahoma City Police Detective Bill Cook testified that they had always believed that Verna was far more involved in the murders than she had admitted during the two trials, and that she well might have taken part in the actual killings.

At the close of the evidence, Judge Freeman hammered Verna with two life sentences to be served consecutively, effectively meaning she would have to be paroled twice to ever have a chance to get out of prison. In rendering his verdict, Judge Freeman told Verna, "I would wager that there's one of the hottest corners of hell vacant with your name right above it."

Verna was devastated. She had convinced herself that she would be set free. She appealed Judge Freeman's ruling, but the decision was upheld. Over the years, Verna would continue to try repeatedly and unsuccessfully for a parole. Her last attempt at parole was denied in June 2011; she is next eligible for parole in 2014.

As of the summer of 2014, after more than three decades, Verna remains in Oklahoma's Mabel Bassett Correctional Center, a women's minimum- and medium-security prison near McCloud, Oklahoma, where she has served almost her entire sentence. In a recent interview, Verna spoke freely about Roger Dale and the murders that had put her in the McCloud prison. Suffering from neurological problems in her feet, she gave the interview from a wheelchair. Throughout the interview she maintained a remarkably passive and unemotional demeanor.

Today Verna's overriding theme is that she participated in the 1978 crimes out of fear of Roger Dale, that he forced her to help by threatening her life and the life of their children. She says that prior to the Lorenz killings, Roger Dale had bragged to her about another murder he had committed and often told her that he was connected with the mafia. She says she continued to receive death threats from Roger Dale even after they were both in prison.

"I'll put it this way," she said. "I did not feel free until the day they executed him."

When asked if there were anything she would like people to know about the cases that had never come out—despite all the trials and headlines—Verna replied: I'm not the meanest person that everybody thinks I am. I mean, I wish I would have had more of a backbone to have stood up to him. You know, I wish it never had happened, but I think until people really realize what type of person he really was, no one's going to understand me. Does that make sense?

It doesn't make sense. Say what she will, in the end Verna's attempt to play victim is far from persuasive. She willingly participated in both of the vicious crimes. She never stepped forward on her own. She knew Roger Dale was a murderer before the Lorenz killings and even after that bloody crime she stayed with him and took part in the Sirloin Stockade murders. And she only helped the authorities after she had been caught and feared the death penalty herself. As for her unemotional appearance it may well reflect her capacity for the cold-blooded killing of innocent people, something Roger Dale shared.

The Oklahoma City Bombing

Oklahoma City
Marathon
By Kent F. Frates

They lived and,
then, they died.

She may have burned the toast
or, he forgot his lunch box
or, heard a good joke on the
car radio,

until one twisted mind
dealt out fiery death
against an enemy
too big to understand,

and, pompous politicians speak
and, self righteous preachers preach
and, many mothers weep
and, we mourn with
10,000 running feet
at dawn
against a pink streaked
Oklahoma sky,

and, the dead stay dead
forever.

CHAPTER SIXTY-TWO

Where Were You

IN EVERY AMERICAN'S LIFE come a few universal "Where were you?" moments. Depending on your age, they might include "Where were you when Pearl Harbor was bombed?" or "Where were you when Kennedy was assassinated?" or, more recently, "Where were you on 9/11?"

In Oklahoma City, such a moment was 9:02 a.m. April 19, 1995, when a car bomb destroyed the Alfred P. Murrah Federal Building in the heart of the city. The worst terrorist attack on U.S. soil at the time, the bombing resulted in the deaths of 168 people, including fifteen children under the age of five who attended daycare in the building.

The blast also caused injury to hundreds more, destroyed millions of dollars worth of property, and shook the confidence of a nation. The triggerman of this horrific act was Timothy McVeigh, a U.S. Army veteran and a self-described "American patriot."

The story of the bombing and subsequent trials begins years before the actual event, and continues today as the citizens of Oklahoma City find new ways to memorialize both the victims and the heroic acts of the many rescue workers, medical personnel, firemen, law enforcement officers, and volunteers who responded that April morning.

The Oklahoma City bombing was a first for the nation, an act of extreme domestic terrorism, but its most lasting effect has been on Oklahoma City and its people. The community has dedicated itself to supporting the survivors and to honoring the victims of this horrific tragedy, always mindful of a promise made in the early days of the tragedy: "We Will Never Forget."

It has been almost twenty years since the heinous act. In those two decades, a national memorial and museum have been erected on the site of the demolished building, and events, such as the Oklahoma City Memorial Marathon, continue to ensure that the 168 people who died are remembered. Voted one the twelve "must-run" marathons in the world by *Runner's World* magazine, the annual race raises funds to support the Oklahoma City National Memorial and Museum.

The bombing, often referred to simply as "Oklahoma City" by law enforcement officers, caused the U.S. government to reassess its security measures at government buildings across the country. Security was tightened to ward off another such an attack; barriers were built to keep vehicles farther away from buildings; and security personnel and the screening of visitors were increased. Even before 9/11, these measures significantly increased safety in federal facilities.

Many books, articles, videos, and films have chronicled the bombing. Not surprisingly in this day and age, a wide range of conspiracy theories have also emerged, some going so far as to suggest the federal government had notice that the bombing would occur or was even involved. Like any complicated and catastrophic event, unknowns and unanswered questions remain. What has been determined beyond a reasonable doubt by three different juries is that Timothy McVeigh built and detonated the bomb and that Terry Nichols helped McVeigh and conspired with him to commit the crime.

McVeigh was executed June 11, 2001, while Nichols remains in a federal supermax prison in Florence, Colorado, serving life without parole. Understanding what motivated McVeigh and Nichols to commit such a violent act against innocent civilians is beyond the comprehension of normal people. However, the evidence collected against them and their personal histories reveal much about the twisted logic that motivated their crime.

CHAPTER SIXTY-THREE

McVeigh & Nichols

BORN APRIL 23, 1968, in the small town of Lockport, New York, Timothy McVeigh grew up in the same place he was born. His hometown is located in northwestern New York, near Niagara Falls and Buffalo. His father, Bill McVeigh, was a factory worker, and his mother, Mildred Noreen "Mickey" McVeigh, was a housewife. He had one older sister, Patty, and one younger sister, Jennifer.

The McVeigh family moved to Pendleton, New York, a neighboring town in 1978 when McVeigh was ten, and shortly thereafter, his parents separated. McVeigh's mother and two sisters then moved to Florida, while he remained with his father. Although his parents attempted reconciliation, they later divorced.

McVeigh's grandfather, Ed McVeigh, helped to raise him and also greatly influenced his life. His grandfather was a farmer who canned vegetables and taught McVeigh how to shoot a rifle.

Early on, McVeigh developed what became a lifelong fascination with guns. After graduating from high school, he briefly attended business school, but found it boring. He quit, opting for a job as an armed security guard and then a guard for an armored car service. McVeigh also developed an ambition to become an Army Ranger. He saw himself as a Rambo-like character, fighting America's enemies. With this in mind in 1988, he joined the U.S. Army. First stationed at Fort Benning, Georgia, for basic training, McVeigh immediately established himself as a competent soldier. He was disciplined, enthusiastic, and committed to earning the right to become a member of Army Special Forces.

After basic training, McVeigh was transferred to Fort Riley, Kansas, where he joined Company C2/16 Infantry Battalion, part of the First Infantry Division known as "The Big Red One." At Fort Riley, McVeigh continued to demonstrate his dedication to the service. He was a superb marksman and impeccable in maintaining his gear and weapons. When his unit was assigned Bradley Fighting Vehicles, McVeigh became a Bradley gunner.

The twenty-five ton Bradley Fighting Vehicle holds nine soldiers, a driver, gunner, commander, and six infantrymen. Designed for the quick movement of troops the Bradley is lightly armored but heavily armed with three highly effective guns. The biggest gun was designed to fire missiles at tanks and other targets more than a mile away. The other two guns included a 7.62 millimeter machine gun that fired a thousand rounds per minute and a versatile 25 millimeter cannon that fired both anti-aircraft and anti-armor shells. McVeigh was a maestro with all three weapons and soon was acknowledged to be the best of the some one hundred and twenty gunners stationed at Fort Riley.

While serving at Fort Riley, McVeigh became friends with Terry Nichols. At thirty-three, Nichols was the oldest private in the company. Nichols shared both McVeigh's right-wing views and his distrust of the government, and their politics made them natural bedfellows. The two soldiers exchanged extremist reading materials and complaints about the policies of the U.S. government. They were particularly critical of any attempt by the federal government to restrain gun ownership.

Although McVeigh and Nichols were similar in their politics, they were different in how they expressed their anger and resentment. McVeigh was a zealot, a true believer, a man who wanted to spread the cause and convince his fellow soldiers of the danger posed by what he believed to be an oppressive government. Nichols, on the other hand, was more of a belligerent separatist, a man who blamed the government for his own failures and who chose to isolate himself from the duties and responsibilities of American citizenship. McVeigh was a positive activist in these years; Nichols, more of a negative complainer. Nichols had been, of course, influenced by his background.

. . . . .

Born April 1, 1955, Nichols grew up on a farm near Lapeer, Michigan. He had two older brothers, Leslie and James, and a younger sister, Suzanne. As a young man Les was badly burned in an accident that disabled him for life, and his accident is said to have haunted Nichols.

Nichols graduated from Lapeer High School in 1973, and his parents divorced in 1974. Nichols attended Central Michigan University, but dropped out after only one semester to help his brother James work a farm near Decker, Michigan, owned by his mother, Joyce. James deeply distrusted the U.S. government and resented paying taxes. Nichols soon adopted his brother's views, which were also prevalent among their friends and neighbors.

Not happy farming, Nichols briefly moved to Colorado where he sold real estate. After he returned to Michigan, he worked as an insurance salesman, carpenter, and grain elevator manager. In 1981, he married Lana Padilla, a two-time divorcee and mother of two children. They had a son, Josh, in 1982. Nichols's older brother, James, married Lana's sister, Kelli, and they also had a son. Before long both marriages were on the rocks and both would end in divorce.

For the most part, Nichols's life was that of a hapless loser. He had tried to change his luck by joining the U.S. Army in 1988, but an Army career didn't suit Nichols either, and in 1989, he obtained a hardship discharge to return home and help care for his young son.

McVeigh, however, thrived as a soldier, and in November 1990, was positioned to fulfill his dream of becoming an Army Ranger. He received orders to report to Special Forces Training at Fort Bragg, North Carolina. Before he could report, however, the U.S. launched Operation Desert Shield. More than 500,000 American troops were to be placed in Saudi Arabia. George H.W. Bush would not declare war on Iraq until January 16, 1991, but the deployment included McVeigh's division, which shipped out to Saudi Arabia, beginning the most defining moments of McVeigh's young life.

Upon its arrival in the Middle East, McVeigh's company was forced to wait for weeks in the harsh conditions of the Saudi Arabian desert. During this time, McVeigh was promoted to sergeant.

When the attack on Iraq began, McVeigh's company was at the forefront of the assault. The offense played out across heavily mined areas of the desert and was led by the Bradley Fighting Vehicles backed by tanks. In four days of fighting, McVeigh's unit saw constant action, and while it was more of a slaughter than a battle there was extreme danger from friendly fire and mines, as well as fire from the Iraqi army.

In one instance of fighting, McVeigh made an incredible long distance shot that took out two Iraqi soldiers over a mile away. He also saved the life of a wounded comrade by racing to the wounded man and temporarily treating his wounds until medical aide arrived.

The war may have ended successfully for the U.S., but for McVeigh, like so many of his fellow soldiers, it was devastating. While proud of his achievements, he is said to have felt sorry for the ragtag Iraqi soldiers, many of whom had been forced to fight against their will. He also felt sympathy for the frightened Iraqi civilians, especially those who did not understand why the U.S. was in Iraq in the first place.

While still in Saudi Arabia, McVeigh again received orders to report to Fort Bragg for Special Forces Training. He hurried home to take advantage of this opportunity, but badly depleted by weeks in the desert, poor food, little sleep, and combat fatigue, he was not prepared for the rigorous demands of Special Forces School. The instructor gave all of the combat veterans the right to defer their training opportunity, but McVeigh and the others opted, unwisely, to proceed. After only a few days, McVeigh and most of the other combat veterans realized that they could not complete the course and dropped out.

Sometime thereafter, McVeigh became determined to leave the military, and in late 1991 mustered out of the service with an Honorable Discharge, a Bronze Star, and a long list of other medals and commendations. His life would never be the same.

. . . . .

McVeigh returned to Pendleton and moved in with his father. Initially he applied for a civil service job. Intelligent and always good at testing, McVeigh scored high on the civil service examination but could not get a job. That failure further alienated him from the government. He was particularly angered because he believed as a veteran, he deserved preference over others who had not served their country.

McVeigh started keeping a diary and writing letters to friends and family expressing his antigovernment opinions. He also took to writing his congressman, Representative John J. LaFalce, and local newspapers about his views. In February 1992, he wrote a letter to the *Lockport Union Sun and Journal* despairing of the condition of the United States and railing against politicians.

The letter concluded:

> Is civil war imminent? Do we have to shed blood to reform the current system? I hope it doesn't come to that but it might.

Frustrated, he took another security guard job, but increasingly was restless and unhappy with his life. Assigned to work security at Calspan, a high-tech research company in Buffalo that did contract work for the government, McVeigh picked up bits of information about a secret law enforcement project that fueled his paranoia against the government. He expressed those fears to a fellow security guard, Carl E. Lebron Jr., and even mentioned a desire to steal guns from the government. Lebron became so concerned about McVeigh's attitude that he recorded some of McVeigh's antigovernment conversations, but he failed to do anything with the recordings.

About this time, McVeigh also reconnected with his Army buddy Nichols, who had come to visit him in Pendleton. The two men seemed to feed off each other, each fueling the other's distrust of the government.

. . . . . .

Back in rural Michigan, Nichols had been struggling financially and developing a militia mindset. He and James had both renounced their citizenship and started to defy the law. Nichols ran up credit card debt of more than $18,000, which he offered to pay with a "certificate of credit" he had created himself. He claimed U.S. currency was worthless because it was no longer backed by gold.

When he had to appear in court in response to a judgment taken against him by the bank because of his failure to pay, he claimed he was "a nonresident alien, non-foreigner, [and] stranger to the current state of the forum." This defense is the mantra of militia groups, such as the Posse Comitatus, and, while it got him nowhere in court, it did serve his need to vent his rage against the system.

Although they worked hard, the farm barely supported the brothers. To supplement his income, Nichols, who had always been interested in guns, began traveling to gun shows all over the country. He started trading firearms, and buying and selling surplus Army equipment and clothing. The gun shows were a hotbed of renegades, gun freaks, and right-wing extremists, and Nichols found many people at them who shared his antigovernment views.

In 1990, Nichols remarried. His second wife, Marife Torres, was a seventeen-year-old "mail order" bride from the Philippines. Marife arrived in Michigan five months pregnant with another man's child. The couple went on to have two children together, but like Nichols's first marriage, this one was far from happy. The couple separated on a number of occasions, and Marife traveled back and forth to the Philippines where she lived off and on with her family. Nichols sometimes visited her in the Philippines, and it was later rumored that while there he met and communicated with communists and the Philippine version of Al-Qaeda.

CHAPTER SIXTY-FOUR

Waco

IN EARLY 1993, McVeigh decided to leave New York. There was really nothing there to keep him and he had convinced himself that New York taxes were too high. In keeping with his desire to escape what he considered government oppression, he became determined to find a place that he felt offered more freedom. Thus began a nomadic life that over the next few years found him crisscrossing the country, never staying more than a few months in any one spot.

McVeigh first moved to Florida where his sister Patty's husband found him a construction job. Then on February 28, 1993, news came that FBI agents had clashed with David Koresh and his followers at the Branch Davidian Complex near Waco, Texas.

Already angered by the 1992 confrontation between the U.S. Marshals Service and the FBI with Randy Weaver at Ruby Ridge, Idaho, McVeigh saw Waco as further confirmation that the real enemy was the federal government. Waco so agitated him that he decided to go there himself. When McVeigh arrived at the scene of the siege, he was rebuffed by law enforcement officers and refused access to the site of the standoff. McVeigh took this not as law enforcement protocol typical at such a confrontation, but rather as further evidence of the arbitrary abuse of power by the federal government. Rather than leaving, he opened up shop in the area and sold bumper stickers with antigovernment slogans such as "When Guns are outlawed, I will become an outlaw" and "Fear the Government that fears you." A reporter for the Southern Methodist University student paper interviewed McVeigh for a story, in which McVeigh harangued against gun control and called for people to take up arms against the government.

After a few days at Waco, McVeigh traveled on to Kingman, Arizona, a small desert town on Interstate 40 near the California border. In Kingman he hooked up with another Army buddy, Michael Fortier, and Michael's girlfriend and soon-to-be wife, Lori Hart. But Fortier was not a zealot like McVeigh, nor an overt renegade like Nichols. Perhaps it was Fortier's affinity for marijuana and methamphetamines, but in any event, he was more of a bitcher and whiner than an activist.

. . . . .

Around this time, McVeigh began to work the gun-show circuit. His routine was to set up a table and sell T-shirts and survivalist gear: canteens, duffle bags, and camouflage pants. He also sold books, like *The Turner Diaries*, and handed out pro-gun and antigovernment literature and bumper stickers.

An avid reader, McVeigh had always himself been particularly fond of gun- and warfare-related magazines, such as *Soldier of Fortune*. One day, while still a teen, he sent off for a book advertised in the back of a gun magazine. That book was *The Turner Diaries*, a novel by white nationalist leader William L. Pearce, written under the pen name of Andrew McDonald, that the *New York Times* once labeled a "bible of the racist right." Written in 1978, the novel was widely popular among gun collectors, militia groups, survivalists, white separatists, and other right-wing radicals. The book chronicles the activities of a gun-owner who rebels against firearm laws by making a truck bomb and destroying the FBI headquarters building in Washington, D.C. McVeigh, like many other fanatic gun enthusiasts, had always related to the plot.

During 1993 and 1994, McVeigh traveled back and forth between Fortier's house in Kingman and the Nichols farm in Michigan, with occasional trips home to New York. When he was on the road at gun shows he mostly slept in his car, as he was only able to eke out a small living from his business.

It was at a gun show in Fort Lauderdale, Florida, that McVeigh met a gun dealer named Roger Moore, who ran a weapon supply business called the American Assault Company. Moore was successful at trading and selling all kinds of weapons and ammunition. Prior to entering the weapons business, he had become wealthy from the sale of a boat-building business he had owned and operated in Florida. Moore had a home and wife in Florida, but also a girlfriend, Karen Anderson, who he lived with on a ranch in Arkansas. Anderson traveled both with Moore and on his behalf to gun shows.

Moore was a controversial character, having already been involved in at least two FBI investigations regarding illegal weapons sales. He had a certain air of mystery about him, and rumors had him involved with the CIA and various foreign connections. Moore, like McVeigh and his buddies, distrusted the government and feared stricter gun control laws. He was attracted to McVeigh and his antigovernment views, and McVeigh respected Moore for his stance on gun control and his business success.

On at least two occasions, McVeigh visited Moore and Anderson at the Arkansas ranch, a hard-to-come-by invitation since Moore was paranoid about security at his ranch, where he kept valuable weapons, cash, and gold and silver bullion. Moore would come to play a role in McVeigh's plot to bomb the Alfred P. Murrah Federal Building in Oklahoma City.

On April 19, 1993, McVeigh's travels found him at the Nichols farm as federal Alcohol, Tobacco, & Firearms agents invaded the

Branch Davidian Complex at Waco. The shootout and subsequent fire that killed David Koresh and many of his followers enraged McVeigh. He had intended to return to Waco, and later he did just that—mainly to see the burned out complex for himself.

As time went by, Waco became an obsession for McVeigh, and helped drive him to action against the government. He ordered a book called *Homemade C-4: A Recipe for Survival* by Ragnar Benson that was basically a bomb-making manual for manufacturing homemade bombs made from ammonium nitrate mixed with fuel oil or nitro-methane. McVeigh also began to add an array of anti-ATF items to his gun show products, including ball caps lettered with "ATF" riddled with bullet holes.

McVeigh was introduced to bomb-making by the Nichols brothers, who had long made bombs to blow up stumps on their farm. He also continued to experiment with bombs made on his own. In Kingman, he made small bombs and took the Fortiers into the desert for demonstrations. All the while the level of McVeigh's rhetoric against the U.S. government was becoming more extreme and violent. He wrote letters to his younger sister, Jennifer, containing stronger and stronger threats about taking action against the government.

Over the same period of time in 1993 and 1994, Nichols was continuing to have domestic problems of his own. His two-year-old stepson suffocated to death in a household accident, and he and Marife fought and separated repeatedly. He moved to Las Vegas to be near his older son, Josh, who was living there with his ex-wife, Lana. The move, like almost everything Nichols did, failed, and he moved again to Herrington, Kansas, near Fort Riley.

Unlike McVeigh, whose dissatisfaction had begun to provoke an aggressive response, Nichols's dissatisfaction with the U.S. government manifested itself in a desire to divorce himself from all forms of authority. In keeping with this, on March 16, 1994, he sent an affidavit to the president, vice president, and attorney general of the United States, together with a long list of local, state, and federal officials.

The affidavit recited a rambling list of grievances, but its main point was that Nichols declared himself to be a "foreign" and "nonresident alien" and, thus, could pick and choose what laws he wanted to abide by. He also sent another affidavit withdrawing his signature on any tax returns he had previously filed with the IRS.

With much fanfare on September 13, 1994, President Clinton signed into law a ban on assault weapons as part of the Crime Control Act of 1994. The bill banned the manufacture, transfer, and possession of a wide range of semiautomatic weapons and large capacity ammunition clips. Many of the weapons banned had been freely traded at gun shows prior to the bill's passage. Rumors spread among gun owners and traders that even more draconian measures were on the way.

That bill seems to be the final event that triggered the paranoid McVeigh to take action against the federal government. From this time forward he would dedicate himself to taking what he deemed to be necessary military action against the government and to formulating and carrying out his plan to bomb the Alfred P. Murrah Federal Building in Oklahoma City.

CHAPTER SIXTY-FIVE

The Plot

HOW MCVEIGH AND NICHOLS went about building and delivering their bomb has been intensely investigated. The FBI logged countless thousands of man-hours gathering evidence against the two suspects. The prosecutors and the defense lawyers in three trials exhaustively reviewed the evidence and pursued alternate theories and leads involving the bombing plot.

Investigative journalists, documentary filmmakers, and conspiracy theorists all took a crack at the case. And a citizens group in Oklahoma investigated and passed a petition forcing a state grand jury to convene and hear witnesses about the crime. As a result, conflicting views emerged as to what parties were involved, what the motives were for the crime, and whether any evidence was "covered up."

Most of these doubts relate to the multiple sightings by seemingly credible witnesses of a third party originally identified by the FBI as John Doe No. 2. This person, who was supposedly with McVeigh in Kansas when he rented the Ryder truck that carried the bomb and accompanied him to Oklahoma City, was never found, and to this day there remains no certainty as to whether he ever existed at all. Regardless of whether anyone else was involved in the bombing, there is no credible evidence to suggest that McVeigh and Nichols were anything except co-conspirators and the perpetrators of the crime and that Michael Fortier was complicit.

For the purposes of this article, the facts relied upon will be those placed in evidence at the McVeigh and Nichols trials, supplemented by findings in the book *American Terrorist: Timothy McVeigh and the Oklahoma City Bombing* by Lou Michael and Dan Herbeck, although multiple other sources were considered. *American Tourist* is based on a series of lengthy personal interviews given by McVeigh to two Buffalo, New York, journalists while he was awaiting execution. Of course, much of what McVeigh said in those interviews was self-serving, but given his mindset, his belief that he had struck a blow for freedom, and his complete admission of having committed the crime this account would seem to have a high level of credibility.

For the most part, the details of this twisted tale of mass murder as told by McVeigh have been documented and verified. There can be an endless argument as to what evidence may have gone undiscovered, but the undisputed facts that remain are more than sufficient to chronicle this infamous case.

Once McVeigh made up his mind to take offensive action against the U.S. government, he had to decide what his target would be and how to attack it. Based in part on the plot of *The Turner Diaries*, he became determined to bomb a federal building. He knew he wanted to do it on April 19—not only because that was the anniversary of the Waco siege, but also because it is the date the first shots were fired in the American Revolution at Lexington and Concord, Massachusetts.

In McVeigh's twisted logic, the government as a whole was not necessarily evil, but the ATF, FBI, and DEA were. He believed these agencies had been corrupted and were independently acting to oppress the American people. Of these agencies, he reserved his strongest hatred for the ATF, which he personally blamed for the unnecessary slaughter of innocent parties at Waco. He also distrusted the U.S. Justice Department, the U.S. Secret Service, and the U.S. Marshals Service. Given this his target should house as many of these federal agencies as possible. With this criteria in mind, he considered a number of government buildings in different cities. He finally selected the Alfred P. Murrah Building in Oklahoma City, which housed the local offices of the ATF, DEA, and Secret Service. Bombing the Murrah building would carry the added shock value of having attacked a seemingly safe location in America's heartland. It would send a message that no one was safe from the coming revolution.

McVeigh calculated that the bombing should occur during business hours to inflict the greatest number of causalities. The fact that innocent people would be killed or injured, he believed, was an unavoidable consequence of war. He considered such loss of life "collateral damage," though McVeigh did later say he had not known a daycare was located in the building. He claimed he would have chosen another target if he had known of the daycare's presence; however, he never showed much remorse over the deaths of the fifteen children.

. . . . .

Once McVeigh had chosen a weapon and a target, he had to acquire the components for a bomb. McVeigh decided to construct the bomb out of ammonium nitrate fertilizer mixed with nitromethane, a racing fuel used by drag racers.

Both of these two ingredients were legal and obtainable. However, in order to detonate the bomb he would need explosives not so easily obtainable. He would also need help in assembling the bomb, and for that he enlisted the aid of Nichols, who was more than willing to join the cause. An attempt to convince Fortier to also take part in the bombing failed. Fortier rebuffed McVeigh, saying, "I would never do anything like that unless there was a U.N. [United Nations] tank in my front yard."

The Oklahoma City Bombing

Nichols and McVeigh began to purchase ammonium nitrate fertilizer. As McVeigh crisscrossed the country to attend gun shows, he picked up a few fifty pound bags of fertilizer at a time. Nichols, on the other hand, made two purchases of two thousand pounds of fertilizer at the Mid Kansas Co-op in McPherson, Kansas. Nichols paid for his purchases in cash under the assumed name of Mike Havens. The fertilizer was loaded into Nichols's pickup and taken to a storage unit in Herrington, Kansas, which McVeigh had rented under the name Shawn Rivers.

The nitromethane necessary to make the bomb was purchased by McVeigh at a racetrack in Ennis, Texas, south of Dallas. Three fifty-five-gallon barrels of fuel were purchased for $2,780 in cash from V.P. Racing Fuels Inc. This was a particularly large order, and Tim Chambers, a V.P. Racing Fuels employee, would remember the transaction.

. . . . .

While the ammonium nitrate and nitromethane had been purchased legally, the explosives to detonate the bomb were not. One night during the first weekend in October, Nichols and McVeigh robbed the Martin Marietta quarry in Marion, Kansas.

Using a self-powered drill owned by Nichols, they drilled out the padlocks on three different storage sheds. The pair stole 299 sticks of the explosive Tovex, 544 blasting caps, and ninety-three lengths of primadet shock tube fitted with non-electric blasting caps. Their take could have been bigger: One of the sheds contained 40,000 pounds of ANFO, an explosive that combines ammonium nitrate and fuel oil.

McVeigh ignored the ANFO because the bomb he intended to make, using nitromethane instead of fuel oil, packed a more powerful punch. McVeigh later also abandoned the idea of using electric blasting caps because he worried that static electricity might prematurely detonate the bomb. In its final form, his bomb utilized the Tovex, the primadet tubes, and hand-lit fuses.

After robbing the quarry, McVeigh and Nichols showed up at Fortier's house in Kingman. McVeigh showed Fortier the boxes of explosives that he planned to store in his storage unit in Kingman. McVeigh also showed Fortier blasting caps and described how they had robbed the quarry.

Now in possession of the components necessary to make the bomb, McVeigh honed his design. At one point while at the Fortier house with Lori present, McVeigh went to the kitchen cabinet, got down a number of soup cans, and began arranging them on the floor like they were fifty-five-gallon drums of explosives. He scribbled out handwritten drawings of how he would construct the bomb. McVeigh continued to try to talk Fortier into helping with the bombing, and while Fortier continued to resist he would later become more involved.

In order to finance their operation McVeigh and Nichols decided to rob their Arkansas buddy Roger Moore. Like many paranoid gun nuts, Moore used an alias, sometimes calling himself Bob Miller. McVeigh and Nichols usually referred to him as "Bob" or "Bob from Arkansas."

Although McVeigh and Moore had once been friends, they had last parted on bad terms when Moore angrily accused McVeigh of stealing and selling Moore's design for a homemade flare launcher. McVeigh still held a grudge over the accusation, and didn't trust Moore to stand up against the federal government in a real crisis.

McVeigh, however, was also concerned that if he took part in the Moore robbery he might be recognized, so it was decided that Nichols had to handle it on his own.

On November 5 at about nine in the morning, with Moore home alone and Anderson away at a gun show, Moore stepped outside to feed his animals. As he walked from his house to the barn a man approached him from behind and ordered him to lie on the ground. The assailant wore a black ski mask and was dressed in camo and combat boots. He was also armed with a pistol-grip shotgun that he kept leveled at Moore's head. The shotgun was equipped with a steel wire for use as a garrote.

Moore did not recognize his assailant, but later would say he was sure it was not McVeigh. At gunpoint, Moore was ordered to crawl back into his house where he was secured with plastic handcuffs, police ties, and a strip of duct tape slapped over his eyes. The gunman then began cleaning out the cash, guns, gold, silver, and jade that Moore kept in his home. In all, he took more than eighty pistols, shotguns, and rifles. Moore later reported a loss of more than $60,000.

At one point during the robbery, Moore complained that his circulation was being cutoff by the handcuffs, and the gunman considerately removed them and secured Moore with duct tape instead. He then loaded the loot into Moore's customized van and left, but not before warning Moore that there was another man outside with a shotgun and that they were coming back soon "for the rest of it."

After the van left, Moore managed to free himself from the duct tape. The telephone line was dead, so he found the only weapon the gunman had not taken, a hidden stainless steel .45 pistol. He walked to a neighbor's house and from there he called the sheriff. Moore's van was later found abandoned about six miles away from his house. Although Moore suspected McVeigh might have been involved in the robbery he knew he was not the actual robber, and Moore had plenty of other associates whom he also mistrusted.

Years after the crime and his convictions in connection with the bombing, Nichols would claim that Moore had willingly financed the bombing. He accused Moore of contriving the robbery story to hide Moore's involvement in the crime. Nichols also said that the FBI never investigated Moore because of his undercover connections with the Bureau. Given Nichols's level of credibility, bitterness, and the fact that Moore had testified against Nichols, his accusation is suspect, although Moore's story and the extent of his loss may well have been exaggerated.

CHAPTER SIXTY-SIX

Leaving a Trail

IN NOVEMBER, McVeigh's grandfather, Ed McVeigh, died. In order to help his father take care of his grandfather's possessions, McVeigh returned to Pendleton. While there he hung out with his younger sister, Jennifer. The two had always been close, and McVeigh confided to her that he had plans to take action against the government soon. McVeigh would not reveal any details about his plan to Jennifer, but he did show her a video about Waco and then proceeded to rail against the overreach of the ATF.

He also wrote a letter addressed to the ATF that he intended to be found after his death. In part, the letter stated:

> ATF all you tyrannical mother-fuckers will swing in the wind one day for your treason actions against the Constitution of the United States. . . .

From then until the bombing, McVeigh would stay in touch with Jennifer by telephone and letters. His theme and tone were always the same, castigating the government for Waco and threatening action to avenge the government's wrongs against the people.

McVeigh also paid a visit to Carl E. Lebron Jr., the security guard with whom he had worked in Buffalo. To Lebron, McVeigh seemed more agitated and hostile to the government than before, and while they parted on good terms, the visit upset Lebron.

More than these contacts, McVeigh and Nichols were leaving a paper trail of their activities leading up to the bombing. In November 1993, Nichols obtained a debit card through the now defunct conservative weekly newspaper *The Spotlight* in Washington, D.C. Nichols used the name Daryl Bridges on the card, but gave the address of James Nichols's farm in Decker, Michigan. Periodically, both McVeigh and Nichols made payments on the card by money order, and the two men routinely used the card for telephone charges, thus establishing a record of their whereabouts and the recipients of their calls.

McVeigh also discussed his intentions with both Michael and Lori Fortier. In December, McVeigh returned to Kingman. He told Fortier about the robbery of "Bob from Arkansas," and asked Fortier to accompany him to retrieve some of the stolen guns in Kansas, so they could bring them to Arizona for storage, and then sell them at gun shows. He told Fortier the gun transactions could net Fortier ten thousand dollars, and coached him on changing the appearance of the guns before they were offered for sale.

Fortier agreed to accompany McVeigh to pick up the stolen guns. On this cross-country drive, McVeigh told Fortier how he planned to build the bomb and deliver it to the target by means of a rental truck. The pair stopped in Oklahoma City where McVeigh showed Fortier the Murrah building. He told Fortier he had previously looked at the building and because of its construction, which included a glass front, he thought he could do maximum damage to the building and the government workers inside.

McVeigh also showed Fortier where he would leave a getaway car, north of the Murrah building, behind the YMCA. Either McVeigh would stash a car there, or Nichols would be waiting to drive him away after he detonated the bomb. Fortier and McVeigh continued on to Kansas where Fortier rented a car, loaded up the stolen guns at a storage facility in Council Grove, and then returned to Arizona. Many of the guns were later sold at gun shows or swapped by Fortier for marijuana and meth.

During this time, Nichols had gone to the Philippines to visit Marife and her family. Before leaving the country, he stopped in Las Vegas at Padilla's house to visit his son, Josh. When he left Las Vegas, Nichols gave Padilla a plastic bag and his truck keys. He told her to only open the bag in the event that he didn't return. Instead, Padilla opened the bag immediately after he left. Inside she found a life insurance policy on Nichols and the combination for the lock on Nichols's Las Vegas storage unit. There were also instructions on how to find another plastic bag Nichols had hidden at Padilla's house behind a drawer.

The second plastic bag contained twenty thousand dollars in cash and a letter to Tim McVeigh. In part, the letter read:

> . . . on your own now; Go for it!! . . . As far as heat—
> none that I know, This letter would be for the purpose
> of my death.

Padilla and her son from a previous marriage, Barry Osentoski, also went and opened Nichols's storage unit. Inside they found gold, silver, jade stones, a black wig, and a ski mask. At the time, Padilla didn't know what to make of her find, but her suspicion that Nichols had been involved in some kind of robbery wasn't far off the mark.

When Nichols returned to Las Vegas from the Philippines in January 1995 and found his cash missing, he was furious. He confronted Padilla, and after a series of heated arguments she returned all but three thousand dollars, which she said she was keeping for Josh. Nichols then left Las Vegas and ended up back in Herrington, Kansas, where he purchased a modest house.

The Oklahoma City Bombing

Throughout the early months of 1995, McVeigh was living in a motel in Kingman. He and Fortier were traveling to gun shows selling Moore's stolen guns. As the date for his attack on the government grew closer, McVeigh fortified his resolve by writing more inflammatory letters to Jennifer and other friends. His letters to his sister referred to a big event that would happen soon but gave no specifics. With the help of the Fortiers, McVeigh also created false identification for himself in the name of Robert Kling. He used a false address and gave himself a birth date of April 19, 1972, the day and month of the Waco attack.

CHAPTER SIXTY-SEVEN

Building the Bomb

O N APRIL 12, TIMOTHY McVeigh left Kingman and headed to Kansas, stopping in Oklahoma City to once again view the Murrah building and finalize his plan. On the way to Kansas, the junker car he was driving began to have serious problems. McVeigh managed to nurse the car to Junction City, Kansas, where he learned the car had a broken crankcase.

In need of a getaway car, McVeigh purchased a yellow 1977 Mercury Grand Marquis for two hundred and fifty dollars. McVeigh got what he paid for as the old beater had its own mechanical problems, but at least it ran, if only barely. McVeigh told the seller of the Marquis to send the paperwork to the address of the Nichols farm in Decker, Michigan.

Friday, April 14, McVeigh checked into the Dreamland Motel in Junction City under his own name.

Using the Bridges debit card he called the local Ryder truck rental agency located in Elliott's Body Shop. He inquired about renting a truck to drive to Omaha, Nebraska, identifying himself as Robert

Kling. On Saturday, he went to Elliott's where he dealt with the owner, Eldon Elliott, and reserved a twenty-foot truck for a trip to Omaha from April 17 through April 21. That evening, McVeigh ordered take-out Chinese food from a local restaurant. Jeff David, the deliveryman who brought McVeigh's order to the Dreamland Motel, would later describe the man who accepted the food as being someone other than McVeigh.

Looking back on McVeigh's stay at the Dreamland, the motel manager and owner, Lea McGown, also recalls hearing the voice of someone besides McVeigh talking in McVeigh's room. Both of these accounts would lead to the theory that at least one other person besides Nichols and McVeigh was involved in the plot.

April 16 was Easter Sunday, but not a day of rest for McVeigh and Nichols. McVeigh drove the Mercury to Oklahoma City, followed by Nichols in his pickup. Nichols's explanation for the trip to Marife was that McVeigh was going to help him retrieve a television set that belonged to him.

The two men left Kansas in the afternoon and arrived in Oklahoma City that evening. When McVeigh reached Oklahoma City he parked the Mercury in a vacant parking lot three blocks north and east of the Murrah building. The location would be blocked from the force of the bomb blast by several intervening buildings. McVeigh removed the Arizona license plate he had previously transferred to the Mercury from his disabled vehicle and placed a note on the windshield that read:

Not abandoned. Please do not tow. Will move by April 23. (Needs battery cable.)

What his plan was if the car was towed away is unknown. And why he removed the license plate is also unexplainable, but he had previously told Fortier that he didn't expect to survive the bombing, figuring he would either die in the explosion or a shootout with the Feds.

After leaving the getaway car in Oklahoma City, Nichols and

McVeigh returned to Kansas in Nichols's pickup. They arrived back in Junction City early the morning of April 17. That afternoon around four o'clock, McVeigh returned to Elliott's and picked up the Ryder truck, still using the name Robert Kling. Eldon Elliott and two of his employees, Vickie Beemer and Tom Kessinger, were present. Each of these three individuals later gave different descriptions of the person who rented the truck. Each of them would also describe a second individual who they said accompanied the renter. The FBI later contended that they were simply confused, and the second person they described was actually Army Private Todd Bunting who was with another soldier who rented a Ryder truck from Elliott's the day after McVeigh did.

After parking the truck at the motel on Monday night, McVeigh rose early Tuesday morning and drove to the storage unit in Herrington, where the components of the bomb were stored. Nichols was to meet McVeigh to help load the bomb materials and make the bomb. Nichols was late and McVeigh was angry. Nichols had already made several halfhearted attempts to back out of the scheme and convince McVeigh to change his mind. This infuriated McVeigh. His wholehearted dedication to his cause increasingly made him view Nichols as weak and cowardly.

Loading the Ryder truck was hard work. It took several hours to haul 108 fifty-pound bags of fertilizer from the storage unit and load them onto the truck. Using a hand truck, the men loaded three fifty-five gallon drums of nitromethane weighing more than four hundred pounds each. They also loaded the Tovex blasting caps, shock tubes, hand-lit fuses, and thirteen empty fifty-five gallon plastic barrels.

After the rental truck was loaded, McVeigh drove it to a paved parking area by Geary Lake, a few miles away from Herrington. Nichols followed in his pickup, and they arrived at the lake about seven-thirty that morning. There they started mixing the bomb, using five-gallon buckets and a scale to measure the components.

This again was a laborious process. Each of the plastic barrels had to be filled with a mixture of ammonium nitrate fertilizer and nitromethane. The barrels were then arranged in the truck, in roughly a T-shape with the top of the T against the forward cargo wall behind the cab, a design created by McVeigh so that the truck would not be overbalanced on either side. Seventeen bags of ANFO, a less powerful, but still lethal explosive were added to the mix.

To finish the bomb McVeigh packed a five-gallon bucket with the sausage-like Tovex. He then ran shock tubes to blasting caps connected to hand-lit igniting fuses. He drilled holes in the back wall of the truck's cab and ran the fuses through the holes so that they could be lit by someone inside the cab of the truck. His design included two fuses: one timed for five minutes, the other for two minutes.

Questions have been raised as to whether two amateurs the likes of McVeigh and Nichols could have on their own designed and constructed a bomb like the one used on the Murrah building. It has also been suggested that the bomb as described would not have been powerful enough to cause the devastation witnessed at the Murrah building. Speculation aside, the type of bomb McVeigh described—weighing more than seven thousand pounds, augmented by the Tovex and ANFO—was a powerful instrument of destruction.

At least two people observed the Ryder truck at Geary Lake on the morning of April 18. A retired military man, Richard Wahl, and his son were fishing at the lake. After launching their fishing boat they floated within twenty-five yards of the shore near the truck. They saw no one about, but its presence seemed odd to them at that time of day, though there was nothing to suggest any kind of criminal activity.

After McVeigh and Nichols finished building the bomb, McVeigh washed off in the lake and changed clothes. Later at his trial, the government offered evidence that traces of the explosives were found on the clothes McVeigh was wearing at the time of his arrest. McVeigh believed this evidence was fabricated.

CHAPTER SIXTY-EIGHT

The Crime

WHAT TIMOTHY McVeigh did between the morning of April 18 and the time he ignited the bomb at 9:02 a.m. on April 19 remains a mystery. According to him, he drove south taking care to follow back roads and keep off interstates. At some point he parked the truck in a gravel lot behind a motel and slept in the cab.

There were numerous McVeigh sightings on the morning of the nineteenth, both on the way to Oklahoma City and in the city before the bombing. Some of these witnesses described a companion with McVeigh; others claimed the Ryder truck was accompanied by a brown pickup. In prosecuting McVeigh, the government either decided the accounts were not credible, or simply elected not to pursue them since McVeigh's supposed companion could not be identified.

A citizens' committee calling itself the Oklahoma Bombing Investigation Committee investigated the bombing but could not confirm or identify a specific person who had accompanied McVeigh, but its members were convinced other unknown persons were involved.

The Oklahoma City Bombing

Whatever route McVeigh took to Oklahoma City that fateful day, he arrived a few minutes before 9:00 a.m. Armed with a 9mm Glock carried in a shoulder holster, he drove the Ryder truck east down Fifth Street into the heart of downtown Oklahoma City.

In front of the Regency Tower apartments, a block west of the Murrah building, the truck was captured on a security camera: As McVeigh drives toward the Murrah building, he lights the five-minute fuse with a cigarette lighter and as he grows closer, the two-minute fuse, proving his willingness to risk his own death to carry out the attack.

Arriving at the Murrah building, McVeigh pulled the truck into a small turnout parking area directly in front of the building on the north side. Assured that the fuses were burning, he left the truck and walked across Fifth Street, heading northeast at a normal pace. He also placed earplugs in his ears. After crossing the street, he turned into an alley, putting the YMCA and other buildings between him and the target, before beginning to run toward his car. When the explosion occurred he was already close to the getaway car several blocks north of the Murrah building.

Behind McVeigh, the bomb exploded with tremendous force, leveling death and destruction on the occupants of the Murrah building and the surrounding community. The force of the bomb reduced approximately one-third of the twenty-year-old building's north face to rubble. The third through ninth floors pancaked and collapsed one atop of the other to street-level, leaving a pile of debris as high as thirty-five feet in some places.

A total of 851 people were injured or killed as a direct result of the bombing. One hundred and sixty-seven people including nineteen children died. Another person, a volunteer nurse, was killed by falling debris attempting to help the victims.

Of the 168 who died, 163 were occupants of the Murrah building, and of these, 118 worked there; fifteen were small children attending daycare; and thirty were visitors in the building, including four more children.

Two deaths also occurred in the Oklahoma Water Resources building and one in the Athenian building, both of which were located across Fifth Street to the north, and another death occurred outdoors near the building.

The blast destroyed automobiles for blocks around ground zero, many others were left smoking and burning after the explosion. More than three hundred buildings located within forty-eight square blocks were damaged, many so seriously that they had to be demolished. About a mile north of the Murrah building on Northwest Twenty-Third Street, store windows were blown out for blocks and people felt the blast at the state capitol complex miles away.

Massive rescue efforts began immediately as firefighters and police rushed to the Murrah building. Oklahoma City firefighters entered the building unsure of whether the building would continue to support its own weight, as most of its steel supports had been destroyed.

Many stories of heroism came to be told of the extraordinary efforts first responders made to extract and save victims from the site that morning. One police officer rushed into the crumbling building to pull children from the rubble that had only minutes before been a daycare, while Daina Bradley endured the amputation of her leg before rescue workers could free her from beneath a massive chunk of concrete. Andy Sullivan, the doctor who crawled through the rubble to perform the amputation, did the surgery lying on the ground using only scalpels and a pocket knife.

The entire Oklahoma City community, under the leadership of Mayor Ron Norick and Governor Frank Keating, mobilized to help the victims and their families.

Nationally, President Clinton oversaw the federal response, including the deployment of a FEMA urban search-and-rescue force and search-and-rescue dogs, while firefighters and others from across the nation poured into Oklahoma City to render help. Across the country in New York City's Times Square, a billboard went up atop a skyscraper in one of the world's most cynical cities, declaring: "NYC [hearts]

OKC." Internationally, people from around the world watched the rescue efforts and prayed for Oklahoma and her people.

The onsite search and rescue continued for days until all hope of finding any further survivors was finally abandoned.

The emotional recovery would take far longer.

CHAPTER SIXTY-NINE

The Arrest

THE MAN WHO HAD caused the mass devastation simply jogged away. McVeigh retrieved the Mercury and drove out of the city headed north on Interstate 35. About sixty miles north of Oklahoma City, McVeigh passed an Oklahoma Highway Patrol car stopped behind a van on the shoulder of the highway. A few minutes later the same patrol car approached McVeigh's vehicle and turned on its flashing lights. McVeigh pulled over and exited his car.

The trooper, Charles Hanger, was a nineteen-year OHP veteran, and when he saw McVeigh exit his car he instinctively proceeded with caution. Hanger advised McVeigh he had stopped him because there was no license plate on the Mercury. As McVeigh pulled his wallet from his pants pocket at Hanger's request, Hanger noticed a bulge under McVeigh's jacket and asked what it was. A gun, McVeigh said.

Hanger then drew his own gun.

"My gun is loaded," said McVeigh.

"So is mine," Hanger replied. Hanger took McVeigh's gun and then searched McVeigh. He found an ammunition clip as well as a knife attached to McVeigh's belt. After disarming McVeigh, Hanger handcuffed him and placed him in the patrol car. McVeigh was carrying his real Michigan driver's license, and Hanger called in McVeigh's information to the Oklahoma Highway Patrol dispatcher for a computer check. The check revealed no arrests or warrants. Hanger also checked to see if the Glock was stolen and found that it was not.

Hanger transported McVeigh to the Noble County Jail in Perry, Oklahoma, only a few miles east off the interstate. The Mercury was left locked by the side of the highway. At the jail, McVeigh was booked on four misdemeanor charges, including transporting a loaded firearm in a vehicle, unlawfully carrying a weapon, failing to display a current license plate, and failing to maintain proof of insurance.

Among McVeigh's possessions inventoried at the jail was a set of earplugs. The jailer, Marsha Mority, also noted McVeigh's T-shirt, which she found unusual. On the front was a drawing of Abraham Lincoln and the words *sic semper tyrranis*, the phrase shouted by John Wilkes Booth when he assassinated Lincoln. It translates, "Thus ever to tyrants." On the back of the shirt was a tree with drops of blood dripping from its branches and a quote attributed to Thomas Jefferson: "The Tree of Liberty must be refreshed from time to time with the blood of patriots and tyrants."

In spite of the proximity to the bombing in Oklahoma City, McVeigh was initially treated as an anyone arrested for minor violations of the law might be. He was kept in the Noble County Jail pending an appearance before a judge, which would normally have taken place within a few days and routinely led to his release on the posting of a nominal bond, perhaps even on his personal agreement to appear for a future hearing.

While McVeigh sat in the Noble County Jail, rescue efforts continued at the bombing site in downtown Oklahoma City. The last survivor was pulled out of the collapsed building at 10:05 p.m. that same day, but the search for bodies continued for sixteen more days.

CHAPTER SEVENTY

The Investigation

AN INVESTIGATION OF THE CRIME was launched immediately by the FBI and local law enforcement agencies. At first, the perpetrators were suspected to be Middle Eastern terrorists linked to the 1993 bombing of the World Trade Center in New York City. This theory led to the detention of a totally innocent American citizen of Jordanian descent. After questioning, however, the suspect was cleared, and the investigation proceeded in other directions.

The FBI agent in charge of the Oklahoma City office, Bob Ricks, had been at Waco as the FBI's public information representative. Ricks immediately noted that the date of the bombing was the anniversary of the Waco siege and focused on a possible connection. Ricks was right about the connection, but his assumption was of no initial value in solving the crime.

The first big break in the case came the day of the bombing with the recovery of an axle from the Ryder truck. The axle had flown a block in the air, smashing into a car parked in front of the Regency Tower.

Within a few hours of the crime, the confidential vehicle identification number on the axle had been traced to a truck registered to Ryder in Miami, Florida. Ryder then traced the truck to Elliott's Body Shop in Junction City, Kansas.

Later that day, part of the truck's bumper and a Florida license plate were found near the Murrah building, confirming the identity of the truck. Witnesses had also reported seeing the truck in front of the building prior to the explosion. A key to the truck was later found in the alley near the YMCA.

The FBI sent agents to Junction City, where they interviewed Eldon Elliott and his employees, Beemer and Kessinger. Elliott and Kessinger described the renter of the truck, "Robert Kling," as a white male, twenty-seven to thirty years old, five-foot-eleven to six feet, weighing about a hundred and seventy-five pounds. With the aid of these witnesses, an FBI forensic artist prepared a drawing of what became known as John Doe No. 1.

Both Beemer and Kessinger also described another man with Kling. The second man, who became known as John Doe No. 2, was also young, twenty-six to twenty-seven years old, and stocky; said to have worn a baseball cap with what looked like lightning bolts on it.

Using the composite drawings, agents then began to canvas the area of Junction City near Elliott's. They hit pay dirt at the Dreamland Motel. Lea McGown, the motel's owner, remembered a man, fitting the description of John Doe No. 1, parking a Ryder truck at the motel. She did not recognize John Doe No. 2.

The motel records identified McVeigh and the address he had given in Decker, Michigan.

. . . . .

By using a computer search, the FBI discovered McVeigh had been arrested and was being held in the Noble County Jail in Perry, Oklahoma, on misdemeanor charges. A call to Noble County Sheriff Jerry

Cook on the morning of April 21 revealed that McVeigh was scheduled for a hearing that day and could have already been released on bond. In fact, when the call came, McVeigh had been taken from his cell and was already in the courtroom. Fortunately, the judge was delayed, the hearing had not started, and McVeigh was returned to jail.

The FBI rushed agents to Perry from Oklahoma City via helicopter while obtaining a warrant for McVeigh's arrest from U.S. Magistrate Judge Ronald Howland.

When the agents confronted McVeigh in Perry and asked if he knew why they were there he responded, "It's probably about that Oklahoma City thing." Like the soldier that he had been not that long ago and envisioned that he still was, McVeigh refused to talk to the agents further and demanded a lawyer.

Perry is a small town and word of McVeigh's arrest traveled fast. By 6:00 p.m. when McVeigh was to leave for Oklahoma City, a hostile crowd had gathered at the courthouse. The media had also been tipped off, and television cameramen and news photographers and reporters were present in force. McVeigh feared for his life, and the FBI was also worried about his safety.

For McVeigh's protection, the FBI placed agents on the roof of the courthouse and also surrounded McVeigh with law enforcement officers as he was hustled into a van backed up as close to the entrance as possible. He was then taken to a helicopter and flown to Tinker Air Force Base in Midwest City where his first court appearance took place before Magistrate Howland. After a brief court appearance in which attorneys were appointed to represent him, McVeigh was taken by a SWAT team to the federal prison in El Reno.

The evidence against McVeigh was already starting to pile up. A search of the Mercury had produced a packet of antigovernment propaganda that McVeigh had intentionally left on the front seat, as well as the handwritten sign McVeigh had left on the car in Oklahoma City asking that it not be towed. Hanger also found a business card for Paulsen's Military Supply, Antigo, Wisconsin, that McVeigh had left in his patrol car. On the back of the card was the notation:

> TNT @ $5/stick. Need More . . . Call after 01 May, see
> if I can get some more.

To add to the growing evidence against McVeigh, Carl E. Lebron Jr., who had worked with McVeigh as a security guard, showed up at the FBI's office in Buffalo, New York, on April 21, offering information. Lebron said he had seen the drawing of John Doe No. 1 on television, and he knew who had blown up the Murrah building. He identified McVeigh as the perpetrator. At first skeptical, the FBI nonetheless followed up the lead when McVeigh was identified in Oklahoma. Lebron furnished the FBI with taped conversations of McVeigh's rants against the federal government, providing a possible motive for the crime.

CHAPTER SEVENTY-ONE

The Arrest of Nichols

WHILE MCVEIGH WAS BEING apprehended and moved to El Reno, the FBI was following leads to determine if anyone else was involved in the crime. The address in Decker, Michigan, on McVeigh's driver's license matched the one he had used at the Dreamland Motel. The FBI quickly identified the Decker address as the Nichols family farm.

Local law enforcement personnel advised the FBI of James and Terry Nichols's antigovernment attitudes, and talks with the Nichols brothers' ex-wives disclosed that McVeigh was an old Army buddy of Terry Nichols and had visited the Michigan farm. The FBI sent surveillance teams to watch both James in Michigan and Terry in Kansas.

After the bombing when McVeigh did not contact Nichols in Herrington, Nichols had feared the worst. He panicked and tried to dispose of the ammonium nitrate in his possession by spreading it on his lawn. A neighbor observed that Nichols had covered the lawn with so much nitrate it looked like snow. He emptied the Herrington storage locker of its remaining bomb materials and hid them under his house.

The Oklahoma City Bombing

By the afternoon of April 21, Nichols realized he was under surveillance. Radio and television reports had also begun to identify both Nichols and his brother as suspects. This was more than Nichols could take, and so, along with Marife and their baby daughter, Nicole, he drove to the Herrington Police Station. There he told the local police chief that he was alarmed that he was a suspect in the Oklahoma City bombing, and he wanted "to talk to someone."

That "someone" turned out to be the FBI agents who had followed the Nicholses to the station. Other agents joined them shortly.

Nichols waived his right to remain silent and the right to an attorney, and then proceeded to give the agents a rambling interview that lasted some nine hours, not concluding until well after midnight. The story was filled with half-truths, lies, fabrications, and some truth.

He denied any part in the bombing, but admitted knowing McVeigh. In Nichols's version of the story, he went to Oklahoma City on Easter Sunday to retrieve a television set McVeigh had picked up for him in Las Vegas. McVeigh's car had broken down, and so he gave McVeigh a ride to Junction City where he dropped him off at a McDonald's. Nichols claimed not to have seen McVeigh since.

Nichols also gave the FBI permission to search his house, and the search began immediately. Nichols's cooperation with the government was uncharacteristic. He must have convinced himself that he could talk his way out of trouble since he had an alibi and could prove he was in Kansas at the time of the explosion. Whether motivated by fear, over confidence, or contempt for law enforcement personnel, his decision to talk was a miserable failure. His story was shot through with obvious lies, and the search of his house only helped to further confirm his involvement in the crime.

In the Nichols home, the FBI discovered all sorts of incriminating evidence, including a receipt for two thousand pounds of ammonium nitrate fertilizer issued to a "Mike Havens," five roles of Primadet blasting caps, the bomb-making instructional book, McVeigh's military issue rucksack and rifle, and a debit calling card and coupon book for the

295

Daryl Bridges debit card. McVeigh's fingerprint was later discovered on the fertilizer receipt. Based on the search of the house and Nichols's own statement, the FBI detained him as a material witness and placed him in the Dickson County Jail in Abilene, Kansas. The next day Nichols was taken to the federal courthouse in Wichita, Kansas, where he was placed in federal custody.

The FBI also suspected James Nichols of being involved in the bombing. They arrested him and kept him in custody for thirty-two days. They also exhaustively searched the Nichols farm. James was an obvious target for the investigation as his antigovernment leanings were well known. His brother and their mutual friend, McVeigh, had been firmly linked to the crime, and ammonium nitrate, fuel oil, and blasting caps were found on his farm. Some of the FBI agents wanted badly to charge and convict him, but the FBI could not find evidence that tied James directly to the crime and finally had to cut him loose. He was never prosecuted, and all his arrest did was intensify his hatred of the federal government.

CHAPTER SEVENTY-TWO

McVeigh's Lawyer

THE FBI CONTINUED its investigation, and a federal grand jury was convened in Oklahoma City to consider the case. The government's key witnesses turned out to be Michael and Lori Fortier. Originally uncooperative, they had experienced a sudden change of heart upon being subpoenaed to appear before the grand jury.

Their testimony implicated them in the crime, but proved so important they were able to work a deal with the prosecutors. Lori Fortier was granted immunity in exchange for her cooperation. After the conclusion of the McVeigh and Nichols trials, Michael Fortier was sentenced to twelve years in prison and fined $200,000. The fine was later reduced to $75,000. The amount of the fine was irrelevant, as Fortier didn't have the means to pay even the reduced amount. He served ten of his twelve-year sentence.

The Bridges debit card was also important to the investigation. It gave the FBI a road map of the activities of McVeigh and Nichols based on the phone calls charged to the card. Their movements and the subject of their calls confirmed the other evidence being gathered against them. The testimony of the Fortiers also tied Nichols and McVeigh to the theft of the explosives from the Martin Marietta quarry as well as the Roger Moore robbery.

Early on, Lana Padilla, Nichols's ex-wife, also cooperated with the FBI. She gave the FBI the letters he had left for her to send upon his death or disappearance and showed them his storage unit and its contents. The letters tended to incriminate both Nichols and McVeigh.

McVeigh was not formally indicted by the federal grand jury until August 10, 1995.

His trial did not take place until March 19, 1997.

In the meantime, however, he needed a lawyer.

Initially, McVeigh was represented by J.W. Coyle, an experienced Oklahoma City criminal attorney, and Susan Otto, the U.S. public defender. The two lawyers met with McVeigh, and appeared on his behalf at the first court hearing in a military courtroom at Tinker Field on April 21. They again represented McVeigh at a bail hearing eight days later. The second hearing was held under tight security in a visitors' room at the El Reno prison. At this hearing, based on the testimony of Patrolman Hanger and FBI Agent Jon Hersley, Magistrate Howland ordered that McVeigh be held pending formal charges and denied bail.

Coyle and Otto had taken the case at the request of Chief U.S. District Judge David Russell. They vigorously represented McVeigh and preserved his legal rights. However, both of these lawyers had personal friends who were victims of the bombing. After careful consideration, they did not feel that they could properly defend McVeigh under these circumstances and requested to withdraw from the case. Judge Russell granted their request. Now a new lawyer for McVeigh had to be found.

On May 8, 1995, Judge Russell appointed Stephen Jones of Enid, Oklahoma. A self-described "small town county seat lawyer," Jones was, in fact, anything but the stereotype this description suggests. Far from being a good ol' country boy, Jones was urbane and somewhat pedantic. In dress and speech he more resembled a college professor or an Ivy league grad than a small town lawyer.

The Oklahoma City Bombing

Politically active in the Republican Party, Jones had been an unsuccessful candidate for the U.S. Senate, U.S. House of Representatives, and Oklahoma Attorney General. He had represented defendants in more than fifteen death penalty cases and was well qualified to represent McVeigh. There was just one big problem: McVeigh disliked Jones almost on sight, and throughout the case their relationship grew increasingly strained. Several times, McVeigh considered firing Jones, but eventually decided to see the case through with Jones as his lawyer. In Jones's defense, a criminal defendant is frequently his own worst enemy, and the relationship between the accused and his attorney is often rocky. In criminal cases, the truth is hard, some defendants don't want to accept it, and it is always easier to blame the lawyer.

In McVeigh's case, his personal theory of his defense posed the first problem. McVeigh was the first to admit that he had done the crime, but he wanted to defend his acts as justifiable resistance to a tyrannical government. It fell to Jones to explain to McVeigh that there was no such defense in U.S. law and that such a stance was tantamount to a guilty plea to a crime punishable by death.

McVeigh finally relented. He had considered pleading guilty, but after learning he would be quizzed about the case and any others that might be involved in it with him, he elected to plead not guilty. He then proceeded to try and make it as hard as possible for the government to prove his guilt. Rather than remorse, his attitude remained one of continued defiance.

Bottom line: McVeigh was guilty. There was no alibi, no persuasive exculpatory evidence to be presented, and McVeigh could not take the stand. Between the evidence in hand and McVeigh's posture, Jones had an insurmountable task.

Jones and McVeigh's conflicting views of the case are well documented in two books: *American Terrorist*, in which McVeigh's position is set out, and *Others Unknown, The Oklahoma City Bombing Case and Conspiracy*, in which Jones gives his version of the case in his own words as the book's author.

After the publication of *American Terrorist*, Jones felt compelled to publish a revised version of his book directly responding to McVeigh's later assertions and criticisms of his work as McVeigh's lawyer. In the second edition of his book, Jones took the position that McVeigh had waived any attorney-client privilege by publicly revealing confidential facts and filing a motion accusing Jones of incompetence. Those actions by McVeigh, Jones contended, meant he was released to talk freely about the case.

Interestingly, it is Jones who somehow concluded that a defense existed for McVeigh. He had begun to question whether the U.S. government could prove its case, and he convinced himself that McVeigh was actually part of a conspiracy including "others unknown." His strategy was to blame the crime on someone else, regardless of the fact that the involvement of others, whether it existed or not, did not exonerate his own client.

As for McVeigh, he viewed himself as a soldier in a war or revolution. He had carried out a mission. He had been captured by the enemy, and there were consequences for that. He fully expected to be convicted and executed. This was part of the commitment he had made to himself from the start. He also continued to deny that others were involved. Whether they were or not, his denial was consistent with the duty he felt to refuse to give any information to the enemy.

The friction between Jones and McVeigh was exacerbated by Jones's refusal to believe McVeigh about the involvement of others in the bombing plot, to the point that Jones convinced McVeigh to take a lie detector test on the issue. The polygraph operator reported McVeigh's answers about his own participation in the bombing were truthful, but that his answers regarding the involvement of others showed signs of evasion. To this day, Jones maintains more participants than just McVeigh and Nichols were involved in the Oklahoma City bombing.

Jones suspected Nichols of making contact with terrorists while in the Philippines, and he also focused on a group of white supremacists located in the tiny northeastern Oklahoma community of Elohim

City. In particular, Jones believed that Dennis Mahon, a former Klu Klux Klan leader, and Andreas Strassmeir, a German citizen, were connected to the crime. McVeigh had made at least one telephone call to the Elohim community on the Bridges debit card. McVeigh also knew Strassmeir from the gun show circuit, but he consistently denied that these two men had anything to do with the bombing.

No hard evidence of involvement by Mahon or Strassmeir could be found, but there was evidence that John Doe No. 2 had taken part in the bombing. Besides the sightings by eyewitnesses, the coroner had found an extra leg after the explosion that did not belong to any of the identified victims. Jones was convinced the leg belonged to the real bomber, whom he believed had been killed by the explosion. No matter how the evidence of John Doe No. 2 developed, however, it would not have been enough to clear McVeigh of his own part in carrying out the bombing; at best, it was a red herring, something perhaps to confuse a jury. But, lacking any other defense for McVeigh, Jones determinedly pursued this theory.

The charges that McVeigh and Nichols had to answer were defined when the grand jury indicted them on eleven counts, including conspiracy to use a weapon of mass destruction, use of a weapon of mass destruction, destruction by use of explosives, and eight counts of first-degree murder. Murder is generally a state crime. However, the murder of certain government officials, including law enforcement officers and military personnel, is a federal crime. Eight of the victims qualified under the federal murder statute. Along with the indictment, the government filed a Notice of Intent to Seek the Death Penalty.

CHAPTER SEVENTY-THREE

The Legal Battle Begins

INITIALLY, THE CASE WAS assigned to U.S. District Judge Wayne Alley, who served in the Western District of Oklahoma. Judge Alley's office was one block from the Murrah building, and was damaged by the bombing. He had friends and acquaintances that were victims of the bombing. As a result, the defendants requested he be removed from the case.

The Tenth Circuit Court of Appeals granted this request and appointed U.S. District Judge Richard P. Matsch of Denver to preside over the trial. Judge Matsch was sixty-seven years old at the time and an experienced and well-respected trial judge. By all accounts, Judge Matsch was known to be even-handed and forceful, without enjoying the reputation as a petty tyrant, shared by a number of federal judges.

Almost immediately the judge was presented with a number of defense motions crucial to how the case would be conducted. For one, the defendants claimed they could not receive a fair trial anywhere in Oklahoma and asked for a change of venue. Judge Matsch granted this motion and moved the trial to Denver.

The defendants also wanted to be tried separately. This issue was particularly crucial to Nichols, who was not in Oklahoma City at the time of the bombing and who wanted to distance himself as far as possible from McVeigh. Once again Matsch ruled in favor of the defendants, severing the trials and ordering that McVeigh be tried first.

A case of this magnitude was too big for one lawyer to handle, and the defense team eventually grew to include thirty-five lawyers, in addition to investigators and support staff. Prominent in the defense, along with Jones, was Rob Nigh of Tulsa, who had experience as a public defender. Nigh developed a much better relationship with McVeigh than Jones, and along with attorney Richard Burr of Houston, later participated in the appeal of the case. Burr handled the defense of the death penalty phase of the trial. Christopher Tritico of Houston also participated in McVeigh's defense as did Jerri Merritt, Cheryl Ramsey, Mandy Welch, Randy Coyne, and Mike Roberts. Bob Wyatt, Jones's Enid law partner, also took part in the defense.

The defense team had a formidable job when it came to preparing for the trial. For one, it had to extract the evidence compiled by the FBI from the U.S. government. As anyone who has ever dealt with the U.S. Justice Department and the FBI knows, these agencies make the discovery of evidence as painful and time consuming as possible; both often refuse to turn over materials and information until forced to do so by a judge, even though furnishing such information is legally appropriate. The McVeigh case was no exception.

Eventually the defense accumulated mountains of documents that had to be examined and analyzed. Jones's theory of the case created even more work for his team. In the name of defending McVeigh, Jones traveled to the Philippines, Israel, England, and Ireland, and his investigators roamed the U.S. searching for a link to any terrorist group no matter how tenuous. Jones has said he went to the Philippines trying to determine why Nichols had traveled there six times; he also wanted to know what evidence the FBI might have found there. Jones went to Israel, England, and Ireland to contact experts on bomb trace analysis and bomb engineering. Although, none of these trips ultimately un-earthed any evidence exonerating McVeigh, Jones felt they were neces-sary to prepare McVeigh's defense. All of this travel took time and the trial was repeatedly delayed. The preparation for McVeigh's defense was also a costly endeavor; some estimates of the costs of the defense ran as high as twenty million dollars, all of it paid for by the same government that McVeigh so reviled.

The federal case was handled by a team of experienced prosecutors. The chief prosecutor was Assistant U.S. Attorney Joseph Hartzler of the Central District of Illinois. Forty-four-years-old, Hartzler had four-teen years experience as a prosecutor. Among his wins was a convic-tion of four terrorists belonging to the now defunct Fuerzas Armadas de Liberacion Nacional, a clandestine paramilitary organization that advocated independence for Puerto Rico.

U.S. District Attorney for the Western District of Oklahoma Pat-rick Ryan remained deeply involved in the case, taking part in both the McVeigh and Nichols trials. Ryan had been sworn into office three weeks after the bombing. A former U.S. Air Force judge advocate gen-eral's officer serving as the chief military justice for Southeast Asia, he had also maintained a successful trial practice in Oklahoma City for more than twenty years.

Working on the McVeigh and Nichols cases, Ryan made it a point to personally talk to the relatives of all of the deceased victims. While the cases were pending, he wore a white cowboy hat, the traditional symbol of a good guy in the American West, in order to remind the relatives of the victims and other survivors that someone from Okla-homa was on their side.

Larry Mackey would also later join the prosecution team. Mackey had fifteen years experience as a U.S. assistant district attorney in Indi-ana and Illinois, and had also been a criminal prosecutor for the Illinois attorney general's office. He was active in the McVeigh case, and would be the chief prosecutor in the Nichols case. Also assisting in the pros-ecution was Beth Wilkinson of Washington, D.C., principal deputy of the U.S. Justice Department's Terrorism and Violent Crimes Section. A number of assistant U.S. district attorneys from Ryan's office also worked on the case, including Vicki Behenna, Kerry Kelly, and Jerome Holmes.

. . . . .

After the McVeigh indictment was handed down by the grand jury, a gag order was issued in the case. But before that, McVeigh agreed in June to give an interview to retired Army Col. David Hackworth, a columnist for *Newsweek*. The magazine interview was supposed to exclude questions about McVeigh's guilt or innocence; however, in the end Hackworth couldn't resist.

"Did you do it?" he asked McVeigh.

"We can't do that," McVeigh responded.

"He's innocent," piped up Jones, who was also present at the interview. Jones then reminded Hackworth the government was not about to drop its case just because McVeigh denied his guilt.

The *Newsweek* interview would be McVeigh's only pretrial personal public pronouncement, but it was not the only pretrial publicity that could have influenced the eventual trial. In May 1995, before the *Newsweek* interview, an article appeared on the front page of the *New York Times*. Attributed to a confidential source, the article stated that McVeigh had admitted committing the crime to his defense lawyers and wanted to take credit for it.

In the second edition of Jones's book about the trial, he reveals that he was the source for that article and that he had released the information at McVeigh's behest. Jones even produced a handwritten authorization from McVeigh to support his actions. Since McVeigh had chosen to plead not guilty and Jones was sworn to defend him, the reasoning behind this leak remains unclear.

The *New York Times* article appeared sometime before the beginning of the trial, and most potential jurors were likely unaware of its existence. A more prejudicial release of information, however, came on March 1, 1997, just a few weeks prior to the beginning of the trial when Peter Stover, a *Dallas Morning News* reporter, broke a story based on confidential internal defense memoranda. According to Stover, McVeigh had confessed to the crime to his lawyers and had also admitted that he bombed the building during office hours because "We needed a body count to make our point."

Judge Matsch lifted the gag order so that Jones could respond to the article. Jones immediately held a news conference calling the newspaper story "irresponsible" and the documents it referenced invalid.

"The documents do not resemble anything that's in our office," he told the press.

McVeigh's problem was that he knew he had made the statements, and he blamed Jones for the leak. Similar allegations were also made by *Playboy* magazine on its website.

As the trial date neared, it became obvious that moving the trial to Denver had created a problem for the bombing survivors and the families of the deceased victims. Understandably, many of them wanted to attend the proceedings; indeed some would be called as witnesses. A time zone away from Oklahoma, Denver is almost seven hundred miles and an eleven-hour drive away from Oklahoma City. Attending the trial would be inconvenient, expensive, and a burden for the very people who had already been victimized by the bombing.

The trial judge also ruled that victims who would appear as witnesses could be excluded from viewing the trial proceedings by the defense. This unpopular ruling was upheld by the Circuit Court.

In response to such rulings, the victims organized and lobbied Congress for help. As a result of their requests, Congress passed two laws regarding victims' rights: A new federal statute required that when a court changed the venue of a trial out of the state where the case was filed and more than three hundred and fifty miles away a closed circuit television broadcast had to be provided to the original location (42 USC § 10608). Second, a judge was prohibited from excluding victims from attending a trial just because they might testify about the impact of the crime on the victim or the victim's family (18 USC § 3593).

A coordinated effort, led by Governor Keating, also helped raise funds to assist victims in attending the trial. Thus, some victims attended parts of the trial in person, while many more watched back home in Oklahoma City on closed-circuit television.

Arrangements also had to be made for McVeigh's security during the trial. Rather than house him in a local jail, the federal government elected to build McVeigh a cell in the federal office building next to the courthouse. Although windowless, McVeigh's cell was furnished like a motel room with a comfortable bed and cable TV. It was, however, also monitored twenty-four hours a day, providing little privacy.

CHAPTER SEVENTY-FOUR

The Trial

JURY SELECTION BEGAN March 31, 1997. The jury pool consisted of 352 people summoned from the Denver Division of the U.S. District Court, encompassing twenty-three counties, spread along the front range of the Rocky Mountains. Both urban and rural areas were included in the pool of jurors, and it was a diverse group, including a self-described witch, a reclusive billionaire, a philosophy professor, and a world-class skier, as well as farmers, ranchers, city dwellers, and people from all walks of life.

Over sixteen days, ninety-nine jurors were questioned by the judge, the prosecutors, and the defense lawyers. That reduced the pool to sixty-eight. The judge dismissed several jurors, and each side exercised twenty-three discretionary challenges, leaving a jury of seven men and five women, with six alternates.

For their protection, the jurors' names were not disclosed; they were identified only by letters and numbers. A wall was also erected shielding the jurors from the view of courtroom spectators. The judge chose not to sequester the jury, and so jurors were allowed to live at home or in Denver during the trial. Hartzler made the opening statement for the government. He outlined the evidence that would tie McVeigh to the bombing and prove McVeigh's motive for committing the crime. He also introduced the tragic story of little Tevin Garrett, one of the toddlers in the nursery killed by the bomb. The heart-rending tales of the victims and lives lost were an important and persuasive part of the government's presentation, and Hartzler wanted to emphasize this aspect of the case early and often. He also wanted to dispel any notion that McVeigh was some kind of soldier or "patriot," preferring instead to paint the defendant for what he was: a man who had killed innocent women and children while running from the scene.

Jones retaliated with a two-and-a-half hour opening statement that was criticized by many lawyers and onlookers. Rather than using the traditional tactic of raising "reasonable doubt" as to McVeigh's guilt, he blatantly stated that McVeigh was innocent, something the facts did not support. He also made the questionable decision to read the names of all of the 168 people killed as a result of the bombing. To Jones, it was a way to show respect for the dead, lament the horror of the tragedy, and acknowledge the need to find the bomber, while also giving him an opportunity to segue into why the bomber was not his client. Whatever its impact on the jury, the tactic angered many of the families of the victims. As to why Jones felt such a long opening statement was warranted or wise, he later said that he felt it necessary, or proportional, given the more than four hundred witnesses the government planned to call.

As it happened, the government called 141 witnesses in thirty-one days. In an interview with PBS after the trial, Hartzler explained, "Well, obviously we put together a case much like you would build a wall of bricks. There was a brick here, a brick there with a lot of mortar in between, and in the end we had a very solid brick wall."

The mortar to which Hartzler referred may well have been the compelling testimony of survivors and victims' family members, which was interspersed with that of witnesses offered to prove McVeigh's guilt.

The survivors' graphic firsthand description of the bloody death and devastation caused by the bomb was excruciatingly painful to hear. Victim impact testimony during the guilt stage of a trial is unusual, but the prosecution was able to convince the judge of the relevance of these witnesses in spite of the objections lodged by the defense. On appeal the Tenth Circuit Court of Appeals affirmed the admission of the victims' testimony. This move by the government served to personalize the grief and terror that resulted from the bombing and elicited the natural human sympathy of the jury. In short, it was devastating to McVeigh.

In his PBS interview, Hartzler was reluctant to give any particular piece of evidence special significance in winning the conviction.

"But obviously the fact that he [was] arrested seventy-eight miles from the scene of the bombing, seventy-seven minutes after the bombing was a pretty significant circumstance," Hartzler observed in one of his classic understatements.

. . . . .

While placing McVeigh in the proximity of the Alfred P. Murrah Federal Building at the right time was, of course, important, the government's case still relied heavily on the testimony of Michael and Lori Fortier.

As the only two witnesses who were aware of McVeigh's intentions to bomb the Murrah building, their testimony was crucial in linking McVeigh to the bombing. What they said was also, however, tainted by their own cowardice and complicity in the crime and, even more so, by the fact that they had both made plea bargains with the government in return for their cooperation and testimony.

Luckily, many of the facts they testified to were also confirmed by other witnesses and the calls made with the Bridges debit card.

Lori Fortier described how McVeigh had demonstrated his design for the bomb using soup cans from her kitchen cupboards. She also told how she and Michael had assisted McVeigh in disguising blasting caps by wrapping them as Christmas presents for transport from King-man to Michigan, and how McVeigh invited the Fortiers to witness the explosion of a test bomb in the desert near Kingman. She also told the jury about helping McVeigh create the false driver's license identifying him as Robert Kling.

Michael Fortier recited McVeigh's description of Nichols's involve-ment in the robbery of "Bob from Arkansas," as well as the robbery of the explosives from the Martin Marietta quarry in Kansas. He also told how he had accompanied McVeigh to Oklahoma City to case the Mur-rah building and look for a spot to stash the getaway car.

On cross-examination, Jones was able to bring out the Fortiers' drug use and the many conflicting false statements they had given the FBI before they cut a deal for a plea bargain. In spite of how unreli-able the Fortiers were themselves, their testimony apparently rang true enough for the jurors.

Another reluctant but powerful witness against McVeigh was his own sister, Jennifer. When the FBI first contacted Jennifer, she had refused to cooperate. It was brought out on cross-examination that the FBI agents had put her in a room displaying a poster with her picture on it. The poster contained a list of all of the charges that could be brought against her, in one instance noting, "penalty equals death." Regardless of what ultimately moved her to testify, what she said estab-lished McVeigh's motive for the crime. She testified as to the content of her brother's letters to her, including both his expressed hatred of the government and his promise that "something big" was about to hap-pen. She also testified McVeigh had told her about carrying a half-ton of explosives in his car and about the hate-filled letter he had left on her computer for the ATF to read after he committed the bombing.

Meanwhile, McVeigh's attorneys were able to score some important points on the cross-examination of some of the government's witnesses, including Oklahoma State Medical Examiner Dr. Fred Jordan, whom the government had called to establish the death of the eight federal officers that were the subject of the trial.

On cross-examination, Jordan had to admit that in the course of identifying the bodies of the persons killed by the bombing, he had discovered an extra leg that did not belong to any victim. There were eight victims with traumatically severed left legs and nine left legs. Since McVeigh was still sporting two legs, the defense's inference was that the unidentified leg must belong to the real bomber who was killed by the explosion

Another weakness in the government's case was the shaky scientific evidence claiming to connect McVeigh to the crime. Just prior to trial the inspector general for the U.S. Justice Department had published a report on the FBI lab savaging the lab's procedures and personnel. Problems with contamination of evidence, the chain of evidence, and testing procedures were pointed out in the 517-page report. Part of the report specifically criticized the handling of the evidence in the McVeigh case as well as the supervisors who worked on the case.

Jones wanted to use the inspector general's report on cross-examination and in the defendant's case. The defense received a major setback, however, when Judge Matsch ruled only six pages of the report directly relevant to the McVeigh evidence were admissible.

In spite of this ruling, the evidence given by the FBI's own expert witness, Steven Burmeister, lacked scientific credibility. Burmeister said that he had found traces of pentaerythritol on McVeigh's T-shirt and jeans. PETN is a component of detonating cords. This conclusion conflicted with the opinion of another FBI chemist, Roger Martz, who did not find any residue on the clothing.

Martz, however, said that he had found PETN on McVeigh's knife. Burmeister, on the other hand, had not found PETN on the knife. Worse still, Burmeister's supervisor, David Williams, highly criticized in the inspector general's report, had changed Burmeister's original report to help support Martz's findings.

Serious questions also existed about the preservation of the evidence and chain of custody. McVeigh's clothes had been sent to the lab in a brown paper bag and could have been contaminated after his capture, rendering a scientific analysis inconclusive. All of these problems were brought out by Chris Tritico on cross-examination. Regardless, the presence or absence of PETN on McVeigh's clothes could not alter the strident antigovernment message printed on the T-shirt itself, including the threat against "tyrants."

Jones's style, not uncommon among criminal lawyers, was to engage in a lengthy and detailed cross-examination searching for any small discrepancy in a witness's testimony. In some instances this exposed problems. In others, he asked one question too many. While cross-examining Yuhua Bai, the owner of the Chinese restaurant in Junction City who had identified the receipt for the food delivered to McVeigh's motel room, Jones inexplicably asked if her Mo Gu Gai Pan was good.

"Ask him," Bai said and pointed at McVeigh.

By the close of the government's case McVeigh had been linked to the Ryder truck and the truck tied to the bombing. His arrest clearly placed him in the vicinity of the bombing at the right time. Based on the testimony of the Fortiers and Jennifer McVeigh, the prosecutors had painted a picture of McVeigh as a rabid domestic terrorist ready to strike the government he hated.

Holes in the government's case did exist. No witnesses were called who actually saw McVeigh in Oklahoma City on the day of the bombing. Eldon Elliott's description of McVeigh was shaky, and the seller of the nitromethane, supposedly used to make the bomb, could not positively identify McVeigh. It was certainly possible that reasonable doubt of McVeigh's guilt might have existed in the minds of the jury, although the victims' testimony had created an atmosphere in which retribution against whoever did the crime seemed mandatory.

In many ways the jury had only been given one choice.

CHAPTER SEVENTY-FIVE

The Defense

WHEN JONES BEGAN McVeigh's defense, he sought to refocus the jury by offering up alternate perpetrators. His efforts in that regard were immediately frustrated by Judge Matsch's ruling barring the testimony of Carol Howe, a key defense witness.

Howe was a controversial character who had lived in the white supremacist community at Elohim City and had acted as an ATF informant. At the time of the McVeigh trial, she had herself been indicted for making a bomb threat and possessing bomb-making materials. In spite of the pending charges against her (she was later cleared in a jury trial), the defense lawyers had arranged for her appearance and brought her to Denver to testify. She was prepared to say that she had heard the white supremacist leader, Dennis Mahon, bragging about blowing up a five-hundred-pound ammonium nitrate bomb in Michigan. She also would have been able to testify that Mahon and Andreas Carl Strassmeir had preached destruction of the U.S. government, and that the two men had made three trips to Oklahoma City in November and

December 1994. But Howe never testified. Judge Matsch ruled her testimony was "not sufficiently relevant to be admissible."

McVeigh was not defenseless. Frederic Whitehurst proved to be a powerful witness called in McVeigh's defense. Whitehurst was the FBI chemist who had blown the whistle on the Bureau's crime lab problems and instigated the inspector general's report. He was able to shoot holes in the prosecution's already weak forensic evidence by thoroughly picking apart both the lab's procedures and conclusions.

Another key defense witness was Daina Bradley, the bombing victim whose leg was amputated on the spot. Bradley had been in the Social Security office at the Murrah building with her family immediately before the bomb exploded. She had looked out the front window of the building and seen the Ryder truck pull up to the curb and two men get out. She described the passenger as an "olive complexion man with short hair, curly, clean cut." The man was not McVeigh, but did fit the description of John Doe No. 2. Although a sympathetic witness, Bradley's testimony was questionable due to medical problems, including lapses of memory caused by the trauma of her experience and medication she was taking.

After all of the evidence was concluded, Larry Mackey made the government's closing argument to the jury. He recalled the pain, suffering, heartbreak, and loss of life caused by the bombing. He also pointed out that the government had proved all of the elements necessary to convict McVeigh, including motive, method, and opportunity.

He told the jury that McVeigh had acted out of hatred for the U.S. government, hatred inflamed by the attack on the Branch Davidian Complex at Waco.

Along with Nichols, McVeigh had accumulated the components of the bomb and constructed it, Mackey said. He had rented the Ryder truck and proceeded to Oklahoma City and detonated the bomb. Mackey emphasized that the crime was not a matter of politics or patriotism and that McVeigh had "committed murder." The seasoned prosecutor summed up his argument by asking the jury to consider one question as it related to the bombing and those involved: "Who are [the] patriots and who is the traitor?"

Jones's final argument on McVeigh's behalf attacked the Fortiers and tried to point out the weaknesses in the government's case, including that the debit card calls could have been made by anyone, that the FBI scientific evidence was flawed and incomplete, and that the extra leg from the scene could have belonged to the actual bomber.

Jones tried to persuade the jury that a crime the magnitude of the Murrah bombing required more people and greater expertise than that possessed by McVeigh and Nichols. Perhaps he even scored some points with the jury, but after four days of deliberation McVeigh was found guilty of all eleven counts against him in a unanimous verdict.

The guilt phase of the trial had ended, but there was still the matter of the death penalty.

In the penalty phase, the defense called McVeigh's friends and family as witnesses in hopes that their memories of the young man might help humanize him before the jury. Some described McVeigh as a decorated soldier; others tried to stress the good points in his character and his life. Richard Burr argued for McVeigh's life, trying to portray McVeigh as someone who did not deserve to die.

Giving the argument for the government, Beth Wilkinson echoed the theme from Hartzler's opening statement: "Tell him he is no patriot. He is a traitor and he deserves to die."

Given the enormity of the crime, the many dead, and the jury's guilty verdict, it was no surprise that after three hours of deliberation the jury returned with a sentence of death.

CHAPTER SEVENTY-SIX

The Case Against Nichols

THE MCVEIGH TRIAL WAS over, but having been severed, the Nichols case still remained. Nichols was represented by two able and experienced criminal defense lawyers, Michael Tigar and Ron Woods. They were assisted by Adam Thurschwell, Reid Neureiter, and Michael's wife, Jane Tigar.

Nichols's lead counsel Michael Tigar was a veteran of controversial cases having represented draft-dodgers and protestors against the Vietnam War. He had also represented Angela Davis, the African-American political activist who was charged with murder for her involvement in the 1970 death of a California judge killed during the sensational armed escape of a Black Panther from the Marin County Courthouse. Tigar's representation of Davis resulted in her acquittal on all charges.

Woods had served four years as an FBI agent and nineteen years as a prosecutor, including a stint as the U.S. attorney for the Southern District of Texas.

Going into his trial, Nichols was certainly in a better position to defend himself than McVeigh. Nichols had been in Kansas at the time of the bombing. He could not be associated with the rental of the Ryder truck and had not announced his intentions to the Fortiers or anyone else. Whereas Ryan had felt that the evidence against McVeigh was "overwhelming," he was concerned about convicting Nichols. In a recent interview, Ryan recalled that going into the Nichols trial, he had judged the chances of success "at about fifty-fifty."

Given the state of the evidence, Nichols's attorneys chose a more traditional defense strategy than that pursued by McVeigh's counsel. They attacked the government's witnesses and evidence, seeking to raise a "reasonable doubt" as to Nichols's guilt. In this regard, they artfully cast doubt on much of the government's case against Nichols. They also focused their attention on saving Nichols from the death penalty.

Of course, when all was said and done, a great deal of evidence did tie Nichols to the crime: His friendship and association with McVeigh and his animosity towards the federal government were well documented and irrefutable. Much of his original statement to the FBI was incriminating. The evidence found in the search of his house, including the bomb-making components and the receipt for two thousand pounds of ammonium nitrate fertilizer, also tied him to the crime, and his use of the Bridges debit card linked him to McVeigh's activities leading up to the bombing. There was also the letter he had left with Lana Padilla telling McVeigh to "go for it," as well as the items found in his Las Vegas storage locker. Still the prosecution became convinced that if it was to successfully tie Nichols to the bombing, it needed to prove that the theft from the Martin Marietta quarry and the Roger Moore robbery had been carried out by Nichols.

The task of prosecuting Nichols fell to Larry Mackey, as the government's lead attorney. Hartzler had gone back to his position in Illinois, but Patrick Ryan remained deeply involved and Sean Connelly, Beth Wilkinson, Geoffrey Means, Jamie Orenstein, Aitan Goelman, and Randy Sengel all assisted on the case.

. . . . .

The Oklahoma City Bombing

Judge Matsch remained the trial judge and the Nichols case went to trial in Denver on September 29, 1997. A jury of seven women and five men was seated October 30, and opening statements were made November 3.

Mackey framed the government's case as a partnership, stating that Nichols had "worked side by side" with McVeigh in planning the crime and building the bomb.

"Terry Nichols was there at the beginning and he was there at the end," Mackey told the jury.

Tigar and Woods countered by pointing out that Nichols had been in Kansas at the time of the bombing and had nothing to do with the renting of the Ryder truck. Woods emphasized the existence of John Doe No. 2 and the description of John Doe No. 2, which did not fit Nichols. Tigar implored the jurors to resist making up their minds until all of the evidence was in.

"You may find reasonable doubt in that last bit of evidence," Tigar told them.

Much of the evidence submitted to the jury by the prosecution in the Nichols case was the same as in the McVeigh trial, but there were significant differences.

The Nichols defense won an important victory when Judge Matsch was convinced to severely limit the use of victims' testimony during the guilt phase. This removed much of the emotion that had built a wave of sentiment for the victims and against McVeigh in the first trial. Also, Tigar and Woods enjoyed the benefit of having witnessed the McVeigh trial and observed the government's witnesses, allowing the defense lawyers to develop effective lines of cross-examination that undermined particularly the testimony of the FBI scientific experts.

The government tried to tie Nichols to the plot through his involvement in the robberies of the Martin Marietta quarry and Roger Moore. Explosives similar to those stolen from the quarry were found at Nichols's home. An electric drill and drill bits found at his house also matched the hole drilled in the padlock that secured the door of the shed from which the explosives were stolen. A number of guns and a comforter stolen in the Moore robbery were also found in Nichols's house.

To establish the Moore robbery and connect its stolen items to Nichols, the prosecutors called Moore and Anderson as witnesses. This was a controversial decision as both were shaky witnesses at best, and Moore was a known antigovernment radical in the mode of McVeigh and Nichols.

Anderson identified the items stolen from Moore and found at Nichols's house as being from the Moore robbery. But on cross-examination by Tigar, Anderson had to retract part of her testimony when one of the guns Anderson had said was stolen was proved to have been legitimately owned by Nichols prior to the robbery. The implication was that Anderson had worked backwards from a list of stolen items supplied by the FBI.

Moore described the robbery, and while he could only describe the robber as a man dressed in a ski mask and camo, armed with a sawed-off shotgun, he gave a description that fit Nichols. Tigar's cross-examination revealed Moore's friendship with McVeigh, his hatred for the government, and his conflicting statements about the robbery. Tigar tried to paint Moore as a co-conspirator with McVeigh, not a victim.

Regardless of how Moore was involved, his association with McVeigh and the presence of the stolen guns and other stolen items at Nichols's house was evidence of Nichols's role in at least that conspiracy. This became even more apparent when Fortier testified about how he and McVeigh had retrieved some of the stolen guns and after selling them, had given Nichols some of the proceeds.

Nichols's ex-wife, Lana, also testified, and placed in evidence the letter that Nichols had left for McVeigh with the "go for it!" language. Two witnesses placed a truck similar to Nichols's pickup at Geary Lake along with the Ryder truck on April 18.

The government was also able to show that Nichols had lied in his statement given at Junction City on April 21, particularly regarding his contact with McVeigh shortly before the bombing. Collectively, these facts built a case that pulled Nichols closer and closer to the crime. Although whether there was enough evidence to convict still remained in doubt when the government rested.

CHAPTER SEVENTY-SEVEN

Nichols's Defense

THE NICHOLS DEFENSE TEAM had won another advantage that had been denied McVeigh. In a reversal of his ruling in the McVeigh trial, Judge Matsch allowed the testimony of Carol Howe and evidence regarding the alleged John Doe No. 2.

Howe turned out to be a flaky witness, but did place McVeigh personally at Elohim City, a few months before the bombing. She also recited a telephone conversation between Mahon and "Tim Tuttle," one of McVeigh's aliases, and managed to at least imply that the white supremacists might have taken part in the bombing.

In order to bolster the defense theory that John Doe No. 2 did exist, was involved in the crime, and was not Nichols, the defense called a long series of witnesses.

Motel Owner Lea McGown again told of hearing the voice of someone else talking to McVeigh in his room. The delivery boy for the Chinese restaurant testified that another man had accepted and paid for the food delivered to McVeigh's room at the Dreamland Motel. Eldon Elliott and his employee, Vickie Beemer, testified again that they had seen another man with McVeigh when he rented the Ryder truck. Another witness claimed to have seen McVeigh and another man in the Ryder truck even prior to the date he rented the truck from Elliott's. Two witnesses testified they had seen a Ryder truck at Geary Lake the day before McVeigh rented the truck. Two witnesses saw another man with McVeigh in Oklahoma City shortly before the bombing.

The defense also tried to present Nichols as someone "who was building a life, not a bomb." They called friends and acquaintances to show that Nichols was trying to find employment and had renewed his car tag, acts ordinarily associated with a normal, ordinary future, not a future that included an act of extreme violence that might jeopardize his freedom and his life. His wife, Marife, also testified on his behalf. A weak and confused witness, she nonetheless tried to portray Nichols as an ordinary guy trying to work and raise a family.

Most importantly, Nichols's lawyers won a crucial legal argument that may have ultimately saved Nichols's life. The lawyers convinced Judge Matsch to instruct the jury that they could return a verdict on the eight murder counts for lesser charges, including involuntary manslaughter.

After the jurors deliberated forty hours over six days, they returned with their verdict on December 23. They found Nichols guilty of conspiracy to use a weapon of mass destruction and eight counts of involuntary manslaughter. They found him not guilty on the crimes of use of a weapon of mass destruction and destruction by explosive.

Because the conspiracy verdict still made Nichols eligible for the death penalty, the trial had to proceed to a penalty stage. At the end of the penalty stage, Tigar made a melodramatic argument on Nichols's behalf. Tigar told the biblical story of the brothers Joseph and Benjamin, ending his closing by embracing Nichols and saying, "My brother is in your hands."

By rendering a verdict of involuntary manslaughter, the jurors had already signaled that they were not convinced as to the extent of Nichols's involvement in the actual bombing. This became even clearer when, after three days of deliberation, they advised the court that they could not reach a unanimous decision on Nichols's sentence. At this point Ryan made a decision that would seal Nichols's fate. Tigar moved for a mistrial based on the jury's inability to reach a decision. Only the jury could sentence Nichols to death. If a mistrial were ordered it would fall to Judge Matsch, who was already responsible for sentencing Nichols on the involuntary manslaughter charges, to also sentence Nichols on the conspiracy count. On the other hand, if the mistrial decision was overruled and the jury continued to deliberate the jury had the authority to give Nichols a much lesser sentence, possibly even a few years.

Mackey's knee-jerk reaction was to oppose the defense motion, but Ryan felt that Matsch had wanted all along to sentence Nichols to life. He asked the judge for a short recess and convinced Mackey to agree to the defense's motion to avoid the possibility that the jury might be lenient towards Nichols. The prosecutors announced that they did not oppose the motion for mistrial, and Matsch immediately declared a mistrial and took over the sentencing personally

On June 4, 1998, Ryan's gut reaction proved correct. Judge Matsch sentenced Nichols to life in prison on the conspiracy count. In the federal system there is no parole, so this sentence put Nichols away for life. He also sentenced Nichols to the maximum sentence of six years on each of the involuntary manslaughter counts and fined him $14.5 million, the original cost of the Murrah building.

In delivering the sentence, Judge Matsch called Nichols "an enemy of the Constitution," and he reminded everyone of the cost of Nichols's choices: "[He] has forfeited the freedoms that this government is designed to protect and defend."

· · · · ·

Though his life had been spared, Nichols was the loser in the end. He had nothing to look forward to but life in prison, a punishment he richly deserved. Still the verdict did not please everyone. Most upset with the outcome of the Nichols case were some of the relatives of people killed in the blast. Darlene Welch, whose four-year-old niece, Ashley Eckles, was killed in the bombing, made it quite clear what she thought of the jury: "They are cowards. Gutless. Gutless. They let us all down. I feel like we owe all 168 people here an apology."

Her sentiments were echoed by many of the other relatives of the deceased victims. How the relatives felt mattered to Oklahoma County District Attorney Bob Macy. Widely known for his cowboy attire and his relentless prosecution of death-penalty cases, Macy vowed to file murder charges in state court against McVeigh and Nichols for the deaths of the one hundred and sixty victims who had not been the subject of the federal trials.

When Macy said, "I have no choice at all ethically or morally but to try this case. I promised the people of this county I would do it. I have every reason to believe that we will have a different result," he was referring to the imposition of the death penalty.

Both McVeigh and Nichols appealed their federal cases to the Tenth Circuit Court of Appeals. While these appeals were pending, the two men were housed in the U.S. penitentiary at Florence, Colorado. Dubbed "Supermax," this facility is considered to be the nation's most secure prison. At Supermax, the two men were held on "Murderer's Row," along with three other notorious murderers: Ted Kaczynski, Ramzi Ahmed Yousef, and Luis Felipe.

Kaczynski, or "The Unabomber," is a mathematics prodigy who terrorized the nation with a letter-bombing campaign spanning two decades, from 1975 to 1995. Yousef is one of the main perpetrators of the 1993 World Trade Center bombing. And Felipe, known as "King Blood" for the many murders he committed, is the infamous founder of New York City's Latin King's Gang. Of the five men, only McVeigh was sentenced to death. The others were all jailed for life.

The Tenth Circuit Court of Appeals rejected McVeigh's appeal, and affirmed the verdict and sentence rendered in the trial. On March 8,

1999, the U.S. Supreme Court refused to grant *certiorari* to review the decision of the appeals court. McVeigh made one more vain attempt to secure his freedom: He had new lawyers file a motion for a new trial in district court, viciously attacking the competency of Jones and his other trial counsel. Judge Matsch overruled the motion in 2000.

In 1999, McVeigh was moved to the federal prison in Terre Haute, Indiana. This was the only federal prison equipped to perform an execution, although the last one carried out had been in 1963.

McVeigh's execution was set for May 16, 2001. Just six days prior to the scheduled execution the government released thousands of pages of documents that had previously been withheld from McVeigh's attorneys. As a result, McVeigh's execution was postponed until June 11.

He made one more attempt to stay his execution, but was rejected by Judge Matsch and the Circuit Court. McVeigh, who had always been willing to die for his cause, accepted his fate and was executed by lethal injection on June 11, 2001, in Terre Haute, Indiana.

To the end, he showed no remorse, maintaining that his acts were justified. He even requested that his execution be televised nationally, but this did not occur, although it was shown on closed-circuit television in Oklahoma City for some 232 survivors, rescuers, and family members of the victims.

CHAPTER SEVENTY-EIGHT

State of Oklahoma v. Nichols

NICHOLS'S SUCCESS ON APPEAL was no better than McVeigh's. The Court of Appeals affirmed Nichols's sentence, and in 2001 the Supreme Court refused to review the decision. Nichols, however, had another problem.

Bob Macy had become obsessed with getting the death penalty for Nichols, and he made good on his promise to the victim's families and filed charges against Nichols in March 1999: one hundred and sixty counts of first-degree murder, one count for each person killed who was not the subject of the federal trial. He also filed a charge of first-degree manslaughter for the death of a fetus.

In anticipation of filing charges, Macy had sent one of his top assistants, Sandra Elliott, to Denver to observe both the McVeigh and Nichols trials. Elliott later represented the State at the Nichols trial along with two other Oklahoma County assistant district attorneys, Lou Keel and Suzanne Lister (now Suzanne Lavenue). Based on these charges, Nichols was moved to the Oklahoma County Jail where he was held in solitary confinement under twenty-four-hour surveillance.

In 2001, Macy resigned as district attorney, and on July 1 of that year, Governor Keating appointed Wes Lane to the post. Initially when he took office, Lane had not been sure if he would proceed with Nichols's prosecution. There was a backlog of murder cases in the district attorney's office, and Nichols had already been tried, convicted, and put away for life. Money was also a question. Prosecuting Nichols was an expensive proposition and would tap already limited county resources. But Lane also felt an obligation to meet with the relatives of the deceased and the survivors of the bombing before making his decision.

He held two mass meetings with those groups and listened to their views. The meetings convinced him to prosecute Nichols. He realized that the people at the meetings, for the most part, simply wanted justice for their loved ones. It was not so much vengeance that motivated them, but rather the sense that no one had ever been held responsible for the death of their family members. This inspired Lane to realize that what existed in the aftermath of the Oklahoma City bombing was one hundred and sixty unprosecuted murder cases. He concluded that in good faith as district attorney, it was his duty to pursue these cases. On September 5, 2001, he made a public announcement to that effect.

Lane's decision was not without controversy. Nichols was already serving a life sentence without possibility of release. To retry him would be costly, time consuming, and put the victims' families through another trial. His appointment to fill the term of Macy was only until the next election, and so he faced a race in 2002. He drew a determined and well-financed opponent, Mickey Homsey, whose principal platform was a promise to dismiss the Nichols case. Homsey's position was popular with much of the public and even some of the families of the victims, who saw no merit in giving Nichols more time in the public eye and felt a new trial would only ruin what little closure they had been able to find since the bombing.

Homsey argued that there was nothing to be gained from trying Nichols again, other than the death penalty, and that such a result was merely vengeance and not worth the taxpayers' money. After a heated campaign, Lane prevailed, handily. The die was cast for another Nichols murder trial.

The Oklahoma Supreme Court appointed Brian Hermanson of Ponca City and Creekmore Wallace of Sapulpa to represent Nichols. Hermanson acted as the lead attorney. The defense team also included University of Oklahoma College of Law professor Rod Uphoff. When Uphoff took another job at an out-of-state university, Barbara Bergman, a professor at the New Mexico University School of Law, joined the defense. Bergman did the legal briefing and argued the defense motions; she also participated in the trial. She brought Mark Ernest and Terri Duncan, two other New Mexico lawyers, with her to aid the defense.

The trial took two years to make it to court. Nichols's lawyers raised the legal issue of double jeopardy, which had to be disposed of prior to trial. Oklahoma Criminal Procedure required a preliminary hearing, and one judge assigned to the case was disqualified and another quit. Additionally, the defense lawyers had to be given time to review the mountains of evidence collected by the federal government, which had been turned over now to the State.

When the preliminary hearing commenced in May 2003, Judge Allen McCall of Lawton conducted the hearing, and ordered Nichols to stand trial after seven days of testimony. Utilizing a statute passed by the legislature in 1994, Judge McCall made his decision before the prosecution had called all of its witnesses or the defense had offered any evidence. The judge found a crime had been committed and there was probable cause to believe Nichols had been involved. Judge McCall's ruling abruptly ended what could have been a lengthy fishing expedition by the defense. His ruling was based in part on the testimony of Padilla and Fortier, who reiterated their stories from the first Nichols trial.

. . . . .

The defense lawyers also argued that in view of Nichols's prior conviction the trial should be postponed indefinitely, until the memories of prospective jurors faded on the subject. Certainly Nichols's prior conviction was a problem. Ordinarily his conviction in the federal trial would not have been admissible evidence that could be heard by the jury unless Nichols testified. However, in this case, as Trial Judge Steven Taylor of McAlester was heard to say, "The whole world knew about Nichols's conviction."

Thus, Taylor, who was then a district judge and is now a justice on the Oklahoma Supreme Court, was faced with the daunting task of trying to ensure that Nichols received a fair trial from an impartial jury in spite of the common knowledge of Nichols's previous federal conviction. He began by advising the attorneys and Nichols that there would either be a fair trial or no trial at all, his intention being to dismiss the case if a jury could not be impaneled that measured up to constitutional standards.

The judge also moved the trial from Oklahoma City to McAlester, figuring it would be almost impossible to find jurors in Oklahoma City who had not somehow been affected by the bombing or already made up their mind about Nichols.

Even though the venue was away from the community attacked in the bombing, picking a jury would still be difficult. With this in mind, Taylor had more than one thousand jurors summoned from Pittsburg County. This created a real hardship on the entire county, which had at the time a total population of only a little more than forty thousand.

The potential jurors filled out written questionnaires and were assembled in the McAlester High School auditorium, where Judge Taylor addressed them from the same podium he had used as president of the school's student body years before.

This process excused about three hundred jurors. The remaining jurors were then brought to the courthouse one hundred at a time. Out of these groups, eighteen were placed in the jury box and adjacent chairs and then questioned further by the judge. After eliminating some, the remaining candidates were questioned individually by the judge, the prosecutors, and Nichols's attorneys.

This laborious process took more than three weeks, but resulted in the selection of twelve jurors and six alternates. One hiccup did occur when it was learned that one juror was the cousin of an Oklahoma County assistant district attorney who had assisted the prosecution with jury selection. Two other jurors also knew the same attorney. These three people were removed from the jury, and the case proceeded with three alternates, as it developed, barely enough to see the trial through to the end.

· · · · ·

The prosecution's case in state court was much the same as the case presented against Nichols in U.S. District Court. Sandra Elliott had attended both the McVeigh and Nichols federal trials, and had the advantage of having observed the witnesses' testimony on direct and cross-examination. In spite of this advantage, it was impossible to avoid presenting a huge amount of information. The state offered 151 witnesses and more than one thousand pieces of evidence. Nothing had developed over the intervening years to substantially alter the evidence against Nichols, although the prosecution was faced with the additional task of establishing the cause of death of all one hundred and sixty victims rather than just the eight victims who were the subject of the federal case.

The defense was also similar to that presented on Nichols's behalf in the federal trial: present evidence of John Doe No. 2 and establish that such a person was not Nichols. The defense called ninety-six witnesses over eleven days. Judge Taylor excluded testimony regarding McVeigh's supposed connection to the Elohim City white supremacists and a Midwestern gang of bank robbers, which he felt the defense was unable to sufficiently tie to the bombing.

In the end, it took the jury four hours to find Nichols guilty of 161 counts of first-degree murder, one count of first-degree arson, and one count of conspiracy to commit arson.

One of the murder convictions was for the death of the unborn child, and the jury determined Nichols's punishment for this conviction would be life without parole. The prosecutors were barred from seeking the death penalty on this count because they had not filed sufficient legal notice.

The trial was not over yet. The jury still had to determine whether Nichols would get the death penalty.

It was in this stage of the trial that the evidence differed most from Nichols's previous trial and where his lawyers most probably saved his life. A number of persuasive witnesses were called to testify on Nichols's behalf, including several of the victims' family members who said that they were willing to forgive Nichols and thought his life was worth saving.

Creekmore Wallace, who gave the closing argument for Nichols in the punishment phase and later was awarded the prestigious Clarence Darrow Award for his representation of Nichols, believes the most powerful witnesses were two Oklahoma City jailers who had observed Nichols reading his Bible and praying in the jail. One of these jailers had talked to Nichols and prayed with him about the jailer's personal problems, and the jailer credited Nichols with helping him save his marriage. Wallace implored the jury not to execute Nichols by painting the defendant as a repentant Christian and appealing to the religious nature of several of the jurors.

As the jury deliberated on Nichols's sentence, a problem created by the loss of the three jurors prior to trial almost caused a mistrial.

Over the course of the trial, three jurors had had to be excused. Now only the requisite twelve remained, with no alternates available. That's when one of the women jurors reported that she had developed a terrible hemorrhoid flare-up and could not continue deliberating. With the okay of the lawyers from both sides, Judge Taylor questioned the woman privately. One could argue his best decision during the trial occurred when he ordered a McAlester policeman to fetch some Preparation H from the drugstore and moved a couch from his office to the jury room, allowing the woman to recline on her side while finishing her jury duties.

After three days of deliberation, the jury deadlocked on Nichols's punishment. *The Oklahoman* reported an eight to four split with the eight favoring the death penalty. Judge Taylor remembers it as seven to five; one lawyer, as six to six; and another, as nine to three. As a result of the deadlock a mistrial was declared with regard to the death penalty stage.

From subsequent conversations with three of the jurors, Judge Taylor learned that some of the jurors were holding out for life without parole because they considered it a worse punishment than death. Wallace later received a call from one juror who inquired if he was "really telling the truth" about Nichols reading the Bible and embracing Christianity. Wallace assured the juror that he had told the truth in court, and was advised that the juror felt his religion called for forgiveness and, thus, he refused to vote for the death penalty.

Based on the mistrial of the penalty phase, Judge Taylor was charged with sentencing Nichols. He gave Nichols one hundred and sixty sentences of life without parole to be served consecutively. The verdict and sentence were never appealed.

Had Nichols sought and been granted a new trial, he would have again been subject to the death penalty. Given this prospect and his previous federal sentence, Nichols elected to live out his life in prison. He remains in the Supermax prison in Colorado where he continues to complain constantly about his treatment, including what he considers to be an unhealthy diet.

And there he will remain until his own death.

CHAPTER SEVENTY-NINE

Conspiracy Theories

B
UT THAT IS STILL NOT the end of the story. From almost the inception of the FBI's investigation, there was criticism from some sources of the scope and thoroughness of the FBI's work. State Representative Charles Key asked for an independent investigation by the Oklahoma legislature, but was denied. He then joined with Glenn Wilburn, the grandfather of two children killed in the Murrah nursery, and spearheaded a drive to convene a state grand jury. The pair filed a request for this in October 1995.

After a battle over the legality of the request, a petition for a grand jury was circulated to the public and 13,500 signatures obtained. This exceeded the requisite five thousand signatures required, and a grand jury was convened in Oklahoma County in June 1997.

Key was also responsible for organizing a group known as the Oklahoma Bombing Investigation Committee. The purpose of this group was to expand the FBI investigation to seek what its members believed was the real truth about the bombing. To Key and company, the real truth included not only a government cover-up, but also prior knowledge of the bombing by the ATF and other federal agencies. When the grand jury failed to do more than issue one indictment, that being for tampering with the grand jurors, OKBIC members were enraged and alleged a further government conspiracy to suppress the truth. Continuing its own investigation, OKBIC issued a report on the bombing in 2001, titled "Final Report." This document sought to discredit the FBI investigation and prove the government was somehow aware of or even involved in the bombing. No formal action of any kind has resulted from the report.

Conspiracy theories similar to those held by OKBIC have also been revived by the book *Oklahoma City*, authored by Andrew Gambel, a British journalist, and Roger G. Charles, a retired Marine lieutenant colonel who worked as an investigator for Stephen Jones, and the documentary film *A Noble Lie*, produced and directed by James Lane. Both of these works are more critical than conclusory, attacking the FBI's handling of the case but raising little more than speculation and conjecture about who else may have been involved.

Jones remains convinced there were others involved in the bombing. In particular, he believes that James Nichols was the actual mastermind behind the whole plot. Jones's opinion is based on telephone calls McVeigh had with James while McVeigh was in custody. Given that the FBI considered James a prime suspect, thoroughly searched his farm, and investigated any links he might have had to the crime, his involvement seems unlikely. Also, the Bridges debit card revealed no calls to James Nichols during time when McVeigh and Nichols were planning and implementing the crime. Nichols, on his part, has since said that Moore was a willing participant, not the subject of a robbery. Nichols's conviction, lifetime imprisonment, and obvious bitterness give this accusation little weight. Certainly the FBI and the prosecutors did not fully trust Moore, but as one of Nichols's defense lawyers put it: "He was a total whack job, but he was probably telling the truth."

Regardless of the involvement of others, the overriding fact is that both McVeigh and Nichols were given fair trials.

Both the federal government and the State of Oklahoma spent millions of dollars to ensure that the rights of these two men were protected. They were given able counsel, supported by investigators, and allowed expert witnesses—a cost to the U.S. and the State of Oklahoma of millions of dollars.

The handling of the McVeigh and Nichols cases is a testament to the inherent fairness of our constitutional system. The irony that these two infamous criminals—responsible for the cold blooded murder of 168 people, the maiming of many more, and the destruction of millions of dollars in property—were so well protected by a system they despised says it all.

Once their destiny was sealed, the two defendants reacted according to their character and personality: McVeigh, the fanatical zealot who chose an evil and violent way to express his convictions, unapologetic to the end, almost welcoming death; Nichols, the whiny underachiever, unable to admit the reality of his own complicit acts.

Two men forever linked by their heinous crime.

Postscript

It is appropriate that this book ends with Oklahoma's most heinous and notorious crime, the bombing of the Alfred P. Murrah Federal Building. Yet the author is aware that notorious cases don't stop happening on any given date, nor is this book complete as to past cases.

Several important historical events are not included in these pages, in particular, the Oklahoma Supreme Court Scandal of the 1960s and the County Commissioner Scandal of the 1980s.

The Supreme Court scandal led to a comprehensive reform of our entire state judicial system, while OKSCAM, a kickback scandal, cleaned up a purchasing system that had disintegrated into rampant corruption and illegal entitled behavior.

OKSCAM saw the conviction of two hundred people, including two-thirds of Oklahoma's sitting county commissioners. In all sixty of the state's seventy-seven counties were involved in the scandal. It went down in history books as the largest local corruption investigation in American history, a particularly dubious achievement for the state. Either of these two events would justify an entire book. Likewise, other older cases such as the "Society Gang Murder" in Tulsa in 1934 and the unsolved Mullendore murder would be worthy subjects for any writer.

Since the Oklahoma City bombing, it probably comes as no surprise that there have been many more controversial trials. The recent trial and conviction of James Ersland, the Oklahoma City pharmacist who killed an armed robber, comes to mind. There have been and will be others. Like past notorious cases, the one thing we can count on is that new cases will be cussed, discussed, and dissected around the dinner table and in coffee shops and bars all across the state. Aided by today's ever-present media, each of us will become an instant expert based on at best a superficial knowledge and accounting of the facts.

In the end, that may well underscore best why we should all be grateful for a judicial system that requires a fair trial and a decision by an impartial jury. As demonstrated by the cases in this book, the actual evidence is often quite different than what the public thinks it has heard or read. When this leads to an unexpected outcome, even more controversy ensues, and accounts often become more subjective than accurate. All of these circumstances make a fertile field for a writer, and I am sure there will be many more chronicles of notorious Oklahoma cases to come.

ACKNOWLEDGMENTS

I would like to acknowledge the help of my son Kurt in finding the photographs included in this book. I would also like to thank my friend, Larry Floyd, who gave me the benefit of his extensive knowledge of historical research. All of the people associated with the Oklahoma Historical Center, particularly in the library and the photo archives department, were extremely helpful. Most importantly, this book would not have been possible without the cooperation of the many lawyers, prosecutors, law enforcement officers, and judges who gave freely of their time to discuss the cases in which they participated and who helped make this book as accurate and insightful as possible.

NOTES

Chapter 1, Machine Gun Kelly and the Urschel Kidnapping
This chapter is based on the following sources.
1. Trial Transcripts:
Excerpts from the transcript of the trial, *United States v. George Kelly and Kathryn Kelly*, beginning October 9, 1933.

2. Original Documents:
Copies of correspondence from the personal files of U.S. District Judge Edgar S. Vaught, including: letters to and from Charles Urschel, letters to and from Pauline Frye (Kathryn Kelly's daughter), and, letters to the United States Board of Parole.

Copies of correspondence from the personal files of Charles Urschel, including: a copy of a letter from George Kelly while in Alcatraz, and a copy of a letter to J. Edgar Hoover.

A petition to the United States Board of Parole in Opposition to the Granting of Parole to Ora L. Shannon and Kathryn Kelly written by FBI Agent Gus Jones. Note: This undated document lays out in detail the facts of the Kelly case and Jones's opinion as to the vicious character of Kathryn Kelly.

A copy of a letter from Herbert Hyde to the United States Parole Board opposing a parole for Kathryn Kelly, Ora Shannon, and George Kelly, dated July 19, 1948.

3. Court Cases:

Bailey v. U.S. 74 F2d 451, 10th Cir. (1934).

Shannon v. U.S. 76 F2d 490, 10th Cir. (1935).

Kelly v. U.S. 76 F2d 284, 10th Cir. (1935).

U.S. v. Kelly and Shannon. 269 F2d 448, 10th Cir. (1959).

4. Newspapers:

The Oklahoman, Fort Worth Star-Telegram, New York Times, Oklahoma City Times, Tulsa World, Washington Post

5. Films:

A videotape of a black-and-white film released after the trial that contains footage from the trial and also re-enactments of parts of the crime. Note: This film was discovered by U.S. District Judge Ralph Thompson when a closet was being cleaned out at the U.S. courthouse in Oklahoma City. He had the film converted to videotape. It appears to be a newsreel made for theatrical showing.

6. Books and Articles:

Barnes, Bruce. *Machine Gun Kelly—To Right a Wrong*. Tipper Publications, 1991.

Frates, Kent F. "Kidnapped." *Oklahoma Today*, January-February 2003.

Hamilton, Stanley. *Machine Gun Kelly's Last Stand*. University Press of Kansas, 2003.

Hoover, J. Edgar. *Persons In Hiding*. Little Brown and Company, 1938.

Kirkpatrick, E.E. *Crimes Paradise*. The Naylor Company, 1934.

Kirkpatrick, E.E. *Voices From Alcatraz*. The Naylor Company, 1947.

Mattix, Rick. *Machine Gun Kelly*, Oklahombres, Inc. 1998 (I).

Miles, Ray. *King of the Wildcatters*. Texas A&M University Press, 1996.

Schuler, D. *Machine Gun Kelly On Camera: The First and Last Federal Criminal Trials on Film* (Unpublished Thesis) University of Oklahoma, Norman, Oklahoma.

7. Author's Notes:

The kidnapping of Charles Urschel has fascinated me ever since, as a child, I became of aware of the story. Known in our family as "Big Charles," Urschel was my uncle, married to my dad's older sister, Berenice. Stories about the kidnapping involving various family members were told and retold and although, largely true, many were no doubt, embellished over the years. Urschel did not like to talk about the event and growing up I never remember him saying much of anything about the kidnapping.

In 1960, I lived for several months in San Antonio and later the same year also ended up stationed there at Lackland Air Force Base. During this period of time I became better acquainted with Charles. He frequently invited me to play golf at his club and to his house for lunch afterwards.

On a few occasions he opened up and talked about the Kelly case. My overriding recollection is his fierce animosity for Kathryn Kelly. He was convinced that she wanted him killed. He seemed to carry little or no grudge for George Kelly, Bates, or Bailey, but his hate for Kathryn was clear and abiding.

I believe that Urschel also feared for his own safety and the safety of his family if Kathryn was ever released from prison. He believed her threats and, therefore, always opposed her attempts at parole. Usually a very calm and unemotional man, the intensity of Urschel's feelings about Kathryn still sticks in my memory.

Urschel's experience also gave him great respect for the FBI, especially Agents Jones and Colvin.

Prior to the trial Judge Vaught had been an acquaintance of Urschel's but as a result of the trial, the judge became a respected lifelong friend.

Chapter 2, *The United States of America v. David Hall*
This chapter is based on the following sources.
1. Trial Transcripts:
The Transcript of the Trial of David Hall, *United States v. David Hall*, United States District Court for the Western District of Oklahoma, beginning February 24, 1975.

2. Personal Interviews:
Bill Burkett, May 9, 2012.
Larry Derryberry, May 10, 2012.
Telephone interview with Frank Keating, May, 2012.

3. Court Cases:
United States of America, Plaintiff /Appellee v. David Hall and W.W. Taylor, Defendants/Appellants, 536 F2d 313, 10th Cir. (1976).

4. Newspapers:
Oklahoma City Times, The Oklahoman, San Diego Union, Tulsa World.

5. Television:
"A Conversation with David Hall," OETA TV, June 7, 2010, *An Interview with Dick Pryor.*

6. Books:
Burke, Bob. *Courage Counts: The Life of Larry Derryberry*. Oklahoma, Heritage Association, 2003.
Burkett, William R. and Alexander, James Edwin. *The Fall of David Hall*. Macedon Publishing Co., 2000.
Hall, David. *Twisted Justice*. Tate Publishing, LLC, 2012

7. Author's Notes:
I served in the Oklahoma House of Representatives as a state leg-

islator representing District 83, Oklahoma City, from 1970 to 1978. As a Republican, I was part of the minority, which during my tenure numbered from 21 to 27, out of 101 Members of the House of Representatives. From 1976 to 1978, I was the minority leader.

David Hall and I were both elected in 1970, and I first met the governor while passing through the receiving line at an official function. Having never met Hall before, my wife and I were impressed when he greeted us on a first name basis and inquired about our three children by name.

Hall was a likeable and charismatic leader, who was an activist as governor. However, very shortly after he took office rumors of his corruption began to circulate at the capitol. The results of investigative reporting by the press and grand jury testimony revealed his corrupt nature. As a result, in 1974, I joined with other Republicans to support the impeachment of Hall. This effort was defeated by the Democratic majority of the House.

Chapter 3, The Girl Scout Murders
This chapter is based on the following sources.
1. Trial Transcripts:
A Partial Transcript of the Preliminary Hearing, *State of Oklahoma v. Gene Leroy Hart*, District Court, Mayes County, June 7, 1978.

2. Personal Interviews:
Garvin Isaacs, April 21, 2012.
Telephone Interview with S.M. "Buddy" Fallis, April 9, 2012.
Telephone Interview with retired District Judge William Whistler, April 23, 2012.
Telephone Interview with Gary Pitchlynn, April 30, 2012.

3. Newspapers:
Oklahoma City Times, The Oklahoman, The Daily Times (Pryor, Oklahoma), *Tulsa Tribune, Tulsa World*

4. Television and Internet:
Website: "The Still Unsolved 1977 Oklahoma Girl Scout Murders." *http://www.girlscoutmurders.com/*.
Television: "Stateline" OETA Special, October 2003.

5. Films:
Someone Cry for the Children, Barrister Productions, LC.

6. Books:
McCoy, Gloyd. *Tent Number Eight. An Investigation of the Girl Scout Murders and the Trail of Gene Leroy Hart.* Tate Publishing, 2011.
Wilkerson, Michael and Wilkerson, Dick. *Someone Cry for the Children. The Unsolved Girl Scout Murders of Oklahoma and the Case of Gene Leroy Hart.* Berkley Publishing Group, 1982.

Chapter 4, The Karen Silkwood Case
This chapter is based on the following sources.

1. Trial Transcripts:
Transcript of *Silkwood v. Kerr McGee Corp*, U.S. District Court for the Western District of Oklahoma, beginning March 6, 1979.

2. Personal Interviews:
James Ikard, August 16, 2012.
Larry Ottaway, September 4, 2012.
Bill Paul, September 14, 2012.

3. Original Documents:
Report by Accident Reconstruction Lab, Dallas, Texas, to Chemical and Atomic Workers International Union, December 15, 1974 and attachments.
Oklahoma Police Traffic Collision Report, Oklahoma Highway Patrol, November 24, 1974, covering the Silkwood Accident of October 31, 1974.

Oklahoma Police Traffic Collision Report, November 15, 1974, Oklahoma Highway Patrol covering the Silkwood accident of November 13, 1974.

Division of Inspection Report, United States Atomic Energy Commission by Kenneth H. Jackson, December 19, 1974.

Files, documents, briefs, and depositions in the case of *Silkwood v. Kerr McGee Corp.*, et al.

4. Court Cases:

Bill M. Silkwood, *Administrator v. The Kerr McGee Corporation*, et al. 667 F.2d 908, 10th Cir. (1981).

Bill M. Silkwood, *Administrator v. Kerr McGee Corp*, et al. 464 US 238, United States Supreme Court (1984).

Bill M. Silkwood, *Administrator v. The Kerr McGee Corporation*, et al. 769 F.2d 1451, 10th Cir. (1985).

5. Newspapers:

Oklahoma City Times, The New York Times, The Oklahoman, Tulsa Tribune, Tulsa World, Wall Street Journal

6. Films:

Silkwood. A Mike Nichols film, 1983.

7. Books:

Ezell, John Samuel. *Innovations and Energy: The Story of Kerr McGee.* University of Oklahoma Press, 1979.

Rashke, Richard. *The Killing of Karen Silkwood.* Cornell University Press, 1981.

Spence, Gerry and Polk, Anthony. *Gunning for Justice.* Doubleday and Company, Inc. 1982.

Srouji, Jacque. *Critical Mass.* Aurora Publishers, Incorporated 1977.

8. Author's Notes:

In 2006, Kerr-McGee Corporation was acquired by Anadarko Petroleum Company. Kerr-McGee Corporation no longer exists as a separate entity. In an effort to get more information on Kerr-McGee's side of the story, I contacted a number of former Kerr-McGee employees. Although, they supplied me with some useful information about the company, they almost, uniformly, referred me to Bill Paul as the person to talk to about the Silkwood case.

Jim Ikard donated all of his files on the Silkwood case to the University of Oklahoma, School of Law. These files, including notes, briefs, legal research, and most of the transcript of the trial are available for review at the OU Law Library.

Chapter 5, The Sirloin Stockade Murders
This chapter is based on the following sources.
1. Trial Transcripts:
Transcript of *State of Oklahoma v. Roger Dale Stafford*, District Court, Oklahoma County, beginning October 8, 1979.

2. Personal Interviews:
Larry Koonce, June 6, 2012.
Andrew Coats, June 11, 2012.
Arthur Linville, July 20, 2012.
Verna Stafford, October 31, 2012.
Telephone Interview with retired District Judge Charles Owens, July 13, 2012.

3. Court Cases:
Stafford v. State, 665 P.2d 1205 (Ok. Cr. 1983).
Stafford v. State, 669 F.3d 285 (Ok. Cr. 1983).
Stafford v. Oklahoma, 467 U.S. 1212 (1984).
Stafford v. State, 700 P.2d 223 (Ok. Cr. 1985).
Stafford v. State, 731 P.2d 1372 (Ok. Cr. 1987).

Stafford v. State, 800 P.2d 738 (Ok. Cr. 1990).
Stafford v. State, 815 P.2d 685 (Ok. Cr. 1991).
Stafford v. Saffle, 34 F.3d 1557 (10th Cir. 1994).
Stafford v. Ward, 60 F.3d 668 (10th Cir. 1995).
Stafford v. Ward, 60 F.3d 837 (10th Cir. 1995).
Stafford v. State, 899 P.2d 657 (Ok. Cr. 1995).
Stafford v. Ward, 115 S.Ct. 1830 (1995).

4. Newspapers:
The Norman Transcript, Oklahoma City Times, The Oklahoman, The Purcell Register

5. Books:
Stover, Emma Gene. *Sirloin Stockade Slaughter, Murder on the Run.* Eloquent Books, an Imprint of Strategic Book Group, 2009.

Chapter 6, The Oklahoma City Bombing
This chapter is based on the following sources.

1. Trial Transcripts:
The Transcript of *United States v. McVeigh*, beginning March 31, 1997.
The Transcript of *United States v. Terry Nichols*, beginning September 29, 1997.

2. Personal Interviews:
Stephen Jones, November 15, 2012.
Pat Ryan, December 4, 2012.
Justice Steven Taylor, December 6, 2012.
Wes Lane, December 14, 2012.
Telephone Interview with Brian Hermanson, December 7, 2012.
Telephone Interview with Creekmore Wallace, December 7, 2012.

3. Court Cases:

United States v. McVeigh, 896 F.Supp. 1549 USDC, Western District of Oklahoma (1995).

United States v. McVeigh, 157 F3d 809 (10th Cir. 1998).

United States v. McVeigh, 153 F3d 1165 (10th Cir. 1998).

United States v. McVeigh, 118 F.Supp 2d 1137, USDC, Colorado (2000).

United States v. McVeigh, No. 01-1273 (10th Cir. 2001).

Nichols v. Alley, District Judge, 71 F3d 347 (10th Cir. 1995).

United States v. Nichols, 77 F3d 1277 (10th Cir. 1996).

United States v. Nichols, 169 F3d 1255 (10th Cir. 1999).

United States v. Nichols, 184 F3d 1169 (10th Cir. 1999).

United States v. McVeigh, Appeal of National Victims Center, et al., 106 F3d 325 (10th Cir. 1997).

United States v. McVeigh and Nichols, Appeal of the *Dallas Morning News*, et al. 119 F3d 806 (10th Cir. 1997).

4. Original Documents:
Terry Nichols's Affidavit, March 16, 1994.
Terry Nichols's Affidavit, November 8, 2006.
Summary of Reportable Injuries, Oklahoma State Department of Health, 1998.
The Oklahoma Department of Civil Emergency After Action Report Alfred P. Murrah Federal Building Bombing 19 April 1995 in Oklahoma City, Oklahoma

5. Newspapers:
Denver Post, Daily Oklahoman, Dallas Morning News, The New York Times, Rocky Mountain News

6. Radio:
PBS Interview with Joseph Hartzler, August 26, 1997.

7. Films:

A Noble Lie. Oklahoma City, 1995 Free Mind Films.

8. Television:
Television footage from KFOR, KOCO, KWTV, and CNN.

9. Books & Reports:

Gumbel, Andrew and Roger, Charles G. *Oklahoma City. What the Investigation Missed—and Why It Still Matters.* William Morrow, an Imprint of HarperCollins (2012).

Hersley, Jon, Tongate, Larry and Burke, Bob. *Simple Truths.* Oklahoma Heritage Association (2004).

Jones, Stephen and Israel, Peter. *Others Unknown. Timothy McVeigh and the Oklahoma City Bombing Conspiracy.* Public Affairs (1998, 2001).

Lane, Wes. *Amazingly Graced.* Wine Press Publishing (2010).

Tigar, Michael E. *Fighting Injustice.* American Bar Association (2002).

Michel, Lou and Herbeck, Dan. *American Terriorist. Timothy McVeigh and the Oklahoma City Bombing.* Regan Books, an Imprint of HarperCollins (2001).

The Oklahoma Bombing Investigation Committee. Final Report On The Bombing Of The Alfred P. Murrah Federal Building April 19, 1995 (2001)

10. Museums:
Oklahoma City National Memorial and Museum, Oklahoma City, Oklahoma.

Author's Notes:
The museum contains multiple exhibits connected with the bombing and the victims of the bombing. It is a fitting memorial to the victims and their families, but also furnishes an historical overview of the entire event.